IDEOLOGY AND SOCIAL SCIENCE

ARCHIVES INTERNATIONALES D'HISTOIRE DES IDEES

INTERNATIONAL ARCHIVES OF THE HISTORY OF IDEAS

112

BRIAN WILLIAM HEAD

IDEOLOGY AND SOCIAL SCIENCE

Destutt de Tracy and French Liberalism

BRIAN WILLIAM HEAD

IDEOLOGY AND SOCIAL SCIENCE

DESTUTT DE TRACY AND FRENCH LIBERALISM

1985 **MARTINUS NIJHOFF PUBLISHERS**
a member of the KLUWER ACADEMIC PUBLISHERS GROUP
DORDRECHT / BOSTON / LANCASTER

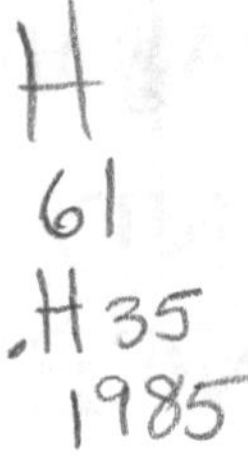

Distributors

for the United States and Canada: Kluwer Academic Publishers, 190 Old Derby Street, Hingham, MA 02043, USA
for the UK and Ireland: Kluwer Academic Publishers, MTP Press Limited, Falcon House, Queen Square, Lancaster LA1 1RN, UK
for all other countries: Kluwer Academic Publishers Group, Distribution Center, P.O. Box 322, 3300 AH Dordrecht, The Netherlands

Library of Congress Cataloging in Publication Data

Head, Brian.
Ideology and social science.

(International archives of the history of ideas ; 112)
Includes bibliographies and index.
1. Ideology--History. 2. Social sciences--Philosophy.
3. Destutt de Tracy, Antoine Louis Claude, comte, 1754-1836. 4. Liberalism--France. I. Title.
II. Series: Archives internationales d'histoire des idées ; 112.
H61.H35 1985 300'.1 85-18796
ISBN 90-247-3228-X

ISBN 90-247-3228-x (this volume)
ISBN 90-247-2433-3 (series)

Copyright

PRINTED IN THE NETHERLANDS

CONTENTS

PREFACE

This book attempts to present a detailed and critical account of the thought of Antoine-Louis-Claude Destutt de Tracy (1754-1836). Major importance has been placed on the analysis of his published writings. Biographical details have been provided only to the extent necessary to elucidate the circumstances of the composition and publication of his writings: in particular, the intellectual and political currents in France during the Revolutionary and Napoleonic periods.

The book has three main themes. The first is Tracy's philosophy of *idéologie*, which was concerned to clarify concepts and provide guarantees of reliable knowledge. The second is Tracy's attempt to elaborate a science of social organisation, *la science sociale*, whose objective was to recommend institutions and policies which could maximise social happiness. The third theme is Tracy's development of liberal and utilitarian approaches to the fields of politics, economics and education.

This study began life as a doctoral dissertation at the London School of Economics and Political Science. I am grateful for the guidance of my supervisor, Professor Ken Minogue, and for helpful comments from Professor Maurice Cranston, Professor Jack Lively, and Dr John Hooper. My research in Paris was aided by a grant from the Central Research Fund of the University of London. I am also pleased to acknowledge a grant by the Research Sub-Committee of the School of Humanities, Griffith University. The drafts were expertly typed by Annette Ritchie and by Jacqui Hurley. Finally, thanks are overdue to Diane for a decade of lively impatience.

1. POLITICAL AND INTELLECTUAL BACKGROUND

PERSPECTIVES ON TRACY AND THE IDEOLOGUES

Tracy and the idéologues have been forgotten and "rediscovered" several times by historians of ideas. In the period around 1800, securely entrenched in the Institut National, the idéologues enjoyed a reputation, which they took care to encourage, as pioneers in the human sciences. They were then relatively ignored for most of the nineteenth century, until reclaimed by liberal intellectuals of the Third Republic.[1] During the early decades of the twentieth century, the idéologues were again generally ignored, except for the attention of a few specialist historians[2]; more recently there has been a marked revival of interest in their work. There are several reasons for their fluctuating fortunes.

In the first place, the degree of attention and sympathy for their work has been partly related to changing currents of ideas in academic circles. Different generations of scholars have been more or less drawn towards certain themes in the idéologues' writings: for example, their liberal republicanism, their anticlericalism, or their scientific pretensions. This is perhaps clearest during the Third Republic, a period whose debates sometimes echoed those of the 1790s, and again in recent years when the character of the social and political sciences has undergone a close reconsideration. The chequered reputation of the idéologues, then, has partly derived from changing tendencies in intellectual life generally. Secondly, the 'great figures' approach to the study of the history of ideas has worked against the idéologues. The hall of fame of the Enlightenment philosophers accommodated many great names, such as Voltaire, Montesquieu, Rousseau, Diderot and Condillac. There was less room for minor disciples, continuators and acolytes, and the idéologues tended to be pushed into these categories. They were often regarded as having contributed nothing original beyond what had already been said by their illustrious predecessors. Moreover, the 1790s era has been deemed notable mainly for its men of action—political and military leaders, rather than philosophers.

Thirdly, there was a strong reaction in the early years of the nineteenth century against the philosophy of idéologie and its rationalist scientism and optimism. A highly unflattering portrait of idéologie emerged, which has influenced subsequent interpretations. On the one hand, the idéologues were taken to have posited a highly reductionist and materialist philosophy of sensations, in which human thought and action could hardly be distinguished from those of other animals, and where moral and religious experiences were dismissed as illusory.[3] There was a movement in philosophical psychology towards a new emphasis on subjective experience (e.g. Maine de Biran), and in literature there was a revival of religious and traditionalist themes (e.g. Chateaubriand). The theory of idéologie was regarded as the last gasp of an intellectually bankrupt sensationalism, a view which still persists.[4]

On the other hand, idéologie was discredited by its association with the political rationalism and faith in human perfectibility which had characterised the spirit of the 1790s. Idéologie was variously charged either with responsibility for the persecutions and turmoil of the Revolutionary period, or simply with a shallow and naive optimism which stemmed from its intellectual abstractionism and *esprit de système*. As if these charges were not enough to destroy the reputation of the idéologues, it has also been suggested that their social and political theory was largely mechanistic, whereas later thinkers increasingly tended to recognise the need to adopt organic models and show more concern for social processes in explaining historical change and continuity. Furthermore, it has been argued by Foucault that the linguistic and social models put forward by Tracy and others were pre-scientific; in other words, that there was a disjunction between the structure of the idéologues' thought in these fields, and the structure of modern linguistics and social science.[5]

For these reasons, it has become arguable that, at least in some fields, the work of Tracy and the idéologues "left no intellectual traces" and that it was destroyed not so much by Napoleon's persecution as by its own "irrelevance" for the new generations of social and political thinkers.[6] In terms of Kuhn's terminology,[7] idéologie had occupied the position of 'normal' science in the 1790s (though it had always been strongly contested, especially outside the institutional stronghold in the Institut National). However, the ideological paradigm was largely abandoned when it was found unable to satisfy the intellectual demands of philosophical and social analysts in the early nineteenth century. The words of Whitehead might be borrowed to describe aptly this perspective:

> Systems, scientific and philosophic, come and go. Each method of limited understanding is at length exhausted. In its prime each system is a triumphant success: in its decay it is an obstructive nuisance.[8]

The degree of attention and sympathy paid to Tracy's work has reflected the fluctuating judgements passed upon the writings of "ces méconnus, les idéologues".[9] F.-A.-M. Mignet, one of the *secrétaires perpétuels* of the Académie des Sciences morales et politiques, wrote a study of Tracy in his series of *éloges* on the idéologues during the 1840s.[10] Mignet had met Tracy and was well acquainted with the family of Tracy's son Victor, and he was able to report a number of family stories about Tracy's beliefs and temperament. Victor's wife, Mme Sarah Newton Destutt de Tracy, wrote a longer essay on the ideas of the old idéologue; this was published privately a few years after Mignet's *éloge*.[11] These two essays long provided the main source of reference upon Tracy's life and ideas although showing a distinct lack of warmth for Tracy's sensationalist doctrines. Their value lay in their "inside" knowledge of the subject and their use of some unpublished notes and papers of the late philosopher. The next landmark was Picavet's large volume on *les Idéologues* in 1891, which included a very long and generous summary of Tracy's writings, and urged a more sympathetic reconsideration of the idéologues' work in relation to their influence upon nineteenth-century philosophical and social thought. Picavet's work remained the major secondary source on Tracy for many decades. A short and very uncritical study of Tracy's writings as a whole by Jean Cruet appeared in 1909; Tracy's close links with the liberal and humanitarian currents of Enlightenment thought were emphasised, but the analysis remained superficial.[12]

Tracy's life and thought continued to be neglected in most works on French history and the history of philosophy. When mentioned, Tracy was introduced as a minor figure in the Assemblée Nationale Constituante of 1789-91 and in Napoleon's Senate, or simply as the inventor of the term "idéologie" and one of a group of sensationalist philosophers and liberal intellectuals known as the "idéologues" However, studies of particular aspects of Tracy's thought began to appear: for example, on his psychological and logical writings,[13] his economic thought,[14] and his political theory.[15] His ideas were also discussed briefly by those historians mainly concerned with the idéologues as a group,[16] including their links with the United States,[17] and their work for the journal *la Décade philosophique*.[18] Few of the idéologues have been the subject of a thorough intellectual biography: excellent studies on the work of Cabanis, Volney, and Sieyès,[19] have not been matched by works of comparable depth on Daunou, Garat, Ginguené, M.-J. Chénier, Andrieux, or J.-B. Say.[20] Research in the general field of French liberalism in the period after 1780 has been growing, partly owing to a new interest in the early development of the social and political sciences and the origins of the theory of industrial society.[21] There have been valuable studies of some influential (and younger) contemporaries of the idéologues such as Benjamin Constant, Mme de Stael, Saint-Simon and Maine de Biran;[22] together with excellent works on important predecessors of the idéologues, including Condillac and Condorcet.[23]

Interest in Tracy's work began to increase in the 1960s and has continued since then. Some of his books were reprinted[24] for the first time since the 1820s, although there was no genuinely critical edition of his writings to complement that devoted to his close friend Cabanis.[25]

The leading commentator on the idéologues, Sergio Moravia, has published several studies which deal with the political and intellectual activities of Tracy's colleagues. His recent volume on the thought of the idéologues[26] includes a substantial discussion of Tracy's "idéologie" from the viewpoint of the materialistic anthropology of Cabanis and contemporary debates on language and sensationalism. But Moravia has nowhere presented a picture of Tracy's theories as a whole, and has instead taken up selected themes, treated with great erudition. All students of Tracy have explicated the concept of "idéologie" at greater or lesser length; but few have attempted to discuss Tracy's work in terms of what I regard as the other central themes: namely, social science and liberalism.[27] The approach of my study is to bring together these three concerns, arguing that they are central not only in Tracy's own conception of his writings, but also as the areas of continuing importance in his work and the sources of his influence.

Tracy's writings, in my view, constitute one of the most comprehensive and interesting attempts at the beginning of the nineteenth century to elaborate a liberal theory of individual, society, education and politics. Tracy's system of ideas operated on three levels. Foremost in his own hierarchy of priorities was his epistemological concern with the nature and limits of knowledge, the basis for certainties in the various sciences, and the possibilities of conceptual reform as the avenue to intellectual progress. Secondly, Tracy participated in the early French discussions about the possibilities of a social science which, he hoped, would be intimately connected with the realm of public policy in government and public instruction. And thirdly, Tracy sought to elaborate a liberal approach to economic, moral and political questions, and to defend what he saw as the liberal gains made by the Revolution.

These various enterprises were not simply echoes of the earlier generation of *philosophes*, whose writings had so inspired his admiration. Nor is it true to say that Tracy's work failed to influence later generations of theorists. Tracy was an important link in the chain of French liberalism in politics and economics; he was a methodological precursor of behaviouralist approaches to the human sciences; and he was a pioneer of new social concepts which became established in a variety of forms throughout the nineteenth century. While confident that his theory was the only solid foundation for the study of man and society, Tracy recognised that his work was not strikingly original. He claimed to be extending certain traditions of thought, in collaboration with other intellectuals whose specialist knowledge of areas like physiology was necessary for the full development of the human sciences. But he did claim to have provided a solid epistemological base for their further development, and to have introduced a greater degree of coherence among these sciences, arguing that they were all dependent on a proper understanding of the intellectual faculties of man, and thence of his needs and capacities.

Specialist research suggests that the degree of Tracy's influence upon later thinkers has been seriously underestimated by many writers, notwithstanding the claims made in his own lifetime that the philosophy of sensations was already moribund. My own view is that Tracy's influence, whether directly upon figures such as Joseph Rey, Henry Beyle (Stendhal), and Augustin Thierry, or indirectly, as with Auguste Comte and the readers of his translated works in Europe and the Americas, was due to the ambitious yet apparently rigorous character of his quest for certainty in the human sciences, and to the liberal currents in his political and economic theories. Tracy is also of interest to the historian concerned with the origins of social and political concepts. Tracy invented terms such as *idéologie* [28] (and its derivatives: *idéologiste*, *idéologique*). He contributed to the currency of other new terms such as *la science sociale*. He anticipated aspects of the theory of *industrialisme*,[29] and the idea of a confederation of Europe.[30] And, according to one learned commentator, Tracy was a precursor of the marginalist conception of economic values.[31]

Tracy's epistemology, social science, and liberalism will be discussed and evaluated throughout this study. The purpose of this introductory chapter is to sketch the biographical and historical context of Tracy's thought, showing the connections between his writings and the political and philosophical debates and problems of his times. In the second section of this chapter, the main events of Tracy's political and intellectual career are briefly traced, before turning in subsequent chapters to the substantive discussion of his theories.

TRACY'S LIFE AND WRITINGS: AN OUTLINE

Antoine-Louis-Claude Destutt de Tracy was born on 20 July 1754, in Paris.[32] He was descended from the Stutt family in Scotland, whose sons had always followed a military career. Four Stutt brothers came to France from Scotland in 1420 to join the cause of the French Dauphin, the future Charles VII, against England. One of the brothers, Walter Stutt, was ennobled by Letters-Patent in 1474 under Louis XI, and settled on estates in the Bourbonnais near Moulins. His descendants acquired by marriage the estate of Tracy in Nivernais in 1586, and that of Paray-le-Frésil in 1640.[33] The father of the future philosopher, Claude-Charles-Louis Destutt de Tracy, born 1723, commanded the King's gendarmerie at the battle of Minden against the Duke of Brunswick in 1759; seriously wounded, the soldier died several years later, leaving only one child, Antoine-Louis-Claude, who was prevailed upon to uphold the military traditions of the family.[34] His education was supervised by his mother, until at about the age of sixteen he went to complete his studies at the *école militaire* in Strasbourg, and also at the University there, which had a liberal and cosmopolitan character and was a training ground for the diplomats of Europe.[35] Tracy's fellow students at that time included Narbonne, Ségur and Talleyrand.[36]

In common with the eldest sons of noble families, Tracy was rapidly promoted through the commissioned ranks of the army.[37] In April 1779, he married the great-niece of the Duc de Penthièvre, and became the colonel of the regiment of Penthièvre Infantry. On the death of his grandfather Antoine-Joseph (1694-1776), Tracy inherited considerable estates in Nivernais and Bourbonnais, and the title of Comte de Tracy.[38] Tracy divided his time between his regiment, his young family and his mother and grandparents at the family home of Paray-le-Frésil.

There is little evidence concerning the reasons that Tracy became dissatisfied with his life as a rich and successful officer of noble birth.[39] However, it appears that he thoroughly read the works of the physiocratic economists, including Quesnay, Dupont de Nemours, and the "revisionist" writings of Turgot. Tracy also read the *encyclopédistes* and philosophes, and formed a particular admiration for Voltaire, whom Tracy had visited at Ferney in 1770.[40] His studies in classical philosophy at Strasbourg confirmed his appreciation of Condillac's sensationalist critique of Scholasticism, but there is no evidence that he became familiar with Kantian philosophy at that time, nor with the particular form of empiricism developed by David Hume.[41] Together with many young nobles, Tracy was enthusiastic about the principles contained in the American Declaration of Independence,[42] supported the administrative reforms undertaken by Turgot and later by Necker, and was generally attracted to the liberal currents of ideas in politics, economics, religion and education. There is no evidence from these years that he frequented any of the *salons* in Paris or that of Mme Helvétius at Auteuil. Nor did he develop a passion for travel, diplomatic service overseas, or modern languages. He remained content to stay in France, and could read books only in French or the ancient languages.

Tracy's career took a new direction after 1788, at the age of thirty-four years. He became a politician and administrator during the early years of the French Revolution. In August 1788, in the midst of a general movement towards new forms of representation, Louis XVI agreed to the establishment in the Bourbonnais of a provincial Assembly, and four local Assemblies in the larger towns. Tracy was the spokesman for the local Assembly at Moulins when it resolved on 27 November to press for the creation of Etats-provinciaux composed of "véritables représentants de la Nation, légitimement et librement élus, au lieu de simples délégués du gouvernement tels que nous sommes".[43] An ordinance on 17 December authorised a meeting of the three *états* (clergy, nobility and *tiers*), to consider the question. Two hundred and twenty-five people from the three *états* met at the Town Hall of Moulins on 22 December and successfully petitioned the King to agree to the creation of Etats-provinciaux on the model of those recently granted in the Dauphiné province. Meetings of the three Orders began on 16 March and each proceeded to nominate commissioners who were to draw up a *cahier* of principles and demands, and then to meet together in order to formulate a single *cahier* for the whole province.[44]

Tracy was one of eight commissioners for the Bourbonnais nobility elected on 18 March 1789. In a series of enthusiastic meetings on 21 March, the nobility and the clergy offered to share the burden of taxation and dispense with their monetary privileges; Tracy was among the deputation sent to the Third Estate informing them of this abnegation. The proposal to draw up a joint *cahier* was strongly endorsed by all three Orders.[45] But after two days of separate meetings to discuss the articles of their own *cahiers*, disagreement arose at a joint meeting on 24 March because the nobility refused to accept a proposal for voting by head at the Etats-généraux rather than voting separately by Orders. The nobility thereby hoped to negate the doubling of the representation of the Third Estate agreed by the King at the end of December 1788. So the plan for a joint *cahier* was abandoned, and each of the *états* elected separate representatives to the Etats-généraux. Tracy was one of three deputies for the Bourbonnais nobility.[46] The majority of the Bourbonnais nobility had ultimately been concerned to avoid making major concessions which would threaten their traditional prerogatives; Tracy emerged in their debates as the leading spokesman for liberal principles and leading critic of their privileges. He had urged voting by head at the Etats-généraux, supported the double representation of the Third Estate, and was in large measure responsible for some relatively liberal provisions in the *cahier* of the Bourbonnais nobility.[47] However, he had not been successful on some important issues. Article 8 of Section III of his *cahier* instructed the representatives of the nobility to support separate debates and voting by Order at the Etats-généraux, and article 15 of Section II declared that the rights and prerogatives of the nobility were never to be renounced.

When the Etats-généraux began meeting on 5 May, Necker, the King's Minister, initially upheld the separation of the three Orders in voting. However, on 17 June the *tiers* renamed itself the National Assembly, and on 20 June its members and some liberal supporters from other Orders took the so-called Tennis Court oath to continue meeting until a new Constitution had been established. Within a few days the National Assembly had been joined by about 170 clergy and 50 nobles. The King eventually reversed his policy on 27 June, and ordered the unification of deputies from the three Orders. Contrary to the accounts given in some biographies,[48] Tracy had not accompanied liberal nobles like La Rochefoucauld into the National Assembly before the King's change of policy, nor had Tracy signed the Tennis Court oath.[49] Indeed, Tracy and his two colleagues had felt bound to seek the approval of their constituents before complying with the King's command to join the National Assembly. The other two Bourbonnais nobles eventually refused to serve in the new Assembly.[50]

Subsequently, Tracy supported the abolition of noble and other privileges on 4 August, the Declaration of the Rights of Man on 26 August, legislation to establish a Civil Constitution of the Clergy in July 1790, and measures to reform public finances. As an inexperienced politician, probably a little bewildered by the rapid turn of events, Tracy remained independent of factions and parties.[51] He adopted a pragmatic and cautious approach in most of his eighty or more interventions in debates, often concerning himself with administrative detail,[52] rather than high-flown rhetoric. He demonstrated no special gifts for leadership or eloquence in more than a few of his contributions. Only two of his speeches from this period were published. The first was a defence of the work of the Assembly against Burke's attack in the House of Commons on 9 February 1790.[53] The second was a major speech in September 1791 in favour of the rights of blacks in the colony of Saint-Domingue to enjoy equal political rights with white colonists.[54] Tracy was clearly in sympathy with the views of the Société des Amis des Noirs (the anti-slavery lobby led by Brissot and Lafayette), but he was never a member of that body.[55]

While living in Paris as a deputy in the National Assembly, Tracy had many opportunities to meet and admire the leading political and intellectual figures who gathered in the various *salons* and clubs. Most important for Tracy's developing intellectual interests, he became a member of the *Société de 1789*, whose main convenors were Sièyes and Condorcet, and whose members included Cabanis, Garat and Bailly.[56] Moderate constitutionalists such as Lafayette and La Rochefoucauld established the Club des Feuillants in opposition to the Jacobins (or Amis de la Constitution); Tracy was a member toward the end of his political career in Paris.[57] In 1789-90, he also frequented the *salon* of Adrien Duport, another foyer of anti-Jacobin opinion.[58]

However, it may be that Tracy's involvement in these clubs was less a matter of doctrinal purity than of friendships and experiment. For in March 1791, he became a foundation member of the Moulins branch of the Société des Amis de la Constitution (affiliated to the Paris Jacobins), alongside the other deputies from Moulins.[59] The membership of this club of liberal patriots at this time was no stronghold for *sans-culottes* and *ouvriers* of egalitarian views. On the contrary, it was "une société de bourgeois et de lettrés",[60] which regarded as a tragedy for the nation the death of the comte de Mirabeau in April 1791. However, after the unsuccessful flight of the King towards the border in June 1791, the Moulins branch shared in the general radicalisation of public opinion: the King's name was struck from their oath of loyalty, and a motion to open their membership was only narrowly defeated. Tracy's regiment had been implicated in protecting the flight of the King, and Tracy felt obliged in the Assembly to declare his devotion to the Constitution and to condemn the complicity of his regiment.[61]

The Assemblée Nationale Constituante completed its work on the new Constitution at the end of September 1791, with great haste and confusion. Tracy was later to argue that a legislative assembly should never take upon itself the dual functions of legislation and constitution-making.[62] The Constituant had declared its members ineligible for the new legislature which met in October 1791, thus depriving the new assembly of all the most experienced politicians, a loss which Tracy regarded as foolhardy.[63] He returned to his home at Paray-le-Frésil, enrolled in the National Guard, and undertook the functions of mayor. Elections for the executive of the Département de l'Allier gave Tracy a place on the administrative Council, and he joined the Commission des Impositions; a few days later (on 19 November) he was elected Président du Département.[64]

The impending war with Austria led to the formation of three French armies in December 1791 by Louis de Narbonne, Minister for War (a friend of Tracy). Tracy returned to active duty as a *maréchal-de-camp* in the Army of the North under Lafayette, and had some skirmishes with Austrian troops in April-June. Meanwhile, the Jacobins in Paris were attacking the loyalty and integrity of Lafayette and of other constitutional moderates.[65] Tracy, with a heavy heart, considered it prudent to resign from the army in July 1792 and seek a quiet life as an ordinary citizen with his family. Contrary to some accounts,[66] Tracy was not among the group of senior officers with whom Lafayette crossed the border into Austrian-held territory on 19 August 1792, after the Jacobin triumph in the Legislative Assembly.[67]

Tracy thus established his residence at Auteuil only in the summer of 1792. There is a strong probability that he had already met, in the Parisian clubs and *salons*, some of the inhabitants of Auteuil: Cabanis, Gallois, La Roche, and others who were the centre of the *salon* of Mme Helvétius. But even if Tracy and Cabanis had already met, it was only after they became neighbours and shared the same intimate circle of political and literary friends that they became intellectual colleagues. Tracy was the debtor in their early exchanges; Cabanis was far more knowledgeable in the physical and biological sciences, and in his understanding of the philosophical heritage of the Enlightenment.

As the Jacobin acendancy grew in Paris and in provincial towns, it became increasingly difficult for erstwhile nobility like Destutt-Tracy[68] to avoid accusations of sympathy for royalism, or lack of *civisme*.[69] The *loi de suspects* in 1793 granted wide powers to local *comités de surveillance* in seeking out people whose zeal for republicanism was not abundantly manifest.[70] The Moulins *comité de surveillance* accused Tracy of *incivisme* and *aristocratie*, and imposed a large "revolutionary tax" which he claimed was too large for him to pay; they accepted instead the revenues of his properties in the Moulins district.[71] Nevertheless, the *commissaire civil* in Paris ordered the arrest of Tracy and other residents of Auteuil on 2 November 1793. Cabanis was involved in hospital administration in Paris and escaped the fate of his colleagues. After a few weeks in l'Abbaye prison, Tracy was transfered on 16 December to Les Carmes, where he shared a cell for many months with Jollivet. His attempts to demonstrate his republicanism and patriotism met with no success, and it was more than three months after the fall of Robespierre before he was freed from prison, after eleven months of detention.[72]

After his retirement from the Assembly, local administration, and the army, Tracy devoted himself to scientific and philosophical studies. In his unpublished manuscripts, Tracy wrote:

> Delivered by circumstances to my penchant for a solitary and contemplative life ... I devoted myself to study, less to extend my knowledge than to become

> aware of its sources and bases. That had been the object of my life-long curiosity. It had always seemed to me that I was living in a mist which restricted me, and the most extreme dissipation had never been able to distract me completely from my desire to know the characteristics of all our surroundings, how we know them, and what we are sure about.[73]

Tracy's studies commenced with the study of nature: the biological and physical sciences. Tracy noted that this emphasis was all the more welcome, under the Jacobin régime, for helping him "forget the history of men".[74] He began with Buffon's vast work on natural history, with its broad evolutionary perspectives, imaginative hypotheses, and detailed classifications.[75] He moved on to the works of Lavoisier and Fourcroy, who were breaking new ground in establishing the methods and nomenclature of modern chemistry.[76] Lavoisier was especially important for Tracy's intellectual development, because Lavoisier claimed to adhere to Condillac's analytical method in his search for the laws governing the combination of the elements in physical nature. "M. de Tracy regarded Lavoisier as a great idéologue, who had perceived most of his discoveries via the chain of his ideas, before confirming them by experience".[77] Tracy himself wrote at this time that:

> Lavoisier led me to Condillac ... I had previously seen only his *Essai sur l'origine des connoissances humaines* ... and had come away without knowing whether I should be satisfied or not with it ... In the prison of Les Carmes, I read all his works, which made me go back to Locke. Taken together they opened my eyes, their conjunction showed me what it was I was seeking. I saw clearly that it was the science of thought (*la science de la pensée*). The *Traité des systèmes* in particular was for me a shaft of light, and, having found the *Traité des sensations* neither complete nor free of errors, I then drew up for myself a short exposition of the main truths which result from the analysis of thought.[78]

According to Mignet, the summary of truths was written on 5 thermidor (23 July 1794), just a few days before Tracy was expected to face the revolutionary tribunal and thence the guillotine; Robespierre, however, was himself overthrown on 9 thermidor and the revolutionary tribunal never pronounced upon Tracy's case. The table of truths took a quasi-algebraic form:

> The product of the faculty of thinking or perceiving = knowledge = truth. In a second treatise on which I am working, I show that three other terms must be added to this equation: = virtue = happiness, sentiment of loving. And in a third work, I will demonstrate that the following must be added: = liberty = equality = philanthropy.
>
> It is for lack of a sufficiently precise analysis that we have not yet managed to find the deductions or mediating propositions needed to make obvious the identity of these ideas. I hope to prove by facts what Locke and Condillac have shown by reasoning, that morality and politics are capable of demonstration.[79]

This strikingly deductivist system of identities provided the germ for a series of papers and volumes written during the following fifteen years, Tracy's most creative period of intellectual activity. Released from prison in October 1794, Tracy returned to his family and friends at Auteuil. Sixteen months later, he had the good fortune to be elected as an associate (non-resident) member of the Class of Moral and Political Sciences in the newly created Institut National. Tracy's nomination on 18 February 1796, to the section entitled *Analyse des sensations et des idées*,[80] was very curious considering that he had not yet published anything in that field. Cabanis, a member of that section, was doubtless responsible for Tracy's election, having inside knowledge of Tracy's work at Auteuil. Cabanis' faith proved justified: two months after his election, Tracy began reading a series of papers in which the concept of idéologie as a fundamental science of ideas was first elaborated.[81] Tracy was also very busy serving on commissions of the Institut responsible for awarding prizes in essay competitions, and investigating ideas put forward by private citizens.[82] Outside the Institut, Tracy helped to edit the literary section of the *Mercure français*, alongside Lenoir-La Roche, Cabanis, Barbier and others (1795-98).[83] He also contributed during the Directory period to the *Moniteur*, to *la Décade philosophique*, and possibly (given Cabanis' involvement) to *le Conservateur*.

Tracy became increasingly involved in educational problems, and eventually was directly involved with the administration of the system of national education established by the law of 3 brumaire an IV (25 October 1795). The Minister of the Interior established a Conseil d'instruction publique in October 1798, composed largely of Tracy's friends at the Institut.[84] Tracy was appointed as a member in February 1799, and drafted a number of circulars designed to improve the quality of teaching in the *écoles centrales* and to standardise the curriculum in accordance with his conceptions of idéologie.[85] He also corresponded privately with a number of teachers sympathetic to his own conception of the "science of ideas", and thereby promoted the diffusion of these doctrines throughout France. By this time, Tracy was confirmed in his new role of *savant* and educator. He had refused Bonaparte's offer of a position as *maréchal-de-camp* in the ill-fated military and scientific expedition to Egypt.[86] Tracy continued to write papers for the Institut on various themes related to idéologie, including criticisms of Kant and of Berkeley.

Tracy also wrote several pamphlets of topical and theoretical interest. The first was an answer to a prize-essay topic "*Quels sont les moyens de fonder la morale chez un peuple?*", offered by the Class of Moral and Political Sciences in 1797 and later withdrawn for lack of response among the literary public. Tracy's answer appeared in three issues of the *Mercure français* in January 1798, and later as a pamphlet. He argued that law and order was of fundamental importance in society, and that wise legislation and education were the keys to instituting public virtue and private happiness.[87] His second pamphlet, an anonymous digest of Charles Dupuis' *l'Origine de Tous les Cultes* (1795), appeared in 1799. Tracy seemed to agree with Dupuis' argument that Christianity was a permutation of prior religious systems, and that all systems of worship of supernatural beings have their origins in worship of the sun and stars.[88] Tracy published a greatly extended second edition of his *Analyse* of Dupuis in 1804, in the midst of the Catholic revival in France.[89] The anonymity of this work was pierced by Napoleon's librarian in 1806, in his *Dictionnaire des ouvrages anonymes*:[90] Barbier and Tracy had worked together ten years earlier on the *Mercure français*.

The final pamphlet to be noted here was a defence of the education system established in 1795, and especially a plea for the retention of the *écoles centrales*. The Consulate government after 1800 had begun an enquiry into the operation of the schools; Tracy's pamphlet, partly based on information obtained from his work on the Conseil d'instruction publique, argued that minor changes could greatly improve the idéologues' educational programme and that drastic reorganisation of the system would be irresponsible.[91] Tracy's plea was ignored: *lycées* came to replace the *écoles centrales*, and all traces of idéologie were removed from the curricula.

Tracy commenced writing in about 1800 a series of philosophical works intended as texts in the *écoles centrales*. This decision was partly a result of his work on the Conseil d'instruction publique, where he became aware of the acute shortage of suitable texts for the new courses in the schools, and partly a fulfilment of his desire, first formulated in 1794, to provide a systematic account of the human understanding in its various manifestations. The first volume in the series, *Projet d'éléments d'idéologie*, appeared in 1801.[92] The second volume on *Grammaire* (1803), and the third volume on *Logique* (1805), completed the first part of the series, devoted to the origin, formation and expression of ideas in general. This third volume was dedicated to his friend Cabanis, whose conversations and whose *Rapports du physique et du moral de l'homme*[93] had guided and inspired Tracy's own studies. Tracy wrote:

> ... the goal that I most desire is that my work might be regarded as a consequence of your own, and that you might see it as a corollary of the principles which you have expounded. Such a result would be extremely advantageous for the science itself (idéologie) which henceforth would be placed on its true foundation: for, if I deserve such praise, the intention of Locke is fulfilled; ... and in accordance with his wish, the detailed history of our intelligence is at last part of and dependent on *la physique humaine*.[94]

In the meantime, the schools and curricula for which these works were written had been abandoned in 1802 by the Consulate government; Tracy's works were read not by students but by the *savants*.

Tracy had intended his three volumes on epistemology and language to form the basis for three further volumes on the moral, economic and political sciences. But works of liberal doctrine could not be published in Napoleonic France owing to the censorship of views critical of the Imperial government. Tracy began to establish closer links with Jefferson in the United

States, who had already met or corresponded with a number of idéologues, and who had been elected in 1802 as a foreign associate member of the Class of Moral and Political Sciences. Tracy sent Jefferson several of his publications, and was subsequently elected a member of the American Philosophical Society in January 1806.[95]

Tracy wrote a critique of Montesquieu in 1806-7 as a basis for his projected volumes on politics and economics. He sent the manuscript of this *Commentaire sur l'Esprit des Lois* to Jefferson in Virginia in June 1809; Jefferson was sufficiently impressed to undertake an English translation, published anonymously as *A Commentary and Review of Montesquieu's Spirit of Laws* (Philadelphia 1811).[96] After writing a manuscript on political economy in 1810-11, Tracy sent it to Jefferson in November 1811, but the translation was seriously delayed and appeared only in 1817 as *A Treatise on Political Economy*.[97] In the meantime, the same work had appeared in France, after the fall of Napoleon, as *Elémens d'idéologie, IV partie, Traité de la Volonté* (Paris 1815). The anonymous manuscript of the *Commentaire* was reprinted in France, apparently without Tracy's permission, in Liège (1817) and Paris (1819). He decided to issue an authorised edition under his own name, which appeared in July 1819.[98] Tracy's volume on *la morale* was never completed. He sketched a few ideas, including a chapter on *l'amour* which was sent to Jefferson for comment in 1821 and had been published in an Italian translation in 1819. Tracy confessed to a certain timidity which prevented him declaring publicly his opinions on such sensitive matters in his own country.[99]

Tracy had re-entered politics, after Bonaparte's *coup* of November 1799, when he was appointed alongside Volney, Cabanis and Garat among the first thirty members of the *Sénat conservateur* on 25 December.[100] It was the Senators who in turn nominated the members of the Tribunate and the Legislative Assembly, and many idéologues were included in these bodies. Having been appointed for life, the Senators did not face the threat of periodic purges which faced their colleagues elsewhere. On the other hand, they had no power to initiate legislative debates or to discuss matters not referred to them by other bodies. They were the "elders" of the Revolution, with high status but little power. Compliance with Bonaparte's wishes was further induced by handsome salaries, and by the creation in 1803 of *sénatoreries*, or revenues from landed estates (none of the idéologues were thus rewarded). The Senate was cajoled into passing a decree on 2 August 1802 proclaiming Bonaparte Consul for Life. This became the pretext for issuing what was really a new Constitution two days later, in which the powers of Bonaparte were greatly extended and the powers of the other legislative bodies were reduced; the epithet *conservateur* was removed from the Senate's title. A further constitutional decree was passed on 18 May 1804 introducing the hereditary principle and, after obtaining approval in a plebiscite, the Empire was proclaimed. The Tribunate was abolished by a further decree in August 1807.[101]

Tracy and his colleagues had long since become silent partners in the growing autocracy, taking little part in the Senate's proceedings or in the pageantry of the Empire. The title of *comte de l'Empire* was bestowed uniformly upon all Senators, even upon Grégoire (who alone had voted against the new nobility in March 1808) and posthumously upon Cabanis (who was granted the title two weeks after his death in May 1808).[102] There was no effective, organised opposition to Bonaparte after 1802, and apart from the theatrical attempted *coups* of General Malet in 1808 and 1812, there was no open rebellion. In December 1813, when a committee of the *Corps législatif*, including Maine de Biran, dared to imply that France would be best served by a policy of peace, their mild protest was met with Imperial rage, and the assembly was dissolved.[103]

The death of Cabanis in May 1808 deprived Tracy of his closest intellectual colleague. Tracy's sense of loss was immense[104] and in some respects he never regained his impetus, for he began to lose his ability to undertake sustained work and he gradually began to lose his eyesight. Tracy was elected on 15 June to fill Cabanis' place in the Classe de langue et de littérature françaises (later the Académie française), and his *discours de réception* on 21 December was an *éloge* of his friend Cabanis.[105] After Cabanis' death, Tracy moved from Auteuil to Paris,[106] where he lived the rest of his life except for visits to his country estates.

Napoleon suffered reverses in March 1814 and the Allied armies occupied Paris. The Senate was invited to appoint a provisional government and draft a new Constitution. Talleyrand organised the Senators to nominate a provisional government of five members (including himself) on 1 April, and Tracy was among the 63 signatories of the Senate's resolution approving this measure.[107] On 2 April, the Senate passed a resolution to remove Napoleon and his family from the throne, and it requested Lambrechts to draft a more detailed resolution for the following day. The Russian Emperor Alexander gave an audience to the Senators, in which he said: "it is just and wise that France be given strong and liberal institutions which are in accord with the present *lumières*. My allies and I only come to protect the liberty of your decisions".[108] The next day, the Senate debated and approved the detailed resolution, drawn up by Lambrechts, specifying the motives for the *déchéance* of Napoleon: fourteen *considérants* were given, listing his infractions against the liberties and good government of the French people.[109] There is some dispute concerning whether Tracy or Lambrechts moved the original resolution to remove Napoleon from office on 2 April. Tracy apparently claimed to friends, including Lafayette, that it was he who had moved the historic decree; if this was the case, it may seem curious that Lambrechts was selected to draw up the detailed resolution for the next meeting. The official reports of proceedings are silent on the matter, noting only that "a member" proposed the *déchéance*.[110]

The provisional government organised informal meetings to consider the general principles for a new constitution; several Senators were invited to attend these meetings. After a preliminary meeting on 3 April, a committee of five Senators (Tracy, Lambrechts, Lebrun, Barbé-Marbois, Emery) was asked to draw up the text of a constitution. The text was debated at these large and informal meetings on 4 and 5 April.[111] It was sent to the Senate where the 29 Articles were referred to a Committee before being passed unanimously. This constitutional project recalled the Bourbons to the throne as if by popular request, rather than by ancient prerogative.[112] The document was seen, however, as extremely self-serving, for the Senators had defended their own positions and revenues as matters of constitutional law (article 6). The royalist party was able to exploit this unpopular aspect of the document, although their main disagreement concerned the Senators' attempt to cast the monarch's authority in terms of social contract theory and national sovereignty. Eventually, in consultation with the provisional government instead of the Senate,[113] Louis XVIII was able to proclaim his own Constitution as a *fait accompli* on 4 June. Its provisions were generally acceptable to the constitutional liberals, despite their dislike for Louis' reassertion of his traditionalist legitimacy.

Tracy was nominated on 6 June a member of the Chambre des Pairs (and retained this position after Napoleon's Hundred Days interrupted the continuity of the restored monarchy). His title of comte was restored on 31 August 1817.[114] Several of his colleagues, however, were excluded from royal favour and thus from official positions: Volney, Garat, Lambrechts, Sieyès, Grégoire. The cynical *Dictionnaire des Girouettes* took to task the political opportunism and vacillations of public figures during the previous decades. Each biographical entry was accompanied by a string of flags indicating how many régimes had been served or accommodated by each subject. Destutt de Tracy received eight "flags". His entry concluded: "M. de Tracy is a quiet person who, while writing brochures to stifle his boredom, allows events to pass by—without, however, forgetting to make use of them to his greatest advantage".[115] The great survivors and opportunists, however, were men like Fouché, Fontanes and Talleyrand who each collected twelve "flags"; together with the Senate ("dit Sénat-Conservateur"), which attracted the particular scorn of the compilers of the *Dictionnaire*.[116]

Tracy attended some of the more important debates in the Chamber, but refused to attend the trial of Marshal Ney.[117] He was more active outside the Chamber, maintaining a distinguished *salon*, frequented by constitutional liberals from the legislature[118] and a variety of young admirers, who included at various times Henri Beyle, Victor Jacquemont, Augustin Thierry, Joseph Rey, and a number of young Academicians including Pierre Flourens. Tracy's only son, Victor (1781-1864), who had resigned from the army in 1818 after many years of active service, entered the lower Chamber in 1822, beginning a political career of some thirty years, mainly among the left-liberal opposition who were attracted to Tracy's *salon*.[119] Tracy was involved with B. Constant, Lafayette and others in establishing a Société des Amis de la Presse in November 1817 to campaign against restrictive censorship.[120] Tracy's four volumes of *Elémens d'idéologie* were reprinted in 1817-18, and again in 1824-25 and 1826-27. Several of his works were translated into Italian, Spanish and German (in addition to the English translations supervised by Jefferson). Through his secretary, Tracy maintained a wide correspondence with several young disciples, and a circle of foreigners who sought his advice on political and other matters.[121] The publication of Tracy's *Commentaire* boosted the liberal cause, and provoked polemical reviews, both flattering[122] and highly critical.[123] Though increasingly given to bouts of melancholy,[124] Tracy made a favourable impression on distinguished visitors, such as David Ricardo in 1822 and Lady Morgan in 1829.[125]

Tracy died in Paris on 9 March 1836, having survived his wife by twelve years. His old friend Daunou, and the young physiologist Flourens (secretary of the Académie des Sciences), delivered *éloges* at his funeral on 12 March. Tracy's place in the Académie française was taken by François Guizot. His place in the section of Philosophy in the Academy of Moral and Political Sciences was taken by J.-P. Damiron[126] (a disciple of Victor Cousin's spiritual eclecticism), whose *Essai sur l'histoire de la philosophie* in 1828 had been severely critical of Tracy and his fellow idéologistes. For Guizot and Damiron, Tracy had been a faithful disciple of eighteenth-century materialism and utilitarianism. But the nineteenth century had, in their opinion, transcended such narrow perspectives, reintegrating the spiritual and the material aspects of human life and thought.

For Daunou and Flourens, on the other hand, Tracy's idéologie pointed the way to a precise knowledge of the human understanding and of economic and political organisation. In Daunou's words, Tracy "devoted his whole life to research into and propagation of those truths which can exercise a happy influence on the intellectual, moral and political habits of peoples".[128] Flourens singled out for special attention Tracy's analytical method:

> ... that instrument of all our progress in every field. It is through it that he (Tracy) has had such a great influence on philosophy, and from there this influence has spread to all the other sciences, which all ultimately draw from philosophy their basic rules; and hence his name, which belongs to two Academies, that of moral and political sciences, and the Académie française, is pronounced with no less respect and acknowledgement in the Academy of physical and mathematical sciences than in the other two.[129]

The partisans and critics of Enlightenment philosophy will always dispute its intellectual value and historical influence. Judgements about Tracy's importance will doubtless be influenced by the observer's position in this debate. Tracy typified a particular strand of late eighteenth-century thought in which reason, truth, liberty and happiness became mutually entwined, as both the means and end of a progressive social and philosophical movement against the forces of ignorance, repression, habit and superstition. In 1798, Tracy wrote: "... la vérité est le seul chemin du bien-être".[130] Tracy's search for fundamental truths about the individual and society, led him back to an enquiry into the operations of the human intellect. The following chapter examines Tracy's quest for a "scientific" understanding of man, together with his concept of idéologie as the key to providing certainty in the human sciences.

Notes

1. Most notably by F. Picavet, whose lengthy study on *Les Idéologues* (Paris, 1891) was the only detailed overview until the recent works of Sergio Moravia and Georges Gusdorf. Other important contributions in the earlier period included J. Simon, *Une Académie sous le Directoire* (Paris, 1885), and A. Guillois, *Le Salon de Mme Helvétius: Cabanis et les Idéologues* (Paris, 1894).
2. For example, G. Chinard, *Jefferson et les Idéologues* (Baltimore, 1925), C.H. Van Duzer, *Contribution of the Idéologues to French Revolutionary Thought* (Baltimore, 1935), and E. Cailliet, *La Tradition littéraire des Idéologues* (Philadelphia, 1943).
3. For example, J.-P. Damiron, *Essai sur l'histoire de la philosophie en France au XIX siècle* (Paris, 1828); A. Franck (ed.), *Dictionnaire des sciences philosophiques* (Paris, 1844-52), articles on "Destutt de Tracy" and "Idéologie".
4. C. Smith, "Destutt de Tracy and the Bankruptcy of Sensationalism", in *Balzac and the Nineteenth Century*, eds. D.G. Charlton, J. Gaudon, A.R. Pugh (Leicester, 1972), pp. 195-207. Contemporary criticisms of *idéologie* are reported below in chapters 2 and 3.
5. M. Foucault, *The Order of Things: An Archaeology of the Human Sciences* (London, 1970). Foucault argued, however, that in the field of medicine and the biological sciences, contemporary figures such as Pinel and Cuvier were pioneers of the modern viewpoint; Cabanis was not specifically evaluated in this context by Foucault.
6. J.N. Shklar, review of K.M. Baker's *Condorcet*, in *Political Theory*, vol. 3 no. 4 (November 1975), pp. 469-474. A more general argument is found in Shklar, *After Utopia: the Decline of Political Faith* (Princeton, 1957).
7. T.S. Kuhn, *The Structure of Scientific Revolutions* (Chicago, 2nd ed. 1970). Cf. S.S. Wolin, "Paradigms and political theories", in *Politics and Experience: Essays presented to Professor Michael Oakeshott*, eds. P.T. King and B.C Parekh (Cambridge, 1968), pp. 125-152; I. Lakatos and A. Musgrave (eds.), *Criticism and the Growth of Knowledge* (Cambridge, 1970).
8. A.N. Whitehead, *Adventures of Ideas* (New York, 1933), p. 159.
9. A. Canivez, "Les Idéologues", in *Histoire de la Philosophie*, tome III (Encyclopédie de la Pléiade, tome XXXVIII) (Paris, 1974), p. 99.
10. "Notice historique sur la vie et les travaux de M. le Comte Destutt de Tracy", in F.-A.-M. Mignet, *Notices et Mémoires historiques* (Paris, 1843), vol. I, pp. 245-288. This essay originally appeared in the *Séances et Travaux* published by the Académie des Sciences morales et politiques, vol. I (1842), pp. 396-434; studies on other idéologues also appeared in this series, and were reprinted in Mignet, *Portraits et Notices historiques et littéraires* (Paris, 2nd ed. 1852).
11. Mme Sarah Newton Destutt de Tracy, "Notice sur M. Destutt de Tracy", first published separately in 1847, and reprinted in *Essais divers, Lettres et Pensées de Madame de Tracy* (Paris, 1852-55), vol. I, pp. 305-404.
12. J. Cruet, *La Philosophie morale et sociale de Destutt de Tracy (1754-1836)* (Tours, 1909).
13. R. Lenoir, "Psychologie et logique de Destutt de Tracy", *Revue philosophique de la France et de l'étranger*, vol. 84 (1917), pp. 527-556; O. Kohler, *Die Logik des Destutt de Tracy* (Borna-Leipzig, 1931); G. Madinier, *Conscience et mouvement* (Paris, 1938), ch. 3; S. Moravia, "Logica e psicologia nel pensiero di D. de Tracy", *Rivista critica di storia della filosofia*, vol. 19 (1964), pp. 169-213.
14. E. Allix, "Destutt de Tracy, économiste", *Revue d'économie politique*, vol. 26 (1912), pp. 424-451.

15. V. Stepanowa, *Destutt de Tracy: eine historisch-psychologishe untersuchung* (Zurich, 1908); P.-M. Imbert, *Destutt de Tracy: Critique de Montesquieu* (Paris, 1974).
16. R.G. Carey, *The Liberals of France and their relation to the development of Bonaparte's dictatorship* (Ph.D. thesis, University of Chicago, 1947); G. Gusdorf, *Introduction aux sciences humaines* (Strasbourg, 1960); J.W. Stein, *The Mind and the Sword* (New York, 1961); S.M. Gruner, *Economic Materialism and Social Moralism* (The Hague, 1973); S. Moravia, *Il tramonto dell'illuminismo* (Bari, 1968); G. Gusdorf, *La Conscience révolutionnaire: les Idéologues* (Paris, 1978).
17. G. Chinard, *Volney et l'Amérique* (Baltimore, 1923); G. Chinard, *Jefferson et les Idéologues* (Baltimore, 1925); D. Echeverria, *Mirage in the West: A History of the French Image of American Society to 1815* (Princeton, 1957).
18. R. Fargher, *The "Décade philosophique" and the defence of philosophy* (D. Phil. thesis, Oxford University, 1940); J. Kitchin, *Un Journal 'philosophique': La Décade* (Paris 1965); M. Régaldo, *Un Milieu intellectuel* (Paris and Lille, 1976).
19. F. Labrousse, *Quelques notes sur un médecin-philosophe, P.-J.-G. Cabanis* (Paris, 1903); M.S. Staum, *Cabanis* (Princeton 1980); J. Gaulmier, *L'idéologue Volney 1757-1820: Contribution à l'histoire de l'Orientalisme en France* (Beyrouth, 1951); P. Bastid, *Sieyès et sa pensée* (Paris, 2nd ed., 1970).
20. These thinkers are discussed by the works cited in footnotes 1,2,10,16,17,18 above.
21. For example, H. Gouhier, *La jeunesse d'Auguste Comte* (Paris, 1933-41).
22. For example, P. Bastid, *Benjamin Constant et sa doctrine* (Paris, 1966); G.E. Gwynne, *Madame de Stael et la Révolution française* (Paris, 1969); F.E. Manuel, *The New World of Henri Saint-Simon* (Notre Dame, 1963); L.A. Siedentop, *The Limits of Enlightenment ... Maine de Biran and Joseph de Maistre* (D. Phil. thesis, Oxford University, 1966); H. Gouhier, *Les Conversions de Maine de Biran* (Paris, 1947).
23. I.F. Knight, *The Geometric Spirit: the abbé de Condillac and the French Enlightenment* (New Haven, 1968); K.M. Baker, *Condorcet: From Natural Philosophy to Social Mathematics* (Chicago, 1975).
24. A.-L.-C. Destutt de Tracy, *A Commentary and Review of Montesquieu's Spirit of Laws* (Philadelphia, 1811) (New York, 1969); Tracy, *A Treatise on Political Economy* (Georgetown, 1817) (New York, 1970); Tracy, *Eléments d'idéologie*, 5 vols. (Paris, 1801-1815) (Stuttgart, 1974); Tracy, *Elémens d'idéologie*, vol. I, *Idéologie proprement dite* (Paris, 1817) and vol. II, *Grammaire* (Paris, 1817) ed. H. Gouhier (Paris, 1970): the later volumes were not reprinted owing to the small demand for the early volumes.
25. P.-J.-G. Cabanis, *Oeuvres philosophiques*, ed. C. Lehec and J. Cazeneuve (Paris, 1956).
26. S. Moravia, *Il pensiero degli idéologues* (Firenze, 1974).
27. In 1973, when I began the present research, there had been no intellectual biography of Tracy since Picavet (1891) and Cruet (1909). It transpired that several students were working independently on Tracy in the 1970s. Dr Barry Garnham's unpublished account of Tracy's thought (B.G. Garnham, *The Social, Moral and Political Thought of Destutt de Tracy*, Ph.D. thesis, University of Durham, 1974) has dealt with some of the same questions as my own study, and there would be general agreement with his view that Tracy's approach was based more on deduction than observation. However, Garnham says little about Tracy's liberalism, and virtually nothing about Tracy's notions of science and social science. A major recent publication by Dr Emmet Kennedy (R.E. Kennedy, *A Philosophe in the Age of Revolution: Destutt de Tracy and the origins of 'Ideology'*, Philadelphia, 1978) has provided a wealth of detail about Tracy's life and times. The book is organised in a strictly chronological structure, seeking to unite the discussion of Tracy's life, writings, and milieu. In its fine detail and use of unpublished sources, it is sure to become the standard *biography* of Tracy. As a discussion of Tracy the *theorist*, it lacks thematic unity and overlaps only slightly with my own work. My own dissertation was completed in 1979: B.W. Head, *The Political and Philosophical Thought of Destutt de Tracy* (Ph.D. thesis, University of London).
28. B.W. Head, "The origins of 'idéologue' and 'idéologie'", *Studies on Voltaire and the Eighteenth Century*, vol. 183 (1980), pp. 257-264.

29. The theory of *industrialisme* was developed by Saint-Simon in 1817-20 during the Restoration (though his theory of the importance of *savants* and *productifs* is considerably earlier); Tracy's ideas on political economy were written in 1806-11 though not published in French before 1815. Both men were working in the economic tradition marked out by the major works of Smith (1776), Sieyès (1789) and Say (1803), as will be established in chapter seven below.
30. Saint-Simon's proposal for a European confederation dates from 1814; Tracy's idea was sketched in 1806, but published in French only after the Restoration.
31. F.A. von Hayek, *The Counter-Revolution of Science* (Glencoe, 1955), p. 115.
32. Unfortunately, the date of birth is misreported as 1762 by M. Leroy, *Histoire des idées sociales* (Paris, 1946-54), II, p. 167, and by M. Prélot, *Histoire des idées politiques* (Paris, 1961), p. 435. Most biographies correctly give Paris as the birthplace. However, the *Biographie universelle et portative*, ed. Rabbe (Paris, 1834), IV, p. 1435, and the *Nouvelle Biographie générale*, ed. Hoefer (Paris, 1853-66), XLV, col. 562, stated that Tracy was born "in the Bourbonnais", that is, at the family château of Paray-le-Frésil outside Moulins. This information was accepted by G. Rougeron, *A.-L.-C. Destutt de Tracy ...* (Montluçon, 1966), p. 4; by H. Gouhier, "Introduction historique" to Tracy, *Elémens d'idéologie*, vol. I (1817; reprint Paris, 1970), p. 5 (with reservations); and by S. Moravia, *Il pensiero degli idéologues*, p. 319. The correct information was given by F. Potiquet, *l'Institut National de France* (Paris, 1871), p. 34; F. Picavet, "Destutt de Tracy", *La Grande Encyclopédie* (Paris 1887-1902), XIV, p. 297; L. de Brotonne, *Les Sénateurs du Consulat et de l'Empire* (Paris, 1895), p. 4; *Biographie Universelle*, ed. Michaud (Paris, n.d.), XLII, p. 77; *Dictionnaire historique et biographique*, ed. Robinet (Paris, 1899), II, p. 790; *Dictionnaire de Biographie française*, ed. Balteau (Paris, 1967), XI, col. 116; E. Kennedy, *A Philosophe in the Age of Revolution*, p.1.
33. F.-A.-A. de La Chesnaye des Bois, *Dictionnaire de la noblesse* (Paris, 1770-86), vol. VI, pp. 201-203, vol. XV, pp. 282f.; F. Michel, *Les écossais en France ...* (London, 1862), I, p. 254.
34. Mignet, "Notice historique sur ... Destutt de Tracy", *Notices et Mémoires historiques* (Paris, 1843), vol. I, p. 247. The death of the marquis de Tracy has been variously estimated at 1761 (when Antoine was less than eight years old) and 1766 (when the boy was at least twelve years).
35. A. Sorel, *Europe and the French Revolution* (London, 1969), p. 188.
36. Louis de Narbonne, his lifelong friend, Minister for War at the end of 1791, and a companion of Mme de Stael. Louis-Philippe de Ségur, who replied to Tracy's *discours de réception* in 1808 on his entry to the Classe de langue et de littérature françaises (later renamed the Académie française). Cf. L. Apt, *Louis-Philippe de Ségur: an intellectual in a revolutionary age* (The Hague, 1969). Charles-Maurice de Talleyrand-Périgord, diplomat and politician, who was influential in almost every régime in France from 1789-1815. Cf. J. Orieux, *Talleyrand, ou le sphinx incompris* (Paris, 1971).
37. Lafayette, *Mémoires* (Paris, 1837-8), III, pp. 276ff; M. Reinhard, "Elite et noblesse dans la seconde moitié du XVIII siècle", *Revue d'histoire moderne et contemporain*, vol. 3 (1956), pp. 5-37; E.-G. Léonard, "La question sociale dans l'armée française au XVIII siècle", *Annales: économies, sociétés, civilisations,* vol. 3 (1948), pp. 135-149; J. McManners, "France", in *The European Nobility in the Eighteenth Century*, ed. A. Goodwin (London, 1967), pp. 22-42.
38. Mignet, "Notice historique sur ... Destutt de Tracy", p. 250. The estate of Paray-le-Frésil itself amounted to 3,600 hectares in the Restoration period, according to the *Dictionnaire de Biographie française*, ed. Balteau, vol. XI, col. 118 (on Tracy's son, Victor).
39. However, see the following remarks by Tracy, cited in J.-P.-M. Flourens, *Discours prononcé aux funérailles de M. le comte Destutt de Tracy ...* (Paris, 1836), p.11: "I was in that period immediately following the end of one's education, and, having no more very important duties to fill in the career I had undertaken, I could leave myself without scruple to my meditations and to the researches towards which my inclination led me. I devoted myself, then, to considering my fellow men in all times and countries, and to

seeking the causes of the most important phenomena such as they offer to the eye of the observer". Tracy's early years have not been well documented, mainly because Tracy's private papers have largely been lost or destroyed. The Cabanis-Tracy correspondence, cited by Guillois, has not come to light. Other collections of correspondence have been disappointingly thin for the understanding of Tracy's theoretical work, with the exception of the letters reprinted in Maine de Biran, *Oeuvres philosophiques*, ed. P. Tisserand (Paris, 1920-), vols. VI and VII. For the best discussion of Tracy's early years, see E. Kennedy, *A Philosophe in the Age of Revolution*, ch. 1.

40. Some of Tracy's biographers seem to have regarded this visit to Voltaire, when Tracy was only sixteen years, as something akin to an intellectual baptism: Mignet, "Notice historique sur ... Destutt de Tracy", pp. 249-250; Mme de Tracy, "Notice sur M. Destutt de Tracy", p. 307 (and also pp. 397-99 for Tracy's defence of Voltaire in the Restoration years); G. Rougeron, *A.-L.-C. Destutt de Tracy*, p. 4. The pilgrimage to visit Voltaire was an enterprise common to many young men of the times. Tracy used to call Voltaire "le héros de la raison humaine": Flourens, *Discours prononcé aux funérailles de ... Tracy*, p. 10, and Mignet, *op.cit.*, p. 284. For one of Tracy's comments in praise of Voltaire, cf. *Logique* (1805), p. 137n.
41. Picavet, "Destutt de Tracy", claimed that Tracy might have come across Kant's philosophy at Strasbourg. In his book *Les Idéologues* (Paris, 1891), Picavet further suggested that Professor Muller discussed Kant and Hume with his students, and that Tracy probably became familiar with Kantian ideas through conversation or through reading the Latin editions of Kant (p. 295). (Cabanis, however, who was able to read German, was definitely familiar with the work of German *savants*.) J.W. Stein, reinterpreting Picavet, asserted that Tracy became familiar with Kant and Hume at Strasbourg, and developed "a respect for thinkers whose theories he later contested" (*The Mind and the Sword*, p. 21). For a broader view of the reception of German literature and philosophy in France, cf. L. Reynaud, *L'influence allemande en France au XVIII et au XIX siècle* (Paris, 1922). As for Hume, it appears that he was far better known in France as an historian than as a philosopher of mind; and even in the latter role he was seen as analysing the "association of ideas" rather than as urging a suspension of belief in "laws".
42. Cf. L. Apt, *Louis-Philippe de Ségur*, chapter 2; Lafayette, *Mémoires*, vol. I. Tracy made frequent reference to American experiences in constitution-making in his *Commentaire*.
43. J. Cornillon, *Le Bourbonnais sous la Révolution française*, vol. I (Vichy, 1888), p. 5.
44. *Ibid.*, pp. 8-40.
45. *Ibid.*, pp. 41-48.
46. *Ibid.*, pp. 49-52.
47. For example, Section I of the *cahier* demanded the concurrence of King and Etats-généraux in all laws (article 3), habeas corpus (article 4), Ministerial responsibility (article 6), liberty of the press (article 11); section II demanded the suppression of certain unpopular taxes (articles 10-13) and reform of public finances; and section III urged the improvement of public education as the best way to "increase the citizens useful to the country" (article 6). Cf. *Cahier de l'Ordre de la Noblesse du Bourbonnais* ... (1789); also reprinted in Cornillon, *op.cit.*, I, pp. 233-243, and in *Archives parlementaires*, première série, vol. II, p. 442 ff.
48. For example, *Dictionnaire de Biographie française*, ed. Balteau, XI, col. 116; *Dictionnaire historique et biographique*, ed. Robinet, II, p. 790; *Biographie universelle*, ed. Michaud, XLII, p. 78; J. Cornillon, *Le Bourbonnais*, I, p. 118.
49. Tracy is absent from the list of signatories to the "serment du jeu de paume" of 20 June, in *Archives parlementaires*, vol. 8, pp. 138-141 and 659-660, and from the list of 47 nobles who were present in the National Assembly on 25 June (*ibid.*, p. 154).
50. F. Picavet, *Les Idéologues*, p. 298; L. Biernawski, *Un département sous la Révolution française: l'Allier* ... (Moulins, 1909), pp. 137-8; Mignet, "Notice historique sur ... Destutt de Tracy", p. 250.
51. On 30 March 1790, Tracy explained that he belonged to no committee of the Assembly because he valued his independence and because he was already very busy as an indepen-

dent: *Archives parlementaires*, vol. XII, p. 443. Subsequently, he served for ten weeks on the Comité des Rapports created in July 1790 (*ibid.*, XXXII, p. 562); and for seven days on the Comité des Colonies in August 1791 (*ibid.*, p. 548) before resigning in disgust, when his argument in favour of the coloured population of the colonies was rejected by the Comité (*ibid.*, XXX, p. 55).

52. One of his early tasks was to serve on a commission of the Assembly in January 1790, to establish the boundaries of the new Department of l'Allier; Moulins was chosen as the capital. Cf. L. Biernawski, *Un département*, pp. 52-69; P. Flament, "Introduction", *Inventaire sommaire des Archives Départementales postérieures à 1790*, ed. F. Claudon and P. Flament, Allier: série L, vol. I (Moulins, 1912), pp. i-ii.
53. *M. de Tracy à M. Burke* (Paris, 1790), a speech of 3 April, rewritten on 26 April.
54. *Opinion de M. de Tracy sur les affaires de Saint-Domingue, en Septembre 1791* (Paris, 1791). See also Tracy's speeches on the same subject in *Archives parlementaires*, XXV, pp. 642-43, 750; XXVI, p. 25; XXVII, p. 214; XXIX, p. 627; XXXI, pp. 259-263. The subject of the rights of coloured residents of the colonies became Tracy's major contribution to the debates in the Assembly. It was the Convention Nationale in 1793-94 which finally voted the suppression of slavery. Bonaparte's reintroduction of policies of colonial annexation and slavery deeply wounded Tracy's sensibilities. In his *Commentaire sur l'Esprit des Lois*, written 1806, Tracy insisted that colonies should be freed as rapidly as practicable: (Paris, 1819), p. 136.
55. Tracy strongly denied any link with the Amis des Noirs, in his speech on *Saint-Domingue*, p. 2. Most Enlightenment thinkers were hostile towards discrimination on 'racial' grounds. However, an interesting exception was Saint-Simon, whose unpublished manuscripts show he was persuaded of the inferiority of blacks on the grounds that their cranial dimensions were smaller. He deduced an inequality of political rights from an alleged physiological difference. (I owe this information to Dr John Hooper.)
56. The *Société de 1789*, a club of *savants*, officials and businessmen, is discussed in more detail by S. Moravia, *Il tramonto*, pp. 152-161, and K.M. Baker, "Politics and Social Science in Eighteenth-Century France: the 'Société de 1789'", in *French Government and Society*, ed. J.F. Bosher (London, 1973), pp. 208-230. The membership list is reprinted in J.-B. Challamel, *Les Clubs contre-révolutionnaires* (Paris, 1895), pp. 400-414 (Tracy's name appears on p. 413). Condorcet and Sieyès later joined the Jacobins when the Société de 1789 collapsed.
57. Challamel, *Les Clubs contre-révolutionnaires*, gives membership lists for the Club des Feuillants, p. 286 ff. (Tracy's name appears on page 302; circumstantial evidence suggests that he joined between July-September 1791). G. Michon, *Essai sur l'histoire du parti feuillant, Adrien Duport* (Paris, 1924), p. 323, cites Tracy as participating in a discussion at the Feuillants.
58. Cf. Lafayette, *Mémoires*, IV, p. 4.
59. J. Cornillon, *Le Bourbonnais*, I, p. 120.
60. *Ibid.*, II, p. 109.
61. *Archives parlementaires*, XXVII, p. 391; cf. p. 547.
62. *Commentaire* (1806) (Paris, 1819), pp. 167-8.
63. *Archives parlementaires*, XXIV, p. 622 (7 April 1791); *Commentaire*, pp. 168-9.
64. G. Rougeron, *A.-L.-C. Destutt de Tracy*, p. 6; *Inventaire sommaire des Archives départementales*, ed. F. Claudon and P. Flament, I, pp. 37-48. Tracy's picturesque address of 1 December 1791, closing the current session of the administrative Council, is reprinted at pp. 47-8.
65. Lafayette, *Mémoires*, III, pp. 291-384.
66. For example: (Anonymous), *Biographie des Quarante de l'Académie française* (Paris, 1826), pp. 102-3 (where Tracy follows Lafayette into Austrian-held territory and both are captured); P. Simon, *L'élaboration de la Charte Constitutionnelle de 1814* (Paris, 1906), p. 205 n.1 (where Tracy deserted the army alongside Lafayette).
67. Lafayette, *Mémoires*, III, pp. 402-5, 490-1.
68. After the abolition of noble titles, the comte de Tracy became the *citoyen* Destutt-Tracy.

69. *Civisme* (like its opposite, *incivisme*) was coined during the early years of the Revolution to denote appropriate sentiments for the citizen who cheerfully performs his duties: cf. F. Brunot, *Histoire de la langue française ...*, tome IX, Part II, pp. 666-7; (Anon.), *Dictionnaire de la Constitution française* (Paris, 1791), p. 75; *Dictionnaire de l'Académie française* (Paris, an X-1802), I, p. 291. Under the Jacobin régime the need to demonstrate one's *civisme* was increasingly identified with support for current policies, and became part of an inquisitorial procedure of popular committees.
70. Cf. R. Cobb, *Paris and its Provinces 1792-1802* (Oxford, 1975), who points out that Auteuil was regarded as an area of suspect loyalties during the Jacobin period (pp. 119, 137-8).
71. F. Picavet, *Les Idéologues*, p. 302; L. Biernawski, *Un département*, p. 139; G. Rougeron cites the report of the Moulins *comité de surveillance*, in *op.cit.*, p. 7.
72. A. Guillois, *Le Salon de Mme Helvétius*, p. 90; Mignet. "Notice historique sur ... Destutt de Tracy", pp. 257-8.
73. Cited in Mignet, "Notice historique sur ... Destutt de Tracy", p. 254.
74. *Ibid.*, p. 255.
75. Cf. G.-L. Buffon, *Oeuvres philosophiques*, ed. J. Piveteau (Paris, 1954).
76. Mignet, *op.cit.*, pp. 255-6.
77. Mme de Tracy, "Notice sur M. Destutt de Tracy", p. 314.
78. Cited in Mignet, "Notice historique sur ... Destutt de Tracy", p. 262.
79. Cited, *ibid.*, p. 266n; repeated in Picavet, *Les Idéologues*, p. 303.
80. Potiquet, *L'Institut national*, p. 34.
81. Tracy, "Mémoire sur la faculté de penser", in *Mémoires de l'Institut National, Classe des Sciences morales et politiques*, vol. I (1798), pp. 283-450.
82. For example, Tracy in 1802 wrote the report awarding the prize on the question of the influence of habit upon thinking to Maine de Biran; earlier, he had assisted in investigating various linguistic systems which claimed to help in perfecting a "universal" language, such as *pasigraphie*. On the problems caused by the large workload for members, see J. Simon, *Une Académie sous le Directoire*, pp. 108-9.
83. A.-A. Barbier, *Dictionnaire des ouvrages anonymes et pseudonymes ...* (Paris, 1806-1808), vol. II, p. 69, item 4500; E. Hatin, *Bibliographie historique et critique de la presse périodique française* (Paris, 1866), p. 26.
84. Cf. A. Duruy, *L'instruction publique et la Révolution* (Paris, 1882), pp. 241n, 266-7.
85. Tracy's letter of appointment, and the text of the circulars, are reprinted in his *Elémens d'idéologie*, 5 vols. (Paris, 1824-26), IV, pp. 265ff, and *ibid.* (Bruxelles, 1826-27), IV, pp. 259ff.
86. Cf. Mignet, "Notice historique sur ... Destutt de Tracy", p. 269. On the Egyptian expedition, cf. H. Blet, *Histoire de la colonisation française* (Paris, 1946-50), vol. II, pp. 28-32; C. Herold, *Bonaparte in Egypt* (London, 1963).
87. Tracy, "Quels sont les moyens de fonder la morale chez un peuple?" (Paris, an VI) (1798), also reprinted as appendix, pp. 435-477, in *Commentaire sur l'Esprit des lois* (Paris, 1819).
88. (Tracy), *Analyse de l'origine de tous les cultes ...* (Paris, an VII) (1799).
89. (Tracy), *Analyse raisonnée de "l'Origine de tous les Cultes ou Religion universelle"* (Paris, an XIII-1804).
90. A.-A. Barbier, *op.cit.*, vol. III, p. 10, item 9165.
91. Tracy, *Observations sur le système actuel d'instruction publique* (Paris, an IX) (1801).
92. It had a second edition in 1804, entitled *Elémens d'idéologie, vol. I: Idéologie proprement dite.*
93. Large parts of this work were originally read as a series of papers at the Institut in 1796-97 and published in the first two volumes of the *Mémoires* of the Class of Moral and Political Sciences. The complete work was published in 1802. Tracy contributed a lengthy summary (Table analytique) for the second edition in 1805.
94. Tracy, *Logique* (1805), p. viii.
95. Cf. G. Chinard, *Jefferson et les idéologues*, pp. 13-15, 20-30; for Tracy's first exchange of

letters and subsequent election, see pp. 35-41.

96. *Ibid.*, pp. 42-85.
97. *Ibid.*, p. 86, and chapter 3 (pp. 97-188).
98. Chinard wrongly reported that the only French edition of the *Commentaire* was in 1817 (*ibid.*, p. 45). Tracy complained in the *Avertissement* to his edition of July 1819 that an "inexact copy" had been printed in Liège and reprinted in Paris, without his permission (p. v).
99. Tracy, *De l'amour* (Paris, 1926), translated from the Italian edition of 1819 by G. Chinard. See Chinard's "Introduction", pp. i-vi, and *Jefferson et les idéologues*, chapter 4.
100. L. de Brotonne, *Les Sénateurs du Consulat et de l'Empire*, pp.2-9.
101. J. Godechot, *Les Constitutions de la France depuis 1789* (Paris, 1970), chapters 4-6.
102. C. Lehec, "Introduction" to Cabanis, *Oeuvres philosophiques* (Paris, 1956), vol. I, p. xix.
103. L. de Villefosse and J. Bouissounouse, *L'Opposition à Napoléon* (Paris, 1969), pp. 320-1.
104. See Tracy's letter of 17 August in Maine de Biran, *Oeuvres philosophiques*, ed. P. Tisserand (Paris, 1930), vol. VII, p. 346: "Ma pauvre tête m'a abandonné avec mon bonheur et ma santé. Je me sens vraiment comme aliéné". The first Malet affair coincided with this grief.
105. Tracy, *Discours ... pour la réception de M. de Tracy, ... 21 décembre 1808* (Paris, 1808). Tracy had unsuccessfully contested a vacancy in the same Class in 1803: see J.F. Reichardt, *Un hiver à Paris sous le Consulat, 1802-1803*, ed. A. Laquiante (Paris, 1896), p. 402 n.2. Tracy had obviously felt slighted when he had been appointed in January 1803 as a corresponding member of the Classe de l'histoire et de littérature anciennes, after the reorganisation of the Institut.
106. Tracy, letter of 15 November 1809, in Maine de Biran, *op.cit.*, VII, p. 352.
107. *Le Moniteur universel*, 2 April 1814, p. 365.
108. *Ibid.*, 3 April 1814, p. 367.
109. *Ibid.*, 4 April 1814, p. 369.
110. The evidence is weighed up in B.W. Head, *The Political and Philosophical Thought of Destutt de Tracy*, pp. 435-6.
111. J. de Soto, "La Constitution Sénatoriale du 6 avril 1814", *Revue internationale d'histoire politique et constitutionnelle*, no. 12 (1953), p. 279; P. Duvergier de Hauranne, *Histoire du gouvernement parlementaire en France 1814-1848* (Paris, 1857-72), vol. II, p. 95; C. Viel-Castel, *Histoire de la Restauration* (Paris, 1860-77), vol. I, p. 241; C.-J.-M. Lambrechts, *Principes politiques ...* (Paris, 1815), pp. 3, 88-89; P. Simon, *L'élaboration de la Charte Constitutionnelle* (Paris, 1906), p. 28ff.; J. Thiry, *Le Sénat de Napoléon*, pp. 330-346; J.-D. Lanjuinais, *Oeuvres* (Paris, 1832), vol. II, pp. 68-69. Lambrechts, *op.cit.*, p. 89, reported that Tracy missed the discussion on 5 April because of a confusion about the time of the meeting.
112. The text of the Senators' constitution appeared in the *Moniteur universel*, 8 April 1814, p. 385.
113. Tracy in May 1814 expressed annoyance with the Senate for allowing itself to be excluded from these negotiations. He also expressed his fear lest the Bourbons should bring about their own downfall just as the Stuarts had done: a possibility made more likely by the foreign occupation and by the fact that "Cromwell" (i.e. Napoleon) was still alive. (Letter to Maine de Biran, *op.cit.*, VII, p. 365.)
114. *Nouvelle biographie générale*, ed. Hoefer, XLV, col. 563.
115. (C. de Proisy d'Eppe), *Dictionnaire des Girouettes ...* (Paris, 3rd ed. 1815), p. 142.
116. *Ibid.*, pp. 182-193, 446-451, 462-466.
117. *Nouvelle biographie générale*, ed. Hoefer, XLV, col. 563; also (Anon.), *Biographie des Quarante de l'Académie française*, p. 104.
118. Cf. A.-L.-V.-C. Broglie, *Souvenirs* (Paris, 1886), vol. I, p. 264; G. Weill, *Histoire du parti républicain* (Paris, 1900), chapter 1.
119. Cf. *Dictionnaire de Biographie française*, ed. Balteau, XI, col. 118.
120. C. Rémusat, *Mémoires* (Paris, 1958), vol. I, p. 388n; Broglie, *Souvenirs*, vol. II, p. 82.

121. Mme de Tracy, "Notice sur M. Destutt de Tracy", pp. 330, 393; E. Kennedy, *A Philosophe in the Age of Revolution*, ch. 8.
122. For example, Thierry's review of the (anonymous) unauthorised 1817 edition, in *Le Censeur européen*, vol. VII (1818), pp. 191-260.
123. Cf. P.-M. Imbert, *Destutt de Tracy, Critique de Montesquieu* (Paris, 1974), pp. 175-76, citing the *Journal des Débats*, 1822. The *Commentaire* was reprinted several times in the 1820s.
124. Cf. P. Maes, *Un ami de Stendhal, Victor Jacquemont* (Paris, n.d. (1953)), p. 306; Mme de Tracy, "Notice sur M. Destutt de Tracy", p. 402.
125. D. Ricardo, *Works and Correspondence*, ed. P. Sraffa (Cambridge, 1962), vol. IX, p. 248: letter to Malthus, 16 December 1822. Lady Morgan, *France in 1829-30* (London, 1830), vol. I, pp. 133-146: "The Count de Tracy".
126. Guizot was elected on 28 April 1836; Damiron was elected on 17 December 1836: Potiquet, *l'Institut National*, pp. 170, 404.
127. Guizot, *Discours ... pour la réception de M. Guizot* (Paris, 1836), pp. 9-11, 15; Damiron, *Essai* (3rd ed. 1829), pp. 77-90 and *passim*.
128. P.-C.-F. Daunou, *Discours prononcé aux funérailles de M. le comte Destutt de Tracy* (Paris, 1836), p. 5.
129. Flourens, *Discours*, p. 13.
130. "Quels sont les moyens de fonder la morale chez un peuple?", reprinted in Tracy's *Commentaire* (Paris, 1819), p. 456.

2. SCIENTIFIC METHOD AND IDEOLOGY

Tracy constantly professed his faith in the importance of facts, observations and rigorous scientific method, and yet his writings often have the appearance of rationalist deduction from basic principles. In exploring this paradox or tension in his work, it is necessary to consider the images of scientific method and scientific laws which were part of Tracy's intellectual borrowings. Why did he believe that methods of observation, analysis, and the search for general causal explanations, were the key to attaining certain or reliable knowledge? What kinds of ideas were to be excluded from the realm of positive knowledge? What was the proper starting-point for reaching a scientific understanding of man and society? Could the models derived from mechanics, optics, astronomy, and the biological sciences be applied directly to the study of man? These and similar questions are the concern of this chapter.

SCIENCE AND CERTAINTY

Enormous intellectual excitement had been generated among *savants* in the eighteenth century by the scientific advances in the natural sciences. It was commonly believed that a revolution in the understanding of nature had commenced after 1600, and that a vast range of useful technological applications of theoretical discoveries were following in the wake of the new outlook. Tracy's remarks on some of the major figures in this confrontation between the moderns and ancients, throws a great deal of light on his conceptions of science and idéologie, and appropriate methods for attaining certainty. The writings of Bacon, Descartes, Newton and Lavoisier, contributed in various ways to Tracy's understanding of science and method. (Condillac, another writer of enormous importance for Tracy, will be considered in the following section.)

Francis Bacon was regarded by Tracy as the first *savant* to insist on experimental and observational methods, as part of his rejection of scholastic philosophy. The *Novum Organum* (1620) was seen as a call for a new starting-point in the search for knowledge of nature and of man. The programme announced by that work had a beneficial effect in encouraging the adoption of experimental approaches, and the rejection of hypotheses founded only on custom and authority. Tracy regarded Bacon's work as so important that he placed a twenty-five page summary of the whole *Instau-*

ratio Magna as an appendix to his own volume on *Logique* in 1805.[1] Moreover, in the historical introduction to his *Logique*, Tracy included a very lengthy discussion in praise of Bacon's views.

No progress had been made after Aristotle in the science of human understanding, wrote Tracy, until the works of Bacon. All the scholastic philosophers had merely spun variations of Aristotle's mode of reasoning.[2] "Profound habits of un-reason" had been implanted, and it was Bacon who first had the "admirable and sublime" idea of our need for a *novum organum*, by which to "re-make entirely the human mind, begin all the sciences again, and submit to a new examination the whole of our acquired knowledge, or what we believed we had acquired under the old so-called *organum*". Bacon's call for a new paradigm, based on observation and experience as the foundation of knowledge, was a "decisive" and "unique" step in human history.[3] There followed, in Tracy's exposition, a discourse of six pages where Bacon was made to express "some ideological and logical principles with more precision than he actually managed".[4] Among the ideas attributed to Bacon are the following elements of idéologie:

> But nature does not present us with general principles: it only offers us facts, impressions we receive, and from which we then draw consequences. These so-called first principles, maxims ... are then already products of human art, creations of our intellect. It is first necessary, then, to go back to their elements ...
>
> ... in this world, you never do anything but see facts and draw consequences from them, receive impressions and notice their circumstances; in a word, sensing and deducing (which is still a form of sensing). These are your only means of instruction, the only sources of all the truths you can ever acquire ... Observation and experience to gather materials, deduction to elaborate them: these are the only good intellectual mechanisms (*machines*). Leave all the others to the pedants and charlatans ...[5]

Tracy clearly identified his own idéologie with the Baconian project of renovating the understanding of man and nature. Bacon's *Novum Organum*, he wrote, had the same objective as his own logic of the sciences, namely, "to show the human intellect the road to be taken to increase its knowledge, and to teach it a sure method of reaching the truth".[6] However, Tracy criticised Bacon's classification of the sciences, his inability to break completely from the natural science assumptions of his day, his approach to seeking out the laws of nature, and his failure to describe accurately the properties and operations of our intellectual faculties.[7] Bacon had pointed the way towards a new and more adequate manner of achieving certain knowledge, upon which the practical arts could safely depend. He was a prophet of a scientific technology. But he had not been able, in his own work, to give a positive content to the new sciences, nor to provide what for Tracy was of fundamental importance: a satisfactory theory of the formation and expression of ideas.

For Tracy and his colleagues, Descartes was also one of the founding fathers of the new scientific outlook. The radical doubt upon which he based his philosophy demanded a new starting-point for certain knowledge, locating it in self-knowledge. The quest for certainty, and the clear rejection of tradition and speculation as a basis for knowledge, were important aspects of the Cartesian heritage. On the other hand, Descartes' rationalist image of the physical universe as an ordered and integrated whole, based on matter and motion, was also very influential: images of the animal-machine, and of the universe as a clockwork mechanism, both found their inspiration in Descartes. He had argued for the unity of the natural sciences, and made mathematics a universal model.[8]

Tracy, however, was mainly concerned with Descartes' contribution to the scientific principles of observational method. Descartes' modest *Discourse on method* (1637), wrote Tracy, had independently developed all the important insights of Bacon's long and complex work, and with greater clarity and simplicity.[9] Moreover, Descartes had made two important additional contributions. First, he had distilled his method into four principles of general application (briefly: insistence on clear and distinct ideas, decomposition of concepts into constituent parts, production of reliable knowledge by proceeding from simple objects to the most complex, and constant reviews of each stage in the chain of thought).[10] Secondly, Descartes had claimed that the first object of our examination should be the intellectual faculties by which we gain all our knowledge, and that the first thing of which we are certain is our own existence.

The phrase *je pense donc je suis*, wrote Tracy, is the most profound utterance, and is "the only true starting-point for all reasonable philosophy".[11] Yet Descartes should have said, more exactly: *je sens, donc j'existe.*[12] This formula, according to Tracy, would have saved Descartes from many of the errors into which he subsequently lapsed in assuming that thought and extension were two utterly different substances, were mutually exclusive. Descartes' rash assumption in separating thought and extension led directly to the hypotheses of innate ideas, on the one hand, and the impossibility of a void in space, on the other. These false doctrines, said Tracy, since disproved by Locke and Newton respectively, could only have arisen from Descartes' failing to follow carefully his own rules of procedure.[13] A more cautious attention to the facts, to the operation of our intellectual faculties, would have shown Descartes that "thinking and existing are ... one and the same thing" for the thinking subject.[14] Nevertheless, added Tracy, it took a genius to be the first to perceive that all our certitudes derive from the "original fact" that we are sure of our own existence.

> By this sublime conception, he (Descartes) replaced all of *la science humaine* on its true and fundamental basis. Therein lies the germ of the true and total renovation desired by Bacon. Bacon said: everything consists of facts deriving from one another, it is necessary to study the facts; and Descartes found the first fact from which all the others are derived.[15]

This alludes to another aspect of Descartes' approach which deserves attention for a full understanding of Tracy's thought: namely, his deductivism. The passage by Descartes which immediately follows the four principles in the *Discourse* illustrates this point:

> These long chains of reasonings, quite simple and easy, which geometers are accustomed to using to teach their most difficult demonstrations, had given me cause to imagine that everything which can be encompassed by man's knowledge is linked in the same way, and that, provided only that one abstains from accepting any for true which is not true, and that one always keeps the right order for one thing to be deduced from that which precedes it, there can be nothing so distant that one does not reach it eventually, or so hidden that one cannot discover it.[16]

Tracy's adoption of this conception that knowledge is reducible to an analytico-deductive schema, is a fundamental characteristic of his thought, as will be shown in more depth when the concept of idéologie is examined. Tracy's borrowings from Condillac have usually been taken as his primary intellectual debt; it is arguable, however, that what Tracy extracted from Condillac, at least in regard to the essentials of *method*, had already been said by Descartes.[17]

Newton, more than any other figure, had become a symbol for the substantive progress of the natural sciences. Where Bacon had merely announced a programme of research, and Descartes had refined the statement of methods (after having made some positive investigations of his own), Newton had achieved a grand mathematised synthesis of the physical laws governing the phenomena of astronomy and mechanics, propounding as his basic principle the attraction of objects in proportion to their mass. According to Tracy, Newton was the great theoretical systematiser of previous empirical research, the man who was able to demonstrate that all the facts, now and in the future, followed the patterns specified by a few simple laws.[18] Newton symbolised what could be achieved by a systematic science of nature, but curiously there is no evidence that Tracy ever tackled Newton's *Principia* or *Opticks* in any detailed manner. Tracy was quite familiar with Newton's place in the development of modern astronomy, mechanics and optics: for example, he had certainly read the summaries and commentaries by Voltaire,[19] Bailly,[20] and Condorcet,[21] and probably several others. Newton's influence on Tracy remained diffuse and indirect.

The heritage of Newton, however, was by no means clear-cut. Some championed Newton by stressing his differences from Cartesianism (where Newton was seen as an empiricist and inductivist, and Descartes, or at least his disciples, was represented as an *a priori* metaphysician). Others found Newton too abstractly mathematical and too close to the old deism; they advocated a greater emphasis in scientific research on direct experimentation with the materials provided by nature.[22] Newton was harnessed to competing, or at least complementary, views of science. Part of the explanation for this may be that Newton's *Opticks* and most of his methodological pronouncements tended to place him as a prudent empiricist, wary of hypotheses and closely guided by experimentation; whereas his *Principia* provided a vast synthesis of the laws governing matter in motion,[23] a theoretical picture of the world which appeared not inconsistent with aspects of Cartesian rationalism.

What Tracy understood by Newtonian science is best illustrated in some relevant remarks made by J.-S. Bailly, in his historical discussion of the development of astronomy:

> A science is a sum of truths. The object of the elements is to connect these truths, to present them in their order, from the most simple through to the most complex. But the connected chain of these truths is not the order of their discovery ...[24]
>
> All the phenomena are connected: the system of our knowledge is ordered just like nature. A single principle serves for us to explain everything, just as a single spring suffices for it to make everything act ... The phenomenon of attraction ... the development of that simple cause will encompass all the present phenomena, and will predict the phenomena to come.[25]

It was the simple structure and the comprehensive scope of the Newtonian system which impressed Tracy, rather than Newton's remarks on the importance of observation (which, after all, had already been said by many thinkers before Newton). Tracy's conception of a "completed" science, such as Newtonian mechanics, dwelt upon its systematic and deductive character, rather than upon the gathering of the observational data which supplied the materials from which the science was fashioned. Knowledge deserved the name of *science*, wrote Tracy, only when its systematic character

> is advanced enough for us to see the links among the facts, their governance by a few common laws, and their explanation by a small number of general truths. Until this stage is reached, our knowledge of a subject is only a collection of isolated facts without connection ... on the contrary, a science matures with the discovery of a general truth which by itself explains all the phenomena as consequences of the principle.[26].

This critique of the adequacy of undirected empiricism is an important feature of Tracy's thought. For him, a science was not properly developed until "we know the relations which unite these facts and the laws which they invariably follow".[27] The simplicity of an explanatory principle was not a sign of scientific immaturity, but, on the contrary, was a product of the precision found in a mature science. The ontological structure of nature (for Tracy, the only reality which was knowable) was itself ordered, simple, and governed by general laws which direct the behaviour of all phenomena. As the sciences have become more advanced, wrote Tracy, they have had the great merit of being reducible to a smaller number of basic propositions. "That is the proof that all the questions to which they are related have reached that high degree of precision which is very near the solution".[28]

Lavoisier was another *savant* whose work influenced Tracy's conception of science and method. The atomistic and corpuscular theory of the universe (where nature is composed of a myriad combinations of elementary particles) had existed since the ancient world. This theory had been developed in various ways, beyond the form given by Democritus and Epicurus, into the modern physical and biological sciences. One important application was in chemistry, where Lavoisier and his colleagues succeeded in developing a theory of the elements of matter and their possible combinations, giving rise to a new nomenclature for the modern science of chemistry.[29] Lavoisier, in his *Traité élémentaire de chimie* (1789), attributed his success to following the rigorous analytical method of Condillac, who had put forward the view that a science is a well-made language, i.e., that scientific truth depends upon conceptual coherence and precision.[30]

Tracy, who had studied Lavoisier and Condillac intensively while in prison in 1794, enthusiastically adopted these conceptions in 1796:

> Every science is reducible to a well-made language; and to advance a science is none other than to perfect this language, whether by changing the words or by making their meaning precise.[31]

Similarly, Tracy wrote that "to make a science is to make its language, and to learn the language of a science is to learn the science itself".[32] However, a few years later, when he wrote his *Logique*, he recognised the ambiguity and paradox implicit in such Condillacian formulae, and found it necessary to clarify the relationship he saw between science and nomenclature. The progress of a science, he said, does not depend simply on providing it with a more methodical nomenclature. The important thing is that the meaning of the concepts should "conform to the facts", and that the meanings should be fixed by men who use the terms in this true and precise manner. The use of new words could sometimes be useful; but the words themselves do not "create the science". Thus, for example, when "our learned French chemists" discovered the theory of combustion, they recognised that "phlogiston", previously believed to be the cause of combustion, was not what it had been thought to be: it was not a property of the combustible objects but something which united with them to produce heat, light, and so forth. Lavoisier and his colleagues "fixed the meaning" of these terms in a way which conformed to the facts. Even if they had retained the term phlogiston, with its new meaning, instead of the new and more useful word oxygen, they would still have "rectified the science" by giving the true meaning to its concepts. In this sense, concluded Tracy, a science is well made to the extent that the "ideas" represented in its terminology are correct.[33] Later in the *Logique*, Tracy went so far as to criticise Condillac for not having sufficiently distinguished between "a science, the method it follows, the language it employs, the ideas it elaborates, and the signs which represent these ideas". Condillac, said Tracy, had been guilty of hyperbolic exaggeration in identifying a science with its language or the signs it employed.[34]

Two other aspects of Tracy's views on science and method should be briefly mentioned. Firstly, in common with his contemporaries, Tracy borrowed various images, analogies and metaphors, in a fairly unsystematic way, from the physical, mathematical and biological sciences. The images are sometimes architectural, arithmetical and geometrical: elementary particles, building blocks, basic faculties, which combine or operate to form more complex wholes. Writing in this mode, Tracy sees it as the task of *analyse* (in the sense defined by Condillac and Condorcet) to decompose complex reality into its constituent units, the better to re-combine them in a more rigorous and coherent manner. Sometimes the analogies are mechanical and chemical: attractions, aversions, affinities. On other occasions, the metaphors of organic constitution, organisation, or system occasionally come to the fore, especially under the influence of the physiological writings of Cabanis and the natural history and zoology of Buffon's successors. Tracy makes use of each of the above modes or idioms, depending on the subject under examination, sometimes using more than one kind of image, especially in his social theory.

Secondly, Tracy argued for the unity of all the sciences, and for the scientific status of the study of human behaviour. He believed that the same procedural methods and logical structure of scientific explanation were applicable to all the positive sciences.[35] For Tracy, the human and social sciences differ from geology and astronomy only in their subject matter, not in their epistemological status or their susceptibility to comprehension in terms of general causal laws. In making these assumptions, Tracy seems to be firmly placed among the founders of a positivist and behaviouralist conception of social science. The behaviouralist aspect of Tracy's work consisted in the assumption that science could only deal with observed effects, and not with first causes. Moreover, in the explanation of social and moral action, Tracy is a considerable distance from those approaches which emphasise the importance of motives, intentions and purposes as causally adequate explanations. Tracy's reductionist account of action in terms of needs and desires all but eliminates intentionality. Tracy's unity of the sciences was achieved on the basis of (i) a deterministic view of human behaviour (the complement of the general determinism of the laws of inorganic nature); and (ii) his argument that the certainty of the sciences could be guaranteed and demonstrated only by a correct understanding of man's intellectual operations, which are the substratum of all his forms of knowledge. This is the role played by the theory of idéologie, as the logos of the sciences and the guarantee of their certainty in all fields of investigation.

THE CONCEPT OF IDEOLOGIE

Destutt de Tracy presented his colleagues in the Class of moral and political sciences on 20 June 1796 with a problem of nomenclature: what would be the most appropriate name for the "new" science of ideas?[36] Inspired by Lavoisier and Condillac on the importance of nomenclature and conceptual reform, Tracy was keen to find a suitable name for a science which, he claimed, "is so new that it does not yet have a name".[37] The birth of a new science evidently required a baptism; and the best place for this was in the presence of that section of the Class devoted to *Analyse des sensations et des idées*, whose task was precisely the further development of this science. In seeking a new name, Tracy was not yet proposing a thorough overhaul of all the working concepts of the science of thought: the desire to reform its whole nomenclature would only become widely felt when the science itself had been more systematically studied by *savants*. The first step was to find a suitable name to mark off the scientific study of ideas from the prescientific "metaphysics" of the past, just as it had been necessary for astronomy to separate itself from astrology.[38]

Condillac had been content to use the term *métaphysique*, albeit with the qualification that scientific or observational procedures should be used in the gathering and analysis of facts.[39] Tracy regarded this term as quite misleading and discredited. The common meaning of *métaphysique*, said Tracy, is

> a science which treats the nature of beings, spirits (*esprits*), different orders of intelligence, the origin of things and their first cause. Now these are certainly not the objects of your research ... Moreover, metaphysics strictly means something other than physics: yet the knowledge of the faculties of man, as Locke believed, is certainly a part—an important part—of physics, whatever (ultimate) cause one wants to ascribe to these faculties.[40]

The legislators establishing the Institut had wisely refrained from using the term "metaphysics". But the term which they had used was not very satisfactory; "analysis of sensations and ideas" was hardly a suitable name for the new science; it was rather like saying "analysis of the sources of wealth in a society" instead of "political economy".[41] Another possibility was the term *psycologie*, which Condillac had sometimes used along with Charles Bonnet.[42] However, Tracy argued that psychology literally meant "science of the soul"; it would not only be presumptuous to claim a knowledge of such an entity, but it would give the false impression that the *savants* of the Institut were investigating first causes. On the contrary, insisted Tracy, "the goal of all your works is the knowledge of effects and their practical consequences".[43] What, then, was to be the name for this behavioural science to which Tracy and his colleagues were devoting their attention?

Tracy recommended his own neologism: "idéologie, ou la science des idées". Idéologie, he said, had a very clear etymological meaning, based on the Greek *eidos* and *logos*, and it made no presuppositions about causes.[44] Hence, it was a suitable word to express "the science of ideas which treats ideas or perceptions, and the faculty of thinking or perceiving".[45] This formulation of the content of idéologie was by no means neutral, however. Tracy had not only defined the content in behaviouralist terms as knowledge of "effects" and "consequences", but he had also imported a whole epistemological doctrine by his equation of ideas with perceptions and of thinking with perceiving. This perspective was reinforced and extended in the following passage:

> This word has still another advantage—namely, that in giving the name idéologie to the science resulting from the analysis of sensations, you at once indicate the goal and the method; and if your doctrine is found to differ from that of certain other philosophers who pursue the same science, the reason is already given—namely, that you seek knowledge of man only through the analysis of his faculties; you agree to ignore everything which it does not uncover for you.[46]

Here we find not only statements which define the procedures and content of idéologie in terms of "analysis of sensations" and "analysis of (intellectual) faculties", but we also find sharp limits placed upon what is knowable, or what is to be taken as reliable knowledge. Such knowledge, according to Tracy, must be derived from analysing man's faculties, i.e. from investigating the operations of the mind in forming and expressing ideas. Let us examine more closely some of the main themes in Tracy's conception of idéologie.

First, we will take his view that the science of ideas is the fundamental science, necessary for guaranteeing reliable knowledge in all the other sciences. Tracy's reasoning seems to be as follows. All knowledge, regardless of subject-matter, consists of ideas, and their accuracy depends on our capacity for making a series of precise judgements. Knowledge of the processes by which errors arise and by which correct judgements may be formed, is the only basis available for ensuring the reliability of knowledge. The primacy of idéologie over the other sciences arises from the fact that in explaining the general operations of our intellectual faculties, it points out the methods for attaining certainty and avoiding error. Or, as Tracy succintly wrote: "it is necessary to know our intellectual faculties in order to be sure we are using them well".[47] In his early mémoires on idéologie, Tracy asserted that it was "the first of all the sciences in the genealogical order".[48] Indeed, he went even further, suggesting that

> knowledge of the human understanding is really the only science (*la science unique*); all the others, without exception, are only applications of this knowledge to the diverse objects of our curiosity, and it must be their guiding light.[49]

Tracy gives two main kinds of reasons for the primacy of idéologie: one relating to scientific method, and the other concerning the nature of human experience. The first argument is straightforward: he asserts that all the sciences require a guarantee of their truth-content; that scientific methods of observation and analysis are the best procedural guarantees of reliable knowledge; that all the sciences should adopt such methods; and that idéologie is central because it clarifies and recommends the logic of scientific method and explanation. The second argument, however, is more contentious and surprising. Here, Tracy argues that the science of ideas is fundamental to all our knowledge because the ideas of an individual are constitutive of his experience of the world and of his self.

> In fact, since nothing exists *for us* except through the ideas we have, since our ideas are our whole being, our very existence, the examination of the manner in which we perceive and combine them is alone able to show us in what consists our knowledge, what it encompasses, what are its limits, and what method we must follow in the pursuit of truths in every field.[50]

This doctrine of the primacy of ideas-as-experience is rather anomalous in what is otherwise a philosophy of monist materialism. The doctrine plays little role in Tracy's overall conception of idéologie and the human sciences, but it does suggest the overwhelming residual influence of the Cartesian *cogito* in French philosophy.[51]

Tracy's view of idéologie as analytically and logically prior to all the other sciences led him to describe it as *la théorie des théories*,[52] and to suggest that the "examination of our intellectual operations is the natural introduction to all the branches of studies".[53] Knowledge of our means of knowing is *la véritable philosophie première ou science première*.[54] But it is quite different from "that first philosophy of which all our ancient authors have spoken so much", for the latter had assumed the truth of their general principles and built their systems on shifting sands.[55] The modern *philosophie première*, the "first of the sciences in their order of mutual dependence", is simply "the history of our intelligence considered in relation to its means of knowing".[56]

Tracy's assumptions about the genealogical and analytical priority of idéologie led him to reconsider the traditional classification of the branches of learning, propounded by Bacon and by d'Alembert. Bacon's classification, said Tracy, was confused and fallacious, and d'Alembert had erred in following Bacon so closely.[57] Not only was it wrong that theology had been accorded the primary place as a general ontology; but the major categories of memory (history), reason (philosophy, including theology and science), and imagination (poetry) showed a faulty understanding of our intellectual faculties. The proper way to classify the sciences, wrote Tracy, was to distribute them in accordance with "the order in which they are derived from one another and through which they are fortified and inter-related". The science of the formation of our ideas "incontestably" came first, closely followed by the science of their expression and of their deduction.[58] Idéologie was to form "the trunk of the tree".[59]

At the end of his *Logique* in 1805, Tracy drew up a plan which summarised the ambitious and ever-broadening scope of his conception of idéologie, as the new *prima philosophia* providing the epistemological groundwork for all the sciences. The scheme was divided into nine parts[60] and an appendix as follows:

Elements of Idéologie

First Section: History of our means of knowing. In three parts.

1st part: On the formation of our ideas, or Ideology strictly defined.
2nd part: On the expression of our ideas, or Grammar.
3rd part: On the combination of our ideas, or Logic.
Second Section: Application of our means of knowing to the study of the will and its effects. In three parts.
1st part: On our actions, or Economics.
2nd part: On our sentiments, or Morality.
3rd part: On the rule of some by others, or Government.
Third Section: Application of our means of knowing to the study of beings other than ourselves. In three parts.
1st part: On bodies and their properties, or Physics.
2nd part: On the properties of extension, or Geometry.
3rd part: On the properties of quantity, or Calculus.
Appendix: On the false sciences, which are abolished by knowledge of our means of knowing and their proper use.

Taken together, these sciences would form "the totality of the trunk of the encyclopedic tree of our real knowledge".[61]

Despite the enormous breadth of his ambitions, it should be evident that Tracy's intention was not to summarise all existing knowledge about man and nature, but to recommend and demonstrate the superiority of a particular method of enquiry: *analyse*. According to this method, as elaborated by Condillac[62] (and adopted by Condorcet,[63] Garat[64] and Tracy), all phenomena are susceptible to explication in terms of their location in an ordered progression from simple to complex facts; this approach is equally applicable to the study of animate and inanimate nature, and to mathematics. Any idea or concept can be "decomposed" by analysis into its constituent simple ideas which are anchored in sense-experience. Analysis demonstrates how complex ideas are built up from simple elements.[65] The programmatic aspect of this doctrine implies that any ideas which cannot, in this way, be melted down and reconstituted on the basis of simple sense-experience must be expelled from scientific discourse as ambiguous or meaningless, and propositions based on such ideas are false or at least unprovable.[66] Tracy asserts that analysis and idéologie are based upon scrupulous observation of the facts, drawing only those conclusions fully warranted by the evidence, and always preferring "absolute ignorance" to any claim which merely appears to be plausible.[67]

The study of the formation of ideas, based on observation of facts and the analysis of their relationships, was for Tracy *une science expérimentale*.[68] The implication was that there were two kinds of "knowledge": that modelled on the physical sciences, and that which could hardly be called reliable knowledge at all. Condillac had claimed that there was really only one *science*—the history of nature—which could be subdivided into two, interdependent, parts: that dealing with facts or experience (*physique*), and that dealing with abstractions or reasoning upon these facts.[69] Tracy, in similar fashion, claimed that there are two kinds of "truths", namely, those of "experience or fact", and those of "reasoning and deduction". The deductive or abstract truths, however, had no validity independently of the facts from which they were abstracted.[70] Idéologie, like all positive sciences, required both types of truths. The scientific genius, wrote Tracy, is one who is able to "discover in the facts those important and very general truths which have not yet been detected—but it can never be a question of creating them out of his own head".[71] When idéologie and the human sciences had become more highly developed, he believed, they would be closer to the positive sciences of nature, especially physiology, than to any purely abstract science such as mathematics whose truths are entirely a deductive system abstracted from the objective world.[72] In idéologie and the human sciences, claimed Tracy, "perfection is not proportional to the number of facts observed, but to the knowledge of the laws which govern these facts".[73]

The problem, in Tracy's conception, was to find a starting-point for structuring "the facts" in accordance with the laws governing their interrelationships. What kind of starting-point was appropriate? Would it be a truth of observation or a truth of deduction? Tracy chose the latter, on the analogy of astronomy, which explained all its phenomena "by starting from this single truth, that attraction acts in direct proportion to mass and in inverse proportion to the square of the distance".[74] Once such a secure starting-point had been found, the rest of the scientific system would be unfolded in a series of rigorous deductions. If this were accomplished, the system of truths would be complete and entirely "certain". On the foundation of idéologie, according to Tracy, the human sciences were capable of certainty in the same manner as the sciences of inanimate nature. A whole system of truths about man and society would follow:

> now that we are certain of the formation and filiation of our ideas, all that will be subsequently said—on the manner of expressing, combining and teaching these ideas, on regulating our sentiments and actions, and directing those of others—will be only the consequences of these preliminaries, and will rest on a constant and invariable base, consistent with the very nature of our being. Now these preliminaries constitute what is strictly designated as idéologie; and all the consequences derived from it are the object of grammar, logic, instruction, private morality, public morality (or the *art social*), education and legislation ... We will go astray in all these sciences only to the extent that we lose sight of the fundamental observations on which they rest.[75]

The secure starting-point for idéologie, the fundamental building-block on which all the "ideological, moral and political sciences" rested, was sense-perception. The methods of empirical observation and analysis (pioneered by Locke and Condillac in particular) had demonstrated to Tracy's satisfaction the truth of the ancient adage "nihil est in intellectu quin prius fuerit in sensu"[76] (literally: there is nothing in the mind which was not previously in the senses). Idéologie was therefore

> a system of truths closely tied together, all stemming from this first indubita-

> ble fact, that we know nothing except through our sensations, and that all our ideas are the product of the various combinations we make from these sensations.[77]

Tracy's insistence on sense-perceptions was, as we saw earlier, a materialised form of the Cartesian *cogito*. Having assumed that the only fact of which we can initially be certain is our own existence as a sensing being, Tracy's whole system is erected upon this *être sensible*. The proposition that "man is a sentient being", is the *première vérité générale* from which he elaborates his entire theory of man and society.[78] Tracy's disingenuous remark that his theories were devoid of presuppositions and that he had elaborated his idéologie purely by observation of man's thinking processes,[79] is clearly misleading. Tracy had accepted the sensationalist paradigm of what constitutes knowledge and what procedures had to be followed to reach the truth, to the exclusion of all other conceptions and procedures.

In Tracy's view, the study of mental phenomena had wrongly been separated in the past from the study of physical phenomena. Descartes, for example, had separated the two spheres, and had concluded that our thinking faculty owed nothing to sense perceptions, and that general principles were the foundation of knowledge. Tracy, following Locke and Condillac, argued that all ideas stem from sense perceptions or simple ideas which are transformed into complex ideas; and that knowledge must be based on particular facts, not upon *a priori* or axiomatic principles. The "artificial" separation of the mental and the physical had been bridged by empiricist writers like Locke, who, according to Tracy, was "the first man to try to observe and describe the human intelligence just as one observes and describes a property of a mineral or a vegetable, or a noteworthy aspect of the life of an animal: he also made this study a part of *la physique*"[80] The study of the human intelligence, as of the human body, is part of natural history: hence Tracy's well-known claim that "idéologie is a part of zoology'.[81]

Tracy's epistemology assumes, then, that sense-experience is primary; and indeed, Tracy goes beyond Locke in asserting that sense perception and thinking are absolutely identical terms.[82] Locke had allowed the mind a certain independent activity in ordering and recalling ideas from among the materials provided by sense experience. Condillac virtually eliminated such independent reflectiveness of the mind by attempting to demonstrate that memory, comparison and desire consist in nothing but modifications of sense impressions.[83] However, Condillac wished to allow that mind was an entity not entirely reducible to physical operations, and spoke of "l'âme oisive". Tracy, noting the redundance of such an entity in a thoroughly reductionist sensationalism, obliterated the distinction between the mind itself and the activities of rearranging sense perceptions by which it was constituted. His purpose was to deny any independent reality to a mental or moral realm, and to assert a naturalistic monism of consciousness and physical environment. Thought (or perceiving and sensing) consisted of four basic faculties or modes of operation: simple sensibility, memory, judgement and desire. "This manner of envisaging it in these (four) elements unveils for us the whole mechanism".[84] All mental phenomena were produced by these modes. Where Condillac had shown that one faculty of the mind gave rise to the next in a generative manner, Tracy collapsed all such operations into aspects of the general sensibility of living creatures, all being "the results of our organisation".[85]

Here, Tracy's physiological emphasis becomes very important. Tracy takes as pre-given the physical structure and operations of the body, including all the sensibilities involved in consciousness. Whereas the *content* of ideas was largely determined by experience, education and environment, the *structure* of the mind itself was stable and predictable owing to its physiological foundation. Even though the innate ideas hypothesis in its Cartesian, Kantian and other versions was incompatible with Tracy's sensationalism, his theory appears to assume that the mind is so structured that its capacities are universally shared throughout the species, owing to a biological or physiological uniformity.[86] Physiology provided, for Tracy, the stable and certain basis which guaranteed that simple sensations were perceived in the same way by men of all ages and epochs.[87] The "certitude of all we know" depended on the physiological necessity that when we perceive simple objects X and Y, they are necessarily perceived as such and not as A and B. The same is true for "all beings who are organised like us".[88]

An important question arises concerning the character of the physiological determinism implied by Tracy's doctrine and the extent to which the physiological substructure is modified by the social-environmental superstructure. This is an area where contradictory elements emerged in Tracy's writings, and he never discussed these problems at sufficient length to become aware of the inconsistencies. We will see below, in the discussion of the will (desires) in chapter four, that, despite Tracy's voluntarist doctrine of *motilité*, his general reductionism allows no role for genuinely independent volition. On the other hand, his educational doctrines (discussed in later chapters) claim that changes in patterns of ideas and behaviour are made possible through a rational system of public instruction and legislation. Tracy was deeply influenced by the views of Cabanis on the interaction between the physical and moral aspects of man,[89] but these doctrines were largely taken for granted rather than argued or elaborated.[90]

Tracy's professions of belief in the physiological basis of the intellect, and in the capacity of the physiologists to resolve many of the outstanding problems in the science of ideas, became quite marked in the years after 1796 when he had first argued that idéologie should be divided into two parts. *Idéologie physiologique* would deal with the physical and biochemical dimensions of human sensibility, and *idéologie rationnelle* would examine the psychological and logical aspects of the intellectual faculties. Tracy claimed he would confine himself to the latter aspects: "I take our faculties such as they are, and concern myself only with their effects''.[91] Nevertheless, a ''complete'' account of the operations of these faculties would require a unified approach, including the knowledge of a physiologist, mathematician, grammarian, and *algébriste philosophe*.[92] That the human sciences would require the co-operation of *savants* of various kinds was partly recognised in the organisation of the Institut, where Tracy and Cabanis were both in the section on ''Analysis of sensations and ideas''. However, the grammarians had, to Tracy's regret,[93] been placed in a different Class; a more strictly ''ideological'' structure would have united them with the physiologists and idéologistes, for in Tracy's doctrine, the study of how ideas are expressed (grammar) is merely one aspect of the general study of the origin and communication of ideas.

Tracy plainly believed that intellectual and moral ideas were dependent upon physical faculties, but the claim remained ambiguous. It could have meant only that sense perceptions are necessary materials for the mind and that without the senses there can be no human consciousness. However, Tracy no doubt intended a stronger relation of dependence than the claim that bodies and brains are preconditions of minds and thoughts. Tracy argued, against theories which posited the existence of innate or intuitive ideas, that ideas have no autonomy, independence, or innate existence in the mind. Further, he asserted that all ideas are nothing but transformed and modified sensations, whose content derives entirely from data provided by the senses. Tracy, however, never attempted to demonstrate how the supposed physiological basis of mind shapes and interacts with the processes involved in reflection, judgement or desire. Tracy's reductionist language (idea = sense perception, thinking = perceiving sensations, idéologie = part of zoology and physics) was partly a methodological polemic against what he saw as ''metaphysical'' systems of ideas, which had misled men about nature and liberty, and which had asserted a dualism between the natural and moral, the physical and intellectual. Tracy's reductionism was also a confused doctrine, asserting a physiological base of human behaviour, without specifying the exact relationship between physiology and mind.

Tracy and Cabanis were rapidly identified as promoting the same materialist monism as La Mettrie and d'Holbach.[94] The only new thing about idéologie, wrote a hostile reviewer in 1802, is the title itself. Idéologie ''substitutes the movement of the brute for human reason, and sees in man nothing but muscles and nerves''. Fortunately, opined the critic, the human heart and the passage of time would leave such demented systems behind, as so much flotsam left on the river bank after a storm.[95] In obliterating reflective reason, claimed the critic, ''the idéologues saw in man nothing more than Condillac's statue'', man being analysed purely in terms of his physical needs.[96] The ideological analysis of mind, wrote another critic, was just like a ''treatise on mechanics'' where all one can see are ''actions and reactions, moving forces and inertia''.[97] The denial of a separate realm for human morality and reason, was to place man in the family of the monkeys. Those who espoused such a view wanted "to lead the moral man to the cemetery".[98]

Tracy's views on the physiological basis of human thought and action remained undeveloped. He did not ask *why* the mind operated in the ways it did: this was a matter for the physiologists to determine (and in any case, they could do little more than re-describe the processes in physical terms, unless they trespassed into the forbidden area of first causes). Tracy focussed his attention on behavioural effects or operations of the mind, and especially upon the connections between thought and language, ideas and words, the signified and the sign. Here was a field where he expected idéologie to make great progress. Idéologie, as the *science des sciences*,[99] was particularly suited to the task of clarifying ideas, making concepts more precise, and thereby promoting scientific understanding of phenomena in every field. The logical priority of idéologie over the positive sciences of man and nature depended on a view of language as a conventionalised set of signs which express our ideas; and a view of scientific advance as dependent on clarification of concepts and the rejection of those not validated by sense-experience. The scientific language of "elements" and "compounds" also had the eminent advantage, for the philosophe and idéologiste, of lending itself to what Gillispie has called a "naturalistic pedagogy".[100] Idéologie was seen to provide a grammar and syntax of *nature*, and a set of procedural rules for finding the basic elements (signs, concepts) of any language.

The analysis of *language* was thus of critical importance for the idéologiste in his role both as scientific observer, and as educator of mankind. The main features of Tracy's conception of language, his view of how language *qua* knowledge can be perfected, and his critique of "metaphysical" and theological forms of knowledge, are examined in the following chapter.

Notes

1. Tracy, *Elémens d'idéologie. Troisième partie. Logique* (Paris, 1805), pp. 563-588. See also *ibid.* (Paris, 1818), pp. 489-514; *Elémens d'idéologie*, 5 vols. (Paris, 1824-26), IV, pp. 7-44; *Elémens d'idéologie*, 5 vols. (Bruxelles, 1826-27), IV, pp. 1-38.
2. Tracy, *Logique* (1805), pp. 4, 46.
3. *Ibid.*, p. 50. The Baconian programme was also extremely prominent in the conception of the *Encyclopédie*: see, for example, d'Alembert's *Preliminary Discourse to the Encyclopedia of Diderot* (1751), trans. R.N. Schwab (New York, 1963). Bacon was also one of the masters of the modern mind identified by D.-J. Garat in his lectures on *l'analyse de l'entendement* at the *école normale* in Paris early in 1795: see *Séances des écoles normales* ... (Paris, 1801), Leçons, vol. I.
4. *Logique*, p. 57.
5. *Ibid.*, pp. 52-54. Tracy added in a note (p. 54); "Bacon uses the word induction instead of deduction. We will see elsewhere the difference between these two terms and why I prefer the latter". Descartes, of course, used the term deduction.
6. *Ibid.*, p. 62.
7. *Ibid.*, pp. 79-82, 87-8, 105-6. See also (Tracy), "Sur les Lettres de Descartes", *La Revue*

philosophique, 1 June 1806, p. 394.

8. On Descartes' views on the physical sciences, cf. A Vartanian, *Diderot and Descartes* (Princeton, 1953); R. McRae, *The Problem of the Unity of the Sciences: Bacon to Kant* (Toronto, 1961).
9. Tracy, *Logique*, p. 109.
10. See chapter 2 of the *Discourse on Method*, trans. F.E. Sutcliffe (Harmondsworth, 1968), p. 41. Tracy cited these principles in *Logique*, p. 109n-110, concluding that "there is nothing as profound nor as just in the whole *grande rénovation*". The continuity between Descartes' four principles and Condillac's methodological position is quite striking. Much of Condillac's polemics are directed against Cartesians such as Malebranche, who developed the "spiritual" side of Cartesian dualism.
11. *Logique*, p. 111. For Descartes' phrase, see *Discourse on Method*, chapter 4, pp. 53-54.
12. *Logique*, p. 133.
13. (Tracy), "Sur les Lettres de Descartes", pp. 395-96; *Principes logiques*, in *Elémens d'idéologie*, 5 vols. (Bruxelles, 1826-27), vol. IV, pp. 200-1.
14. *Logique*, p. 189.
15. *Ibid.*, pp. 189-190.
16. Descartes, *Discourse on Method*, p. 41.
17. Cf. Tracy, *Logique*, p. 126. Of course, Condillac substituted sensationalism for Descartes' spiritualised dualism, in explaining the operations of the intellect. The influence of Descartes upon the idéologues has seldom been raised: exceptions include the brief remarks by F. Bouillier, *Histoire de la philosophie cartesienne* (Paris, 3rd ed. 1868), vol. II, pp. 641-46; F. Picavet, *Les Idéologues*, pp. 1-10.
18. Cf. Tracy, "Mémoire sur la faculté de penser", *Mémoires de l'Institut National, Classe des Sciences morales et politiques*, vol. I (1798), p. 320.
19. See Voltaire's *Lettres philosophiques* (1734); Voltaire also wrote a more detailed *Eléments de la philosophie de Newton* (1737).
20. J.-S. Bailly, *Histoire de l'astronomie moderne*, 3 vols. (Paris, 1779-82), especially vol. I, p. xvi, vol. II, pp. 469-471, vol. III, p. 331.
21. Condorcet, *Sketch for a historical picture of the progress of the human mind* (1793) (London 1955), pp. 148-151. Some of Condillac's views on Bacon, Descartes and Newton may be briefly seen in his *Histoire Moderne*, in Condillac, *Oeuvres philosophiques*, vol. II, pp. 220-1, 230-3.
22. Cf. H. Guerlac, "Newton's changing reputation in the eighteenth-century", in *Carl Becker's Heavenly City Revisited*, ed. R.O. Rockwood (New York, 1958), especially pp. 21-24; for a detailed account of the early phase of Newton's reception in France (before 1738), cf. P. Brunet, *l'Introduction des théories de Newton en France au XVIII siècle* (Paris, 1931). The modern account of Newton by A. Koyré stresses the abstract theoretico-mathematical character of his work upon an idealised nature, rather than his empiricism and positivism: cf. *Newtonian Studies* (London, 1965), and "The Origins of Modern Science", *Diogenes*, vol. 16 (1956), especially pp. 20-22.
23. Cf. G. Buchdahl, *The image of Newton and Locke in the age of reason* (London, 1961), especially pp. 4-5, 11-14; A Koyré, *Newtonian Studies*, chapter 2.
24. J.-S. Bailly, *Histoire de l'astronomie moderne*, vol. I, p. xi.
25. *Ibid.*, vol. III, pp. 330-1. That Tracy was familiar with Bailly's work is shown in "Mémoire sur la faculté de penser", pp. 319-320.
26. Tracy, "Mémoire sur la faculté de penser", p. 387.
27. *Ibid.*, p. 391.
28. Tracy, *Elémens d'idéologie. Seconde Partie. Grammaire* (Paris, 2nd ed. 1817), pp. x-xi.
29. A.-L. Lavoisier, Guyton de Morveau, et al., *Méthode de nomenclature chimique* (Paris, 1787).
30. Lavoisier, *Traité élémentaire de chimie* (Paris, 1789), "Discours préliminaire". Like Tracy, Saint-Simon was very enthusiastic about this profession of faith in *analyse* and observation by a successful investigator of nature.
31. Tracy, "Mémoire sur la faculté de penser", pp. 325-6. This phrasing was repeated in

Grammaire (1803) (Paris, 2nd ed. 1817), p. 386.
32. Tracy, "Mémoire sur la faculté de penser", p. 416.
33. Tracy, *Logique*, pp. 32n-33.
34. *Ibid.*, pp. 503-9.
35. Cf. E. Kennedy, "Destutt de Tracy and the Unity of the Sciences", *Studies on Voltaire and the Eighteenth Century*, vol. 171 (1977), pp. 223-239.
36. The question was posed in the second of a series of mémoires, later collected under the name "Mémoire sur la faculté de penser", and published in *Mémoires de l'Institut National, Classe des Sciences morales et politiques*, vol. I (1798), pp. 283-450. Evidence for the date of the original usage of the term idéologie is given in B.W. Head, "The origin of 'idéologue' and 'idéologie'", *Studies on Voltaire and the Eighteenth Century*, vol. 183 (1980), p. 263-4.
37. Tracy, *op.cit.*, p. 322.
38. *Ibid.*, p. 323.
39. Cf. Condillac, *Oeuvres philosophiques*, vol. I, pp. 3, 619; and vol. II, p. 229.
40. Tracy, "Mémoire sur la faculté de penser", pp. 322-3.
41. *Ibid.*, p. 322. Cf. Garat's lectures at the école normale in 1795, entitled "analyse de l'entendement"—a slightly more Lockean phrase than the Condillacian title of Tracy's section at the Institut.
42. Cf. Condillac, *Oeuvres philosophiques*, vol. II, p. 229; Bonnet, *Essai analytique sur les facultés de l'âme* (1760). Bonnet had sought to develop "une psychologie expérimentale": see H. Gouhier, *Les Conversions de Maine de Biran* (Paris, 1947), p. 89.
43. Tracy, "Mémoire sur la faculté de penser", p. 324.
44. *Ibid.*, p. 324.
45. *Ibid.*, p. 325.
46. *Ibid.*, p. 325.
47. *Logique*, p. 55. See also p. 81n: "all that we know, is only an application of the science which shows us what we can know and how we can know it".
48. "Mémoire sur la faculté de penser", p. 286.
49. *Ibidem*.
50. *Ibidem*. (emphasis added)
51. One might be tempted to call the above doctrine a form of phenomeno-logical Cartesianism, which is distantly related to some aspects of modern existentialism via Maine de Biran.
52. *Elémens d'idéologie*, vol. I (1801) (3rd ed. 1817), p. 307.
53. *Ibid.*, p. 207.
54. *Logique*, p. vi.
55. *Ibid.*, p. 397.
56. *Ibid.*, p. 425.
57. *Ibid.*, pp. 79-82, and Tracy, "Sur un systême méthodique de bibliographie", *Moniteur universel*, 8 and 9 brumaire an VI (29 and 30 October 1797), pp. 151-152, 155-156. Cf. d'Alembert, *Preliminary Discourse*, pp. 143-164.
58. *Logique*, p. 80n. These three areas corresponded to the first three volumes of his *Elémens d'idéologie* (1801-1805).
59. *Logique*, p. 81n.
60. *Ibid.*, pp. 520-1. Of these nine parts, Tracy completed four, sketched a small part of the fifth, and wrote a preliminary work (the *Commentaire*) for the sixth. Some aspects of his conception of the final three parts were summarised in chapter 9 of the *Logique*.
61. *Ibid.*, p. 519.
62. Cf. Condillac, *Essai sur l'origine des connaissances humaines* (1746), in *Oeuvres philosophiques*, vol. I, especially pp. 24-27; *l'Art de penser*, in *ibid.*, vol. I, especially pp. 747, 769-774; and *Dictionnaire des synonymes*, article "Décomposer", in *ibid.*, vol. III, p. 179.
63. Cf. Condorcet's manuscript on the meaning of *analyse*, published by K.M. Baker, "Un 'éloge' officieux de Condorcet", *Revue de synthèse*, vol. 88 (1967), especially pp. 247-251.
64. Cf. Garat's lectures at the *école normale*: note 3 above.

65. Cf. Tracy, "Mémoire sur la faculté de penser", pp. 307, 327, 339, 341-2, 355; *Elémens*, vol. I, chapter 6; *Principes logiques*, in *Elémens*, 5 vols. (Bruxelles, 1826-1827), vol. IV, pp. 208-9.
66. Cf. Tracy, "De la métaphysique de Kant", *Mémoires de l'Institut* ..., Vol. IV, pp. 569, 580. See also the second section of the following chapter, on "metaphysics and religion".
67. "De la métaphysique de Kant", pp. 550-1; "Mémoire sur la faculté de penser", p. 386.
68. "Mémoire sur la faculté de penser", p. 349. Cf. article "expérimentale", in *The Encyclopédie*, ed. J. Lough (Cambridge, 1969), pp. 68-81. See also note 42 above.
69. Condillac, *Art de raisonner*, in *Oeuvres philosophiques*, vol. I, p. 619.
70. "Mémoire sur la faculté de penser", pp. 377-8, 384. Tracy also used the dichotomy "positive" and "conjectural", in his "Supplément à la première section des Elémens d'idéologie" (1805), in *Elémens ... IV et V parties. Traité de la volonté et de ses effets* (Paris, 1815), pp. 46-7.
71. "Mémoire sur la faculté de penser", p. 378.
72. *Ibid.*, pp. 389-390. Cf. Condorcet, *Sketch*, pp. 133, 173, 185-6 on the unity of methods among all the sciences.
73. "Mémoire sur la faculté de penser", p. 390.
74. *Ibid.*, p. 388.
75. *Elémens*, vol. I, pp. 212-213.
76. This was one of the handful of favourable citations by the idéologistes from ancient Greek philosophy: cf. Degérando, *Histoire comparée des systèmes de philosophie* (Paris 1804), vol. II, p. 375, and vol. I, p. 51n; and Cabanis, *Rapports*, in *Oeuvres philosophiques*, vol. I, p. 137.
77. "Mémoire sur la faculté de penser", p. 317; also p. 290.
78. *Ibid.*, p. 389. Cf. the anonymous review (signed "P.M.") of Cabanis' *Rapports du physique et du moral de l'homme*, in *Mercure de France*, 2 pluviose an XI, p. 219: "The rational-analytical philosophy (claims to) depend solely on facts and experiences. But what is one to make of the principal fact (all ideas deriving from the senses) when one invokes witnesses who disavow it?".
79. *Logique*, p. 424.
80. *Elémens*, vol. I, p. xv. The idéologiste Pierre Laboulinière claimed that the science of the understanding should be termed *la physique morale*, because "idéologie" was too restricted in meaning: *Précis de l'idéologie* (Paris, 1805), p. 10. Auguste Comte later made famous the phrase *la physique sociale* before coining the term *sociologie*.
81. *Elémens*, vol. I, p. xiii.
82. *Ibid.*, pp. 24-25; and "Mémoire sur la faculté de penser", p. 326.
83. Condillac, *Extrait raisonné du Traité des Sensations*, in *Oeuvres philosophiques*, vol. I, p. 325.
84. "Mémoire sur la faculté de penser", p. 327; cf. p.336.
85. *Elémens*, vol. I, p. 53.
86. This seemed to imply that where particular individuals were not capable of performing these common intellectual operations, the immediate cause was physiological. In fact the physiological 'dysfunction' could have been induced by factors in the individuals' social environment (or indeed, by the very absence of a social environment: see the wolf-children example mentioned in the following chapter).
87. "Mémoire sur la faculté de penser", p. 414.
88. *Ibid.*, p. 347.
89. Cf. Cabanis, *Rapports du physique et du moral de l'homme*, in *Oeuvres philosophiques*, vol. I, p. 126: physiology should be *la base commune* for the research of the Class of moral and political sciences, to avoid elaborating "a vain scaffolding which is inconsistent with the eternal laws of nature".
90. Cf. *Principes logiques*, in *Elémens d'idéologie*, 5 vols. (Bruxelles, 1826-27), vol. IV, pp. 251-3; *Logique*, p. viii. Tracy had provided an analytical summary for the 1805 edition of Cabanis' *Rapports*, where he attributed to Cabanis the view that the brain is "le digesteur spécial ou l'organe sécréteur de la pensée" (1830 ed., vol. I, p. 29: cf. Cabanis, *Oeuvres*

philosophiques, vol. I, pp. 195-6 for Cabanis' more extended analogy). Tracy repeated that the brain is "l'organe sécréteur de la pensée", in *Principes logiques* (*Elémens*, 1826-27, vol. IV, p. 212). On one occasion Tracy slips into a monist materialist ontology in speaking of "matière animée" (*Logique*, p. 190), but this is rare.

91. "Mémoire sur la faculté de penser", pp. 344-5.
92. "De la métaphysique de Kant", p. 604. Moreau de la Sarthe proposed a different division of labour in the general science of man or *anthropologie*: physical anthropology and moral anthropology, each divided into four sub-sections. Cf. *la Décade philosophique*, 20 prairial an IX (9 June 1801), pp. 458-9.
93. "Mémoire sur la faculté de penser", p. 326.
94. Cf. J. La Mettrie, *l'Homme-Machine* (1748) and Paul Thiry d'Holbach, *Système de la Nature* (1770).
95. Anon. review (signed "G") of Tracy's *Projet d'éléments d'idéologie* (1801), in *Mercure de France*, 16 nivose an X (6 January 1802), p. 102.
96. *Ibid.*, p. 101.
97. Anon. review (signed "D.M.") of Chateaubriand's *Génie du Christianisme*, in *Mercure de France*, 4 thermidor an XI (23 July 1803), p. 214.
98. *Mercure de France*, 8 prairial an XI (28 May 1803), pp. 461, 463.
99. *Grammaire* (1803) (Paris, 2nd ed. 1817), pp. viii-ix.
100. C.C. Gillispie, *The Edge of Objectivity* (Princeton, 1959), p. 203.

3. SIGNS, LANGUAGE, AND THE CRITIQUE OF METAPHYSICS

A language, for Tracy, is a system of signs whose meanings have been fixed or formalised by the attribution of conventional meaning to each symbol.[1] Some languages or sign-systems are more specialised than others (algebraic notation, for example, or the symbols of chemistry), but all share certain characteristics. First, language is created and sustained as a social phenomenon: it is a kind of collective network through which individuals share experiences and perhaps even contribute to the enlargement of knowledge. Secondly, a mastery of language involves a mastery of knowledge, of which the words are signifiers. In Tracy's view, the ability to manipulate an appropriate language was the avenue to understanding man and nature. The problem was to ensure that the words actually designated precise and observable facts, and that general ideas were squarely based on such facts.

THE SCIENCE OF SIGNS

The analytical method of idéologie was invoked to perform the function of making language more precise and scientific: to ensure that the vocabulary and syntax of languages were consistent with the facts discovered by observation, and with a rigorous interrelationship of concepts. As Gillispie has aptly remarked, the Baconian project of a renovation of learning became, in Condillac's work, identified with a "linguistic reform, redesignating words where necessary to make them speak facts, recombining them in a syntax of experience, lending reality to the expression used of the ancient atomists that theirs was an alphabet of nature".[2] Tracy's inspiration was the same, and his model of language was no less atomistic and naturalistic. In the generation of ideas, he claimed, a small number of basic elements, combined in various ways, produce "an almost infinite multitude of ideas, just as a small number of letters variously arranged suffice to represent those ideas. Here as elsewhere, nature shows a remarkable economy of means and profusion of effects".[3]

Tracy's interest in theories of language and the usage of signs was quite different from that of historical philology or pure linguistics. His purpose was far more practical. Ideological analysis was designed primarily to clarify our existing stock of ideas, eliminate vague concepts and false propositions, and provide criteria for rebuilding the human sciences. Tracy rejected all theories which attributed the form or content of language to any divine or supernatural agency. Rousseau had seen language as a divine spark planted in the mind, though its forms were developed by the passions; Maistre and Bonald had proposed a theory of innate ideas, and ridiculed the Locke-Condillac account of the development of language through association of simple perceptions. In his desire to establish idéologie as an empirical science, Tracy believed it necessary to overthrow the "innatist" theories, and to base the principle of language on its instrumental functions for satisfying human needs. Having established in this way how language evolved and functioned, it would become possible to improve its value as a precise instrument for codifying, communicating and enlarging our knowledge. Tracy's model of language was derived primarily from Condillac, whom Tracy therefore praised as the founder and creator of idéologie.[4]

Condillac had argued that all animate beings have sense impressions or perceptions, and are attracted or repelled by them. But only human beings have the capacity to reflect upon these simple ideas, to compare, combine and judge them.[5] The human faculties of reflection and judgement evolved very slowly over time, but rapidly outstripped those of the animal world when men began to invent and manipulate artificial signs to designate their ideas. The earliest signs were gestural and verbal, closely connected with immediate desires or passions. Gradually, various graphic forms of communication were developed, of which modern written languages are the highest form. The earliest signs designated sensible objects; gradually more general terms were derived or abstracted from the particular terms.[6] Condillac regarded the use of language as a process which assigned conventional meanings to given signs or words. The use of concrete particular terms was unambiguous because the objects designated were immediately apparent. But the use of more abstract terms was bound to involve confusion and imprecision, because the objects designated were not immediately obvious, and because clear meanings for general ideas depended on a rigorous chain of conceptual relationships founded upon simple ideas.[7] Finally, Condillac noted the importance of repetition and habit, which not only strengthen our intellectual operations, but also unfortunately confirm us just as much in our badly-formed judgements as in our properly-formed judgements.

Tracy took up these four points concerning the origins of language, the usage of signs, the role of habitual judgements, and the problems of making language more precise. In the first place, Tracy was little concerned to assemble fresh historical evidence on the origin of language, or to engage in any detailed comparative studies of living languages. He was generally content to rely on the research of Gébelin and others in regard to the ancient non-European languages,[8] and on the large number of grammarians who had considered the development of the European languages. The earliest form of communication, Tracy surmised, was a "language of action" by which one's desires were made known. Gestures and movements would usually be complemented by articulated sounds of various kinds. Many animals could rightly be seen to have reached this level of communication.[9]

Wherein lay the distinction between men and other animate creatures? Was this not a major difficulty for sensationalist philosophy, given that all animate creatures were defined by their sensibility? Was not Tracy's definition of man as *l'homme sensible* a denial of a qualitative leap between human and other creatures? Certainly Tracy's critics believed that his emphasis upon sensibility (rather than morality and reason) was to condemn mankind to a search for purely material satisfactions and a life without the consolations and inspirations of religion.[10] As Aimé-Martin wrote:

> To reduce man to his body, is to reduce him to his senses. It results from this idea that the brute would have an intelligence superior to his own, because the senses of a great number of animals are more perfect than those of man. This single objection destroys the system of the materialists.[11]

Tracy had anticipated this line of criticism in his earliest mémoires at the Institut. Man is superior even at the level of communication through gestures or movements: "the organisation of man is so superior to all others that even his language of action can become much more advanced than that of any animal".[12] It was true that ideas, understood as sense perceptions, were experienced by all animate species; perceptions or thinking exist before language, insisted Tracy.[13] But although animals rapidly attain the degree of intellectual development they require for their survival, they seldom surpass that level: their instinct is fixed and limited.[14] No doubt there are many animals whose physical sensibilities are more highly developed in certain fields than human sensibilities. This, however, does not confer a general superiority among such animals over the human species, for the animals have only very limited means of communication with their own species. The fact that our ideas originate in our sense perception, in no way proves that intelligence is the same thing as a refined capacity to perceive sensations: "the perfection of the senses is very far from being the measure of our intellectual capacity".[15]

The superiority of the human species consisted in the ability to make use of conventional and durable signs, to give permanent form to ideas, enabling men to combine and multiply their ideas in a variety of ways in cooperation with their fellows. Tracy no doubt believed that there was a physiological basis for this human capacity to create and manipulate signs representing ideas. He assumed, as a given feature of our physical organisation, the capacity of the brain to deal with complex operations: comparison, recollection, judgement, desire, etc. More immediately, however, he pointed out the importance of the human ability to vocalise a vast range of distinctive sounds (a kind of oral-aural alphabet) which made available a more flexible and extensive system of signs than those given by gesture or movement.[16]

Tracy claimed that Condillac was the first philosopher to have clearly demonstrated our dependence on signs in developing and communicating our ideas.[17] Hobbes was also praised for having understood the difficulties and the importance of establishing clear connections between words and meanings.[18] Signs are necessary to fix in our memory the meanings of and the relations between our ideas; without signs, says Tracy, we could hardly remember our ideas nor combine them.[19] The use of consciously developed language sets man apart from the beast, and makes it possible for him to emerge from that historical stage where he was dominated by his immediate needs.[20] Language, the symbolic embodiment of rationality, is the instrument of man's perfectibility. Having begun in total ignorance, the human species profited by shared experience and knowledge, and eventually reached a point where the desire to increase and propagate knowledge developed its own dynamic.[21] Knowledge becomes a cultural possession only by virtue of sign-systems or languages, which are entirely a product of social interaction over many centuries. It is a slow process: our means of knowledge require considerable exercise before they are developed more fully.

> And so we are entirely the product of art (rather than nature), that is, of our work; and we resemble the natural man, or our original mode of existence, as little as an oak resembles an acorn or a chicken resembles an egg.[22]

If signs were the instruments of human progress and reason, it followed that an individual who was denied the opportunity to participate in a linguistic communication system, would be unable to develop his mental capacities to more than an "animal" level.[23] Eighteenth-century materialists and sensationalists, including Diderot, La Mettrie and Condillac, had taken this to be a clear refutation of any innate-ideas hypothesis. Two examples were of particular interest to them, and were widely discussed: the case of deaf-mutes, and the case of so-called "wolf children". The deaf-mute from birth, said Tracy, cannot share in advanced forms of communication, and his intellectual capacities will reach only a limited level, even though he may be considered helped by instruction in gestural language.[24] The *enfant abandonné* was in a similar position: deprived of social interaction and advanced language skills, his intellect was seriously deficient.[25] The example of *le sauvage de l'Aveyron*, captured in 1799 shortly after Tracy's early mémoires at the Institut, provoked great interest among the idéologistes. The famous Dr Philippe Pinel, who was pioneering more humanitarian forms of treatment for the insane, wrote a report on the boy in 1800, on behalf of a committee of the Société des Observateurs de l'Homme, and concluded that the boy was an idiot, who had been abandoned because he was incapable of reaching more than a mediocre degree of intelligence. Dr Jean Itard subsequently spent several years, with very modest success, training the boy through techniques developed by Sicard at the Institute for deaf-mutes.[26]

According to Tracy, men in primitive societies learn to make certain judgements with great facility and precision, but only in a limited area, beyond which they encounter enormous difficulties. Progress beyond this stage depends on improvements in language as an instrument for communication, knowledge, and mastery of the environment. Without language, said Tracy, "the human species would be condemned to an eternal infancy".[27] Our communication through the use of signs, according to Tracy, "is the origin of all our social relations, and has thus given rise to all our sentiments and all our moral pleasures".[28]

Every language is based on conventional attributions of meaning to a set of signs. But a convention, according to Tracy, must rest on a prior mutual understanding between men. The main foundation for this mutual understanding is the universality of sensible experience. Each individual is affected similarly by feelings of joy, grief, surprise, tenderness, tiredness; the individual observes these feelings in others, and understands the causes. A shared language of action thus arises from our sentiments. From this "natural and necessary" language of action based on our desires, there gradually develops a more "artificial and voluntary" language in which we invent a multitude of signs to represent a wider range of ideas and relationships.[29] It is necessary, for continued progress, that some way is found to "render durable these first artificial signs which are all transient and fleeting".[30] Written languages thus mark a further stage in the development of human understanding.

But the practical consequences of adopting a written language are not uniform, because there are two main kinds of *écriture*: that based on pictorial representation of ideas (such as the complex hieroglyphic languages of China, Japan and the Middle East), and that based on notation of the tonal qualities of the oral language (such as the European languages). Tracy argues for the superiority of the second type, mainly because it is more flexible, simple, and readily learned by the mass of the people.[31] Even when the vocabulary is very extensive, all the words of an alphabetical language "are the result of the frequent repetition of a fairly restricted number of sounds".[32] Tracy could find no obvious reasons why some civilisations have used hieroglyphic writing and others alphabetical writing, for such forms were not the result of calculative choice or deliberation. The consequences, however, were irrevocable. Once a society had adopted one of these forms, it was virtually impossible to change to the other, since the changes involved would amount to a complete uprooting of customs, traditions, habits and institutions.[33] Societies which have adopted the hieroglyphic symbols, said Tracy, are condemned, as a direct result of their complex and inaccessible language, and their inevitably rigid social ranks, to achieving very little further progress.[34]

The alphabetical languages, on the other hand, are more easily taught to everyone. They facilitate the propagation of knowledge through the development of the printing press, for their small number of mobile characters are very flexible.[35] The scientific outlook could be transmitted more readily in alphabetical script, via textbooks and journals which could reach a mass audience. This last factor was an infinite advantage in the eyes of the idéologues, in the Baconian and *encyclopédiste* tradition, for whom the diffusion of ideas and the combatting of existing prejudices was as crucial as the discovery of new knowledge.

Tracy emphasised that the development of intellectual faculties depended greatly upon the repetition of ideas in given circumstances, an exercise which made our judgements more or less rapid and habitual. It is a "general law" of all our movements, mental and physical, that

> the more they are repeated, the easier and quicker they become; and that, the easier and quicker they are, the less they are perceptible, that is to say the perceptions they cause in us are diminished, even to the point of vanishing, though the movement itself still occurs.[36]

Our intellectual development depends on our judgements becoming easier, more rapid and less perceptible; and these operations are enormously facilitated by a shared language composed of a multitude of signs, whose meanings are fixed by conventional usage. However, while familiarity with the ideas contained in a language is the source of our cultural progress, there are certain inherent defects in the use of signs, said Tracy, which prevent us from ever achieving perfect communication, the implicit goal of idéologie.

There is a major problem in ensuring that the same meaning is always given to a sign by different people. Constancy in meanings is impossible to guarantee, said Tracy. On the contrary, it is strictly true that the exact meaning of a sign is known only to the first user; and even for him, only on the first occasion, because he may be mistaken in believing that later circumstances correspond exactly with the first situation.[37] Few people are inventors of signs and of meanings. Language is generally learned as part of our education in a particular society. Tracy assumes that there is always a degree of uncertainty and vagueness in using conventional signs,[38] especially in ordinary language where the sign system is more subject to individual variability in usage. To some extent, we can overcome the difficulty by gaining personal experience of the idea represented by the sign, especially in the case of simple sensations. But this becomes very difficult with complex ideas, for it would be necessary for each individual to analyse all the elements composing such ideas, examining their relations step by step, to be sure that the idea had the same content for that person as it had for others.[39] Condillac and Tracy believed that brute facts, immediately striking the senses, are unambiguous and given directly to man by nature, so to speak. A simple sensation, they assumed, would be experienced in the same way by all individuals owing to their identical organic faculties, and presumably owing to the passivity of the perception.

Complex ideas allowed more possibilities for vagueness, error, or variability in meaning, and for the intrusion of faulty memory. Language in use, therefore, is necessarily individualised to some extent, owing to the improbability of each individual attaching exactly the same meanings to the same words.[40] This, thought Tracy, was an inherent problem in complex communications and the use of abstract ideas.[41] Ambiguity could never be eliminated; but idéologie could do much to reduce the problem by showing how to avoid precipitate judgements,[42] at least in those specialised languages claiming to be systems of scientific knowledge. Fortunately, the defects of language are not all *inherent* in complex communication. Some defects are caused by ignorance, and by habitual errors of judgement: these could be overcome by education and by correcting certain anomalies in the written language.[43]

In searching out the possibilities for improving the accuracy of concepts and knowledge, Tracy considered the difference between language in general and algebraic analysis in particular. In 1796, he had confidently urged his colleagues to "imitate the mathematicians", since the latter had achieved a rigorous system of certain knowledge, beginning from a "palpable" first truth and proceeding slowly "from the known to the unknown".[44] Before long, Tracy recognised that the analogy was misleading,[45] and in so doing rejected Condillac's tendency to posit algebraic equations as the epitomé of linguistic exactitude. Tracy's comparison of language and algebra throws light upon the ideals of his reformist enterprise in conceptual reform, and also upon the impossibility of attaining a perfect language for expressing truths about man and society.

Tracy began by asserting:

> ... we can regard as proven that the general effect of signs is, in summing up prior judgements, to make easier the subsequent analyses; that this effect is exactly that of the symbols and formulae of algebra; and that, consequently, languages are true instruments of analysis, and algebra is simply a language which directs the mind with more certainty than others, because it expresses only very precise relations of a single type. Grammatical rules have just the same effect as the rules of calculus; in both cases, it is only the signs which we combine; and, without our being aware of it, we are guided by words just as by algebraic symbols.[46]

Tracy immediately qualified his analogy, by insisting on the distinctive characteristics of algebra. It is confined to ideas of quantity, which are invariable and distinct units whose relations are very precise and certain: providing one follows the rules, one always reaches a correct conclusion. But, he pointed out, most of our ideas are not quantitative, and it would be mistaken to take algebra as the desired model in our reforms of ordinary language, whose signs and relationships can never have the simplicity and precision of quantitative signs.[47] Algebraic signs are a particularly clear and limited group of precise symbols; ordinary language is relatively untidy and imprecise.

> Words are ... formulae which depict in an abridged way the results of previous combinations and which relieve our memory of the obligation of having these combinations presented ceaselessly in all their details ... (B)ut the results which these words express are not of a kind as simple or precise as those represented by algebraic symbols; and the modifications which we make them undergo in discourse ... are much more varied and much less measurable than

> those undergone by algebraic symbols ... (which) are all perceptible in numerical terms; those of words are not so, and that is an immense difference.[48]

In rejecting the model of algebra for a perfected language, Tracy rejected Condillac's notion that correct judgements are nothing but statements of identity between the two terms of a judgement.[49] Tracy also unwittingly cast doubt upon the very possibility of a deductivist science of man, and upon his own assumption that the human sciences could be brought to the same degree of certainty as the mathematical sciences.

Tracy was determined, above all, to show how the study of intellectual faculties could throw light on the correct operation of our judgements. The problem was to understand the mind sufficiently to enable us to make correct judgements. Given Tracy's view that language consists of signs and the combinations we make of them, the reform of language consisted in making our ideas (and their signs) more precise, and in making the links between them more certain. His ultimate practical objective was "ideological" education: "to make correct judgements habitual".[50] This would be a substantial and long-term project of public instruction, which would never be completely successful, given the inherent defects of signs. However, some progress could be made.

> ... a complete reform (of words and syntax) is almost impossible, for too many habits resist it. To change completely a usage which is tied at so many points to all our social institutions, would require a unanimous consent which cannot even be conjectured, and would be a real revolution in society. (But) ... while letting this usage subsist, since it cannot be destroyed, it would be very useful to point out properly its defects, their causes and consequences, and to place alongside our existing written language a perfected model of what it should be.[51]

Tracy assumes that, for maximum clarity, the written language should represent as exactly as possible the *sounds* of the spoken language. The latter should be examined carefully by a learned body of experts who would draw up a *phonetic* alphabet, containing all the sounds and inflections of spoken discourse, and would publish extracts from local and foreign literature in the new phonetic form for the edification of the public. This would fix the pronunciation and prose form of languages as precisely as possible, while leaving their everyday variations "in the grip of routine and (customary) usage". At least the *savants* of every nation might wish to consult with profit such an *écriture universelle*.[52] Tracy also hoped that a learned group from within the Institut might desire to take up the matter of perfecting the spelling, pronunciation and syntax of the French language.[53]

Tracy's hopes in these areas were neither unfounded nor ignored. Indeed, many of the problems of language raised by Tracy had been examined by grammarians and idéologistes towards the end of the eighteenth century.[54] Discussions at the Institut on questions concerning the development and reform of language were very common between 1796 and 1803, and some of the idéologistes were involved in revising the *Dictionnaire de l'Académie française*. One of the most notable initiatives was the series of prize essay topics proposed by the Class of moral and political sciences, including three concerned with language. The first, proposed in 1796, was addressed to the question of determining "the influence of signs on the formation of ideas".[55] The second, in 1799, asked candidates to "determine the influence of habit on the faculty of thinking, or in other words, clarify the effects on each of our intellectual faculties produced by the frequent repetition of the same operations".[56] The third such competition, announced in 1802, sought essays on the topic: "Determine how one should de-compose the faculty of thinking, and what are the elementary faculties which are to be recognised?"[57] Tracy himself was also active at the Institut pursuing related questions. For example, he was a member of a commission of the Institut appointed to examine the merits of a lexicological system devised by a M. Buttet, who sought to devise rules for giving exact meanings to words by the perfecting of our language. He was also appointed to a commission investigating the systems of *pasigraphie*, invented by de Maimeux and others, who sought to discover a "universal language" in which ideas were directly represented in symbolic forms other than the verbal forms of conventional languages.[58] Tracy in 1800 presented to the Institut his own critical assessment of pasigraphy. Such a system, he claimed, had all the defects of hieroglyphic languages, and thus could not resolve the problems it set out to overcome.[59]

Tracy had argued earlier, in his "Mémoire sur la faculté de penser", that a perfect language of any type was "a chimera, like perfection in any field".[60] Existing languages had developed in a haphazard manner over many centuries; they were far from methodical or systematic. For a perfect language to be created, it would have to be composed all at once, by a genius with universal knowledge, and devoid of all particular passions but love of truth.[61] A perfected language would in principle be able to represent our ideas precisely in a way which prevented misunderstanding, and might impart to our deductions the same certainty which exists in the languages of quantity.[62] There would be no way, however, that such a language would be widely adopted, by other than a few *savants*. Moreover, even if it were adopted, it would immediately become disfigured by the conventional usages of spoken language, and by the inherent weaknesses or limitations of our intellectual faculties.[63]

A less ambitious series of reforms would try to improve spelling and pronunciation; make syntax follow more closely the "natural progression of ideas in deductions"; eliminate vague and euphemistic expressions;[64] encourage the adoption of new terms wherever needed; formulate properly methodical nomenclatures in all the sciences; and correct our ideas by the discovery of new truths, especially in idéologie.[65] All these things could be done to the French language, making it the nearest approximation to the needs of *savants* for precise expression.[66] But while some such reforms could be made in each conventional language, Tracy concluded that a universal perfected language (*la langue universelle*) is bound to remain a "dream": indeed, it is "as impossible as perpetual motion".[67]

The idéologistes of the 1790s had placed great faith in the progressive consequences of conceptual reform; it was central to their conceptions of public instruction and the production of enlightened and virtuous citizens.[68] This explains why the *écoles centrales*, created in the law of October 1795, included a course on *grammaire générale*, a subject which, according to Tracy, would demonstrate that "all languages have common rules which are derived from the nature of our intellectual faculties", and that this knowledge is necessary "not simply for the study of languages but is also the only solid basis of the moral and political sciences, (on which ...) all citizens should have sound ideas".[69] The science of language was intended to have important and beneficial consequences for social and moral behaviour.

While Tracy believed that great improvements could be made by linguistic and conceptual reforms introduced into the education system by enlightened teachers and administrators, the other side of the problem was to combat the sources of error and mystification which were institutionalised in positions of influence. The major source of illusions in France, according to Tracy, was the Catholic Church. In the following section, we therefore examine Tracy's views on religion and theological metaphysics, in terms of his desire to reduce the influence of "metaphysical" and "unscientific" thought.

METAPHYSICS AND RELIGION

Tracy wanted to establish a clear separation between sciences based upon observation and analysis, and bodies of doctrine whose object was

> not to discover the sources of our knowledge, their certitude and their limits, but to determine the principle and the purpose of all things, to divine the origin and destiny of the world. That is the object of metaphysics. We place it among the arts of imagination, designed to satisfy us and not to inform us.[70]

There could be nothing more different in approach, insisted Tracy, between the "old theological metaphysics, or metaphysics strictly defined", and the "modern philosophical metaphysics or idéologie". The latter was the "remedy for all these infirmities" of the mind.[71] *Idéologistes* and *métaphysiciens* were engaged in distinct enterprises. As an "experimental" science dealing with facts and observation, idéologie avoided the "metaphysical" error of believing that general ideas gave meaning to particular ideas, instead of vice versa.[72] Metaphysics tended to separate the mental and material worlds, whereas they should be studied in their essential unity. Metaphysics tended to derogate the reality of man's natural objectivity, and see him as moving in a world of pure thought.[73] Condillac wrote that:

> Nature itself points out the order we ought to follow in the communication of truth; for if all our knowledge comes from the senses, it is evident that the perception of abstract notions must be prepared by sensible ideas ... If philos-

> ophers do not care to acknowledge this truth, it is because they are prejudiced in favour either of innate ideas, or of a customary usage which seems to have been consecrated by time.[74]

The "metaphysics" of Descartes and others who located the origins of ideas in pre-given categories of the mind, was thus contrasted by Tracy with idéologie, whose basic assumption was that a scientific epistemology could demonstrate the unity of mind and body, of the physical and moral realms, and could prove that all ideas were derived from our sense perceptions. Tracy did not attempt to refute in detail the various theories of innate and intuitive ideas. His procedure was to assert fundamental differences of principle between *a priori* "metaphysics" (in which Plato and Aristotle rubbed shoulders with Descartes, Malebranche, Leibnitz, Berkeley and Kant) and the philosophy of sensations and experience (whose key figures included Bacon, Hobbes, Locke, Helvétius and Condillac). As a behavioural science, concerned with effects and not ultimate causes,[75] idéologie was utterly opposed to pronouncements by philosophers and theologians claiming to know the purpose of creation or the destiny of man. Such matters could not be resolved by science; they could only be answered in accordance with revealed religion or private faith. The idéologiste's faith in the benevolent powers of reason in social life was contrasted to the mystifications inherent in acceptance of unverifiable dogmas about man, nature and God. Tracy likened the difference between the old metaphysics and the new science of ideas, to that between astrology and astronomy, or between alchemy and chemistry.[76]

The idéologues, like the philosophes before them, were involved in a bitter contest with Catholic orthodoxy for political and cultural influence. The Church had been a rich and powerful institution, supported by state authority and the censorship system, until it was disestablished from its official status and priests were obliged to swear loyalty to the civil constitution in 1790. In the following years, the goods of the Church were confiscated, convents were closed, and refractory priests were forced to emigrate or face execution. After the Terror and its forcible de-christianisation, there was a slight return towards religious toleration in 1795-97, before the Directory moved against "royalists" and anti-republicans in its efforts to bolster its precarious authority. The separation of Church and State had been formalised in a decree of February 1795.[77] Tracy and the idéologues strongly supported such moves to reduce the influence of the Church, not only in politics but especially in education. However, as opponents of clerical influence and as sensationalist philosophers, they were accused by orthodox believers of destroying the moral stature of the human species by degrading it to the level of animal sensations and appetites. Idéologie was accused of being materialist, atheist, and destructive of morality.[78] These critical claims, however, require certain qualifications.

In the first place, the idéologues, like most utilitarian social theorists,[79] did not want to destroy morality as such, but sought to reduce the authority of the Church in prescribing moral rules and sought to found morality upon a rational consideration of human desires and interests. For Volney and others, moral behaviour was based on natural laws, or rational principles inherent in social life.[80] The moral injunctions of the idéologues were indeed not very distant from certain principles in the Sermon on the Mount.[81]

Secondly, most of the idéologues were deists or agnostics rather than atheists.[82] They occasionally spoke of a divine providence which had ordered the universe; and some were active supporters of deist cults such as *théophilanthropie*[83] which flourished briefly under the Directory. Tracy and his colleagues were predisposed, by their scientific outlook and by their Voltairian ancestry, to be sceptical and agnostic towards theological revelations about the nature of the universe and the moral duties of man, and to be distrustful of claims by the Church to have privileged knowledge of the forms of authority and moral virtue prescribed by God for mankind.

Thirdly, the idéologues' view of man as anchored in natural history may be understood not so much as a denial of man's paramount place in the hierarchy of animal life, but more as a methodological strategy for a positivist science of human behaviour.[84] The idéologues were perfectly willing to agree that the human species had a unique capacity for reason, sentiment and morality. But they wished to demonstrate that these qualities had a physiological dimension (bordering on determinism, in one or two cases), and that these qualities were historically developed through language and social interaction (rather than being a divine gift). There would seem to be a clear line of continuity between the idéologues and Auguste Comte, not only in regard to a thorough-going scientism in their methodological pronouncements, but also in regard to the three stages theory of knowledge.

Tracy argued in his *Commentaire* (1806-7) that there have been three main stages in the development of reason and civilisation. The first was typified by despotism, force and ignorance; the second, aristocratic rule buttressed by religious opinions; and the third, representative government and the full flowering of reason. Comte's three stages were the theological, metaphysical and positive stages.[85] The pattern of evolutionary progress is similar; both systems obviously owe a great deal to Condorcet's ten-stage *Esquisse* of 1793 (and the conception can be traced back even to Turgot). What is common to Condorcet and his successors is a view of religion, theology and abstract ontology as obsolete and pre-scientific explanations of man. Moreover, such systems of belief are seen as institutional obstacles to the development of scientific reason. Condillac had therefore been wrong, in Tracy's view, to retain "natural theology" among the philosophical principles needed to explain man's place in society and history. Indeed, Tracy completely excluded theology from the hierarchy of sciences, where it had traditionally occupied a pivotal position.[86]

In considering theology and institutionalised religion in their dual aspect, as systems of knowledge/belief and systems of authority, Tracy made three kinds of criticism. Firstly, he asserted that many of the doctrines of revealed religion were not merely unverifiable, but had actually been disproved and exposed by science as mystifications and illusions about the operations of natural phenomena. Secondly, he criticised the Church for having resisted and obstructed the search for scientific knowledge about nature, and for attempting to impose a dogmatic and illiberal view of morality and the social order. Thirdly, he argued for a separation of Church and State, and in favour of religious tolerance, claiming that no religious beliefs should have the status of official doctrine, supported by public authority.[87] Religious beliefs, in his view, should be essentially matters of private conscience and faith, not matters of orthodoxy and authority. Taken together, Tracy's criticisms led him to support policies designed to reduce the influence of the Catholic Church in France; and especially in public education, where so many impressionable young minds could be distorted by unscientific dogmas and superstitions.

The anticlericalism of the 1790s changed after the Consulate was established by Bonaparte, who decided that the traditional religion was a necessary basis for the social order.[88] Catholicism was recognised as the official religion of France by the Concordat of 1802, and Chateaubriand's *Génie du Christianisme* simultaneously provided a spiritual defence of the Church. The idéologues were outraged by Bonaparte's policies whereby the Church regained a great deal of its erstwhile influence. It was not possible to mount a strong attack upon the Concordat and the revival of Catholicism (owing to censorship), although Chateaubriand's work was ridiculed in the pages of *la Décade philosophique* and oblique criticisms of the Church and the Concordat were made in articles defending "la philosophie rationnelle" and "la saine morale".

Tracy had observed the changing fortunes of the Church with a watchful eye; he adopted a staunchly and sometimes bitterly anti-clerical position. He had welcomed in 1795 the publication of Charles Dupuis' voluminous *l'Origine de tous les cultes*, which attempted to reduce religious doctrines to allegories or myths about nature, and especially about astronomical phenomena.[89] Tracy was so impressed by the thrust of Dupuis' erudite volumes, that he wrote some articles for the *Mercure français* giving a concise summary of the main arguments. The journal ceased publication in January 1798 before all of Tracy's remarks had appeared. Soon afterwards, Dupuis published a 600-page *Abrégé* of the multi-volume work (1798); but Tracy was not satisfied that Dupuis' summary was sufficiently analytical and didactic to serve the purpose of enlightening the wider reading public. Tracy therefore published, as an anonymous pamphlet, his summary of Dupuis: *Analyse de l'Origine de tous les cultes*.[90] A second and expanded edition, also anonymous, appeared in 1804: in the light of the revived influence of Catholicism, it was a veritable political tract.[91]

Dupuis' main argument, wrote Tracy, was that the ancient fables had never been properly understood, because it was not recognised that "all religions are never anything but the worship of nature and its main agents, the stars, fire and other elements; and because it was not seen that myths are only the allegorical and symbolic expressions of that first religion and its celestial aspects''.[92] Christianity could be understood, in these terms, as essentially the worship of nature and of the sun, under a variety of different names and symbols.[93]

The perspective adopted by Tracy and Dupuis was that religious dogmas were a product of a non-scientific world-view, a product of ignorance, and had been propagated by priests who preached servility and fear. The empirical methods of science were foreign to the priests and theologians, who set themselves up as authorities on the moral and the natural world.

> Let us conclude, then, that every religious system is, at the theoretical level, a supposition without proof, a veritable lapse of reason; and, at the practical level, it is a powerful force for making men follow certain rules of conduct but a sure means of giving them false rules, and emanating from an illegitimate authority; hence, that all religion may be defined as an obstacle to good logic and to sound morality both private and public.[94]

In some lines added to the 1804 edition, implicitly referring to Bonaparte, Tracy said that a man ''convinced of the utility and the sanctity of religion, if he wanted to be just and did not aspire to become domineering and oppressive'', would desire that no religion be taught in the public education system, for that would impose a uniform doctrine on people of contrary views.[95] In writing his *Commentaire* on Montesquieu two years later, Tracy asserted that ''any government which wants to oppress, is attached to priests and works to make them powerful enough to serve it''.[96] These critical references to Bonaparte are unmistakable. Tracy concluded his pamphlet in 1804 by asserting that

> theology is the philosophy of the infancy of the world, (but) it is time that it gave way to the philosophy of its age of reason; theology is the work of the imagination, like the bad physics or poor metaphysics which are born with it in times of ignorance and serve as its base; whereas the other philosophy is founded on observation and experience, and is closely tied to true physics and rational logic, which are all the product of the work of enlightened centuries; finally, a theologian is nothing but a bad philosopher who is rash enough to dogmatise on things he does not and cannot know.[97]

Tracy's identification of religion with speculative metaphysics and imagination was joined to an explanation of the historical origins of religious beliefs. Despite the apparent diversity and mutual antagonism of religious cults and sects, they all had a common basis, namely, that they were

> founded on the same idea—fear of invisible forces. Saint-Lambert said with good reason: *superstition is fear of invisible forces*. That is how he defined it; he could have added: *and it is the source of all religions*.[98]

In seeking the causes of natural phenomena, primitive societies invented various spirits whose task was to ensure that the sun and planets, the rivers and the winds, continued to be activated in their customary way. The worship by men of these multitudinous spirits who presided over everyday life was inevitable for primitive men, with their unsophisticated knowledge of the processes of nature. Later, they imagined a superior being who supervised all the lesser spirits and gave an overarching order to the whole universe.[99] But it was only ignorance of the real causes of phenomena which led man to explain events without a known cause as the product of the will of an unseen being.[100]

Dupuis had especially emphasised the religious significance of primitive astronomy and the mythology of the constellations and signs of the zodiac. "The adventures of all these gods are only allegorical tales about the movements of celestial bodies and their various relations; and thus it is in the heavens that we must find the source and application of all the mythological and theological fables".[101] These myths should not be dismissed without first seeking out their symbolic meanings. Dupuis had claimed that the key to decoding such myths lay in astronomical and physical phenomena.[102] Analysis of these myths showed that the two main sources of human unreason are the personification of abstractions, and the use of metaphorical and metaphysical terminology.[103] In such cases, wrote Tracy, ignorance is preferable to false ideas.[104]

Tracy also elaborated a critique or religion as a social institution in terms of the historical development of a priesthood.[105] In each primitive society there emerged people claiming to recognise more powerful spirits than those currently worshipped, or to know the best means of influencing such spirits, and who thus held sway over credulous people in their locality. Insofar as they did not join with other priests in founding a total religious system and theology, their social effect was relatively harmless.[106] Tracy took a different view of a more powerful priesthood which emerged with the growth of societies: religious doctrines became more systematic and the priesthood became an organised and hierarchical body. Priests then became "an integrating and important part of the constitution of the state".[107]

At the height of their power, the priests made their doctrines into a "science" which stifled all other forms of inquiry.[108] They propounded that *mauvaise philosophie* which is based on imagination rather than observation, conjecture rather than doubt, and which endowed abstractions and essences with reality instead of studying the actual operation of our intellectual faculties.[109] Theologians began to assert the complete spiritualisation of the gods and of souls, depriving them of all material attributes. They could then attribute to these "purely imaginary beings" whatever qualities they chose, without fear of contradiction. The only way to disagree would be to deny the very existence of spiritual powers, and to do so would invite severe punishment.[110] Theologians established a complete separation of the realm of ideas and judgements, from the realm of nature and material existence. Hence, they concluded that all our ideas and sentiments have their source not in our sensibilities but in another immaterial being, the universal spirit of God.[111] By giving free rein to their favourite errors (belief in the real existence of abstract ideas, and belief in the reality of a being deprived of all its sensible qualities) the theologians generated "a host of shocking absurdities", in which the Christian religion is especially prolific.[112]

The early Christian religion, claimed Tracy, consisted largely of practices and precepts; not dogmas, mysteries and sacraments. But by the thirteenth century, and throughout the "barbaric" Middle Ages, Christianity suffered an "excess of theological delirium", full of "far-fetched dogmas which are truly *non-sense*" and sustained by a sophistical language.[113] Such a system of beliefs began to lose ground, however, when the spirit of observation, experience, and doubt emerged alongside that of credulity and supposition. The truths based on observation and on the questioning of received opinion, began to replace the mass of accumulated errors. Once the facts of man and nature have been properly explained, Tracy asserted with more hope than conviction, the human mind would not abandon them again. Theology is like a child's imagination, destined to give way to a mature reason.[114] Tracy expressed a desire to be rid of

> this multitude of different religious systems, which have done so much harm in the world, caused so often the spilling of men's blood, divided people into what amounts to hostile groups, prevented commercial and social interaction among them, especially the communication of knowledge, made some people into objects of aversion and malediction for others, and prescribed so many duties so contrary to their happiness and to reason, particularly that of hating and detesting those who think differently from themselves.[115]

Dupuis' work had shown, to Tracy's satisfaction, that all the ancient and modern religions of Asia and Europe, which denounced one another so fiercely, were exactly the same apart from some changes in nomenclature. There could be no more bitter truth for the priests than this underlying unity of doctrine, for their great passion, he wrote, was hatred of their competitors. In that respect, said Tracy, priests are more like charlatans than thieves: for thieves keep a strong loyalty among themselves for their common security, whereas charlatans denigrate their fellows in trying to attract the crowd exclusively to themselves.[116]

Tracy noted that it would be easier for modern Europeans to see that the ancient religions and myths were based on the worship of nature and the stars, than to see that Christianity was in the same mould.

> Christianity is so close to us, it still rules over *the least enlightened part of* our surroundings, it seems to have so little relationship to these brilliant fictions: how are we to be persuaded that Christ too is only a fantastic being, just one of a thousand versions of the sun-god?[117]

Tracy further agreed with Dupuis that Christ was no more a historical figure than were Hercules, Bacchus or Osiris.[118] Nevertheless, Tracy surmised, it would require a great deal of scientific analysis and demystification to destroy the influence of religious illusions "for the absurdities have a very strong hold on the human mind when they have an ancient priority over reason''.[119] How could this ''ancient mass of prejudices and errors'' be overturned? The exact analysis of our intellectual operations could demonstrate to educated men that we only truly know whatever falls under our senses, and that all other supposed beings are nothing but ''personified abstractions, creations of our imagination''. It was necessary to open the eyes of the common man by tracing the origin and evolution of these myths, showing their fundamental similarity and basis in astronomical allegories.[120]

Tracy's ultimate objections to established religions were moral. Priests who claimed authority over the people, prescribing rules of belief and conduct, demanded blind faith in their own pronouncements. But it was a grave moral error, according to Tracy, to ''make a virtue of stupid servility'', and it was an even greater error to ''accustom men to seek their rules of conduct in the will of an unknown being'' instead of finding them in a rational understanding of their own human needs.[121] Priests hindered men from recognising the inherent link between virtue and happiness, and thus deprived men of the strongest motives for seeking out the good.[122]

> When I see religious men proclaiming almost unanimously that detestable maxim—that without the idea of the life to come, man has no motive for being good—I wonder in dread if they really want to degrade virtue, if they have sworn to pervert all moral ideas, and if their very devil could invent a principle better able to cover the world in misery and crime.[123]

In the place of religion, a defective moral system based on false assumptions and reasoning, Tracy advocated what he termed a morality ''guided by reason'' and based on the observation of man's intellectual faculties. In such a rational morality, we would rouse a man's personal interest in fulfilling his ''true'' duties, instead of employing fear to induce him to fulfil his ''imaginary'' duties.[124] (We will examine the character of this rational morality of needs and interests in chapter five.)

Finally, Tracy argued that religions are ''essentially subversive of true principles of social order or of public morality'', for it is the responsibility of the *civil* legislature to prescribe the duties of citizens. When priests claim for themselves this right, they usurp the sovereignty of the legislature and are often in conflict with it. So they are necessarily the enemies of all governments which they do not already control; and where the clergy does control the state, the liberty of all other citizens is violated, and equity and social equality are destroyed.[125]

Theologians should not, then, be accorded special privileges; the truth of their doctrines should not be protected from criticism by authority; they should not have special rights to exercise public authority or to form a collective body.[126] Their false doctrines, wrote Tracy, deserved to perish along with the false physics and logic which had so long supported them. Science, believed Tracy, would spell the demise of illusions about man and nature. All the ''subtleties of the old theological metaphysics will vanish as soon as we specify the proper meaning of the word, to *exist*''.[127] As soon as the unity of man and nature was fully appreciated, the influence of supernatural explanations of reality would decline,[128] and it would become possible to educate people in the ideological art of forming correct judgements about reality on the basis of observation.

Tracy, despite his fierce condemnation of priests and supernatural doctrines, wanted to avoid being taken for a ''materialist'' and ''atheist''. When Cabanis was accused of holding such positions by Mme de Stael, Tracy replied that such terms were not appropriate to describe

> men who loudly proclaim not to know what is spirit, nor what is matter, and who often repeat that they have never been, and never will be, occupied in determining the (ultimate) character of the principle of thought, for that is irrelevant to everything they have to say about it.[129]

The behavioural scientist of mental operations did not wish to be seen as propounding a materialist ontology; that would also have been a false metaphysics, for it dealt with the ''first causes'' of the universe. On the other hand, he could not resist making anticlerical jibes whenever the occasion arose, as in his remark that ''the religion of the Court of Rome ... is a commodity for export and not for consumption''.[130]

Chapters two and three have outlined in some detail the main themes in Tracy's epistemology: his views on science and method, his concept of idéologie as a logic of discovery and explanation, his views on the centrality of language in human experience and progress, and his critique of metaphysical idealism. Tracy's thinking subject, certain of his own existence and perceptions, must now be placed in the sphere of action. In the following chapter, we examine *l'homme sensible* as actor, and Tracy's account of how the individual becomes a social creature.

Notes

1. Cf. Tracy, *Logique*, p. 504; ''Mémoire sur la faculté de penser'', pp. 401-428; *Elémens*, vol. I, chapters 15, 16, 17.
2. C.C. Gillispie, *The Edge of Objectivity*, p. 169.
3. Tracy, ''Mémoire sur la faculté de penser'', p. 327. A very similar formulation was repeated in Tracy's manuscript of 1806, the so-called ''Mémoire de Berlin'', published by P. Tisserand in *Revue philosophique*, vol. 116 (1933), p. 172.
4. *Elémens*, vol. I, pp. xvi, 214, 322; *Logique*, pp. 121-129; ''Mémoire sur la faculté de penser'', p. 290. Tracy was nevertheless critical of several aspects of Condillac's work: cf. *Elémens*, chapter XI. For Tracy's remarks on Rousseau's recourse to divine agency in explaining language, cf. *ibid.*, pp. 302-3.
5. Condillac, *Essai* (1746), in *Oeuvres philosophiques*, vol. I, pp. 10-53.
6. *Ibid.*, pp. 60-103.
7. *Ibid.*, pp. 104-115; *Art de penser*, in *Oeuvres philosophiques*, vol. I, pp. 720, 727-730, 738-741.
8. Tracy, ''Mémoire sur la faculté de penser'', p. 325n. Cf. the erudite studies on non-European languages by Tracy's contemporaries: Volney, *Oeuvres* (Paris, 1821), vol. VIII, and Lanjuinais, *Oeuvres* (Paris, 1832), vol. IV.
9. ''Mémoire sur la faculté de penser'', p. 407.

10. Cf. Bernardin de Saint-Pierre, *Harmonies de la nature*, in *Oeuvres*, ed. Aimé-Martin (Paris, 1818), vol. IX, p. 435, and vol. X, pp. 10-24, 30-34, 54-55, 58-59, 78-89.
11. L.-A. Aimé-Martin, "Préambule", to Bernardin de Saint-Pierre, *op.cit.*, vol. VIII, p. vi.
12. "Mémoire sur la faculté de penser", p. 408.
13. *Ibid.*, p. 411; *Elémens*, vol. I, p. 361.
14. *Elémens*, vol. I, p. 295.
15. "Mémoire sur la faculté de penser", p. 428. The same point is made, in more detail, in *Elémens*, vol. I, p. 388, where Tracy concluded that "we are, on the contrary, almost entirely the product of the circumstances surrounding us ... (hence) the importance of education, taking this word in its widest sense".
16. *Grammaire*, p. 383; *Elémens*, vol. I, pp. 308, 369-371.
17. *Elémens*, vol. I, p. 322.
18. Tracy's respect for Hobbes' views on language and logic (as against his social and political doctrines) may be judged from the discussions in *Logique*, pp. 112-117; and the French translation of Hobbes' *Logic*, (Part I of *De Corpore*), appended to *ibid.*, pp. 589-667.
19. *Elémens*, vol. I, pp. 324-25, 335; "Mémoire sur la faculté de penser", pp. 425-6.
20. *Elémens*, vol. I, p. 294. Cf. V. Cousin, *Fragmens philosophiques* (Paris, 1826), pp. 168-9.
21. *Elémens*, vol. I, pp. 297-8.
22. *Ibid.*, p. 289; cf. p. 388. The teleological metaphor in this quotation is not typical of Tracy, since his conception of progress does not usually imply foreknowledge of the final destiny of man.
23. *Ibid.*, pp. 292-3.
24. "Mémoire sur la faculté de penser", pp. 408-410.
25. *Ibid.*, pp. 402-3.
26. Cf. Lucien Malson, *Wolf Children* (London, 1972), which reprints J.-M.-G. Itard's reports of 1801 and 1806 on *le sauvage de l'Aveyron*, pp. 91-179. See also Harlan Lane, *The Wild Boy of Aveyron* (London, 1977), which contains the reports on the boy by the naturalist P.-J. Bonnaterre, pp. 33-48, and by the psychiatrist P. Pinel, pp. 57-69, as well as those of Itard. Pinel's report was published by Georges Hervé in *Revue d'Anthropologie*, vol. 21 (1911), pp. 441-454. See also the anonymous article in *la Décade philosophique*, 10 vendémiaire an 9 (2 October 1800), pp. 8-18; and Leroy's essay in *la Revue philosophique*, 21 March 1807, pp. 513-523.
27. *Elémens*, vol. I, p. 378.
28. *Ibid.*, pp. 377-8. Cf. "Mémoire sur la faculté de penser", p. 420.
29. *Elémens*, vol. I, pp. 316-318.
30. *Grammaire*, p. 273.
31. *Ibid.*, chapter 5, especially pp. 264-270 and 277-280.
32. *Ibid.*, p. 261.
33. *Ibid.*, pp. 281-4, 288.
34. *Ibid.*, p. 291; and *Commentaire* (1806) (Paris, 1819), bk. 19, p. 308 (or *Commentary* (1811), p. 202).
35. *Grammaire*, p. 292. Cf. Condorcet, *Sketch*, pp. 99-102, on the importance of printing for the spread of rationality and the destruction of prejudice and oppression.
36. *Elémens*, vol. I, p. 266. For a parody of this so-called "law", see the hostile review of Tracy's *Projet d'Eléments d'idéologie* (1801), in *Mercure de France*, 16 nivose an X (6 January 1802), pp. 99-100: here, the critic applies this "law" to "explain" how a habitual thief acts to satisfy his desires, against all the evidence of reason.
37. "Mémoire sur la faculté de penser", p. 412; *Elémens*, vol. I, p. 384.
38. *Elémens*, vol. I, p. 383.
39. *Ibid.*, p. 379; "Mémoire sur la faculté de penser", pp. 327, 342.
40. *Logique*, pp. 57-8, 420-1; *Elémens*, vol. I, p. 386. Tracy does not seem to acknowledge that perception of simple sensation could itself be highly selective, not to mention erroneous.
41. "Mémoire sur la faculté de penser", pp. 400, 435.
42. *Logique*, pp. 166ff.

43. *Elémens*, vol. I, p. 387; cf. Condillac, *Traité des animaux*, in *Oeuvres philosophiques*, vol. I, p. 375.
44. "Mémoire sur la faculté de penser", p. 288.
45. *Ibid.*, pp. 384-5, 390.
46. *Elémens*, vol. I, pp. 339-340; a similar point emerges on p. 323.
47. *Ibid.*, pp. 340n-349.
48. *Ibid.*, p. 342n.
49. Cf. Condillac, *Art de penser*, in *Oeuvres philosophiques*, vol. I, p. 748. Tracy began his "Mémoire sur la faculté de penser" by agreeing with Condillac's view (p. 314), but gradually began to criticise it (p. 382) and soon rejected it entirely (p. 392), a critique he continued to make in his *Logique*, pp. 104, 155, 158f. Maine de Biran also strongly attacked Condillac on this point, as did most of the "revisionists" including Degérando.
50. "Mémoire sur la faculté de penser", pp. 442-3.
51. *Grammaire*, pp. 359-360.
52. *Ibid.*, pp. 361-3.
53. *Ibid.*, p. 366.
54. Cf. G. Harnois, *Les théories du langage en France de 1660 à 1821* (Paris, 1929); P. Kuehner, *Theories on the origin and formation of language in the eighteenth century in France* (Philadelphia, 1944); P. Juliard, *Philosophies of language in eighteenth-century France* (The Hague, 1970); R. Grimsley, "Maupertuis, Turgot and Maine de Biran on the origin of language", *Studies on Voltaire and the Eighteenth Century*, vol. 62 (1968), pp. 285-307; H.N. Bakalar, "The Cartesian legacy to the eighteenth-century grammarians", *Modern Language Notes*, vol. 91 (1976), pp. 698-721.
55. *Mémoires de l'Institut*, tome II, p. 2. The winner was Degérando, who expanded his essay into the four volumes of *Des Signes et de l'art de penser*, (Paris, 1800). On this work, cf. H.B. Acton, "The Philosophy of language in Revolutionary France", in *Studies in Philosophy*, ed. J.N. Findlay (Oxford, 1966), pp. 143-167.
56. *Mémoires de l'Institut*, tome IV, p. 11. The winner in 1802 was Maine de Biran; Tracy drafted the judges' report granting him the prize, reprinted pp. 207-224 in Maine de Biran, *L'Influence de l'habitude sur la faculté de penser*, ed. P. Tisserand (Paris, 1954).
57. *Mémoires de l'Institut*, tome V, p. 60. The winner in 1805 was Maine de Biran: cf. his *Mémoire sur la décomposition de la pensée*, ed. P. Tisserand (Paris, 1952), p. xv.
58. *Mémoires de l'Institut*, tome III, pp. 1-3.
59. "Réflexions sur les projets de pasigraphie", *Mémoires de l'Institut, Classe des sciences morales et politiques*, tome III (1801), pp. 535-551. See also *Grammaire*, p. 367n.
60. "Mémoire sur la faculté de penser", p. 416.
61. *Ibid.*, p. 415.
62. *Grammaire*, p. 378.
63. *Ibid.*, pp. 369-380.
64. Tracy evidently is unconcerned about the fate of literature, poetry, and works relying upon subtle imagery. He is concerned essentially with obtaining a standardised language for the expression of scientific truths.
65. *Ibid.*, pp. 382-389; "Mémoire sur la faculté de penser", pp. 417, 414.
66. "Réflexions sur les projets de pasigraphie", pp. 549-550.
67. *Grammaire*, p. 369. J. Simon, *Une Académie sous le Directoire*, p. 220, wrongly claimed that Tracy did believe in the possibility of a perfect and universal language. Condorcet, on the other hand, had certainly entertained the idea very seriously: see *Sketch*, pp. 197-199. On the background to the universal language schemes of the 1790s, see L. Couturat and L. Leau, *Histoire de la langue universalle* (Paris, 1907), and the excellent work of James Knowlson, *Universal language schemes in England and France, 1600-1800* (Toronto, 1975), especially chapters 5-8.
68. Cf. Condorcet, *Sketch*, p. 191; Talleyrand, "Rapport sur l'instruction publique" (September 1791), in C. Hippeau (ed.), *L'instruction publique en France pendant la Révolution: discours et rapports* ... (Paris, 1881), pp. 146ff.
69. *Elémens*, vol. I, pp. xxiii-xxiv. In claiming that "all languages have common rules" owing

to our common physiology, Tracy seems to be implying a physiological version of innate ideas, at least in Chomsky's sense of "deep structures". Tracy's claim may strike the reader as an example of rationalist faith, rather than as a product of empirical observation.

70. *Elémens*, vol. I, p. xvi. Cf "Mémoire sur la faculté de penser", pp. 369, 322-3.
71. Tracy, "Dissertation sur l'existence", *Mémoires de l'Institut, Classe des Sciences morales et politiques*, tome III (1801), pp. 516-517; see also pp. 529-530.
72. "De la métaphysique de Kant", pp. 596, 569, 580.
73. *Ibid.*, *passim*; "Dissertation sur l'existence", *passim*; and "Dissertation sur quelques questions d'idéologie", *Mémoires de l'Institut, Classe des Sciences morales et politiques*, tome III, pp. 500, 514.
74. Condillac, *Essai* (1746), in *Oeuvres philosophiques*, vol. I, p. 117.
75. Cf. Voltaire's work *Le Philosophe ignorant* (1765); and Volney, *Les Ruines* (1791), in *Oeuvres complètes* (Paris, 1821), vol. I, pp. 244-5.
76. Tracy, *Logique*, p. 143.
77. A. Dansette, *Histoire religieuse de la France contemporaine* (Paris, 1948), vol. I, pp. 65-158; J. McManners, *The French Revolution and the Church* (London, 1969); and F.-V.-A. Aulard, *Christianity and the French Revolution* (London, 1927).
78. See also J.-P. Damiron, *Essai sur l'histoire de la philosophie*, pp. 25, 88-89; L. de Bonald, *Mélanges littéraires, politiques et philosophiques* (Paris, 1819), vol. I, p. 339.
79. Helvétius and Bentham are clear examples in this context: Cf. C. Kiernan, "Helvétius and a science of ethics", *Studies on Voltaire and the Eighteenth Century*, vol. 60 (1968), pp. 229-243.
80. Volney, *La loi naturelle* (1793), ed. Gaston-Martin (Paris, 1934), especially pp. 104-118.
81. Cf. Tracy, *Traité de la Volonté* (Paris, 1815), pp. 79-80; Mme Sarah Newton Destutt de Tracy, "Notice sur M. Destutt de Tracy", p. 335.
82. J. Kitchin, *Un journal 'philosophique'*, pp. 158-177. Aimé-Martin reported that during a deist peroration by Bernardin de Saint-Pierre at the Institut, Cabanis denounced the use of the word 'God': *Essai sur la vie et les ouvrages de B. de Saint-Pierre* (Paris, 1818), pp. 244-5. Guillois, in *Le Salon de Mme Helvétius*, p. 197, defended Cabanis' reputation. Cabanis' personal views were clearly deist in 1807, in his *Lettre à (Fauriel) sur les causes premières*, in *Oeuvres philosophiques*, vol. II, pp. 256-298.
83. Cf. A. Mathiez, *La théophilanthropie et le culte décadaire, 1796-1801* (Paris, 1904).
84. Cf. Tracy, *Traité de la Volonté* (Paris, 2nd ed. 1818), p. 499; and below, note 129.
85. Tracy, *Commentaire*, bk. 6, pp. 62-78, and p. 223. Cf. Comte, *The Crisis of Industrial Civilization: Early Essays*, ed. Fletcher (London, 1974), p. 134 (written 1822).
86. Cf. Condillac, *Traité des Animaux*, in *Oeuvres philosophiques*, vol. I, pp. 367, 371, and *Art de raisonner*, in *ibid.*, p. 619. Tracy, "Sur un système méthodique de bibliographie"; *Logique*, pp. 520-1.
87. Cf. *Commentaire*, pp. 232, 387-390.
88. Bonaparte's functionalist view of the integrative power of traditional religion, is reported in *Voix de Napoléon*, ed. P.-L. Couchoud (Genève, 1949), pp. 42, 49; *Entretiens avec Napoléon*, ed. L. Pautré (Paris, 1969), pp. 23-26; L. de Villefosse and J. Bouissounouse, *L'Opposition à Napoléon*, pp. 174-5.
89. Cf. Chateaubriand, *Mémoires d'outre-tombe* (Genève, 1946), vol. I, p. 390: Bonaparte exclaimed: "Christianity! Didn't the idéologues want to make of it a system of astronomy?".
90. (Tracy), *Analyse de l'Origine de Tous les Cultes, par le citoyen Dupuis, et de l'Abrégé qu'il a donné de cet ouvrage* (Paris, an VII: 1799).
91. (Tracy), *Analyse raisonnée de "l'Origine de Tous les Cultes ou Religion Universelle"* (Paris an XII: 1804). I noted in chapter 1 that Tracy's authorship was revealed in 1806 by A.-A. Barbier.
92. *Analyse* (1799), p. 2.
93. *Analyse* (1799), p. 3 and pp. 62-77; 1804 ed., pp. 94-116.
94. *Analyse* (1799), p. 100; 1804 ed., p. 148.
95. *Analyse* (1804), p. 149.

96. *Commentaire*, pp. 389-390.
97. *Analyse* (1804), pp. 158-9.
98. *Ibid.*, pp. xi-xii (emphasis in original).
99. *Ibid.*, pp. xii-xxiii.
100. "Mémoire sur la faculté de penser", p.367.
101. *Analyse* (1804), p. 22.
102. *Ibid.*, pp.23, 69.
103. *Ibid.*, p. 27; cf. 1799 ed., p. 17 for slightly different terminology.
104. *Analyse* (1804), pp. 24-25; "De la métaphysique de Kant", p. 551.
105. Cf. *Commentaire*, pp. 388-9.
106. *Analyse* (1804), pp. xxiii-xxiv.
107. *Ibid.*, p. xxv; cf. *Commentaire*, pp. 35-40, on religion as a form of social control.
108. Cf. *Grammaire*, p. 6, where Tracy condemns "the despotism of religious opinions".
109. *Analyse* (1804), pp. xxvi-xxvii; cf. "Sur les Lettres de Descartes", p. 397.
110. *Ibid.*, pp. xxviii-xxx.
111. *Ibid.*, pp. xxxii-xxxiii.
112. *Ibid.*, pp. xxxv-xxxvii.
113. *Ibid.*, p. xxxviii (emphasis in original). This depressing view of the Middle Ages is also found in Condorcet, *Sketch*, pp. 72-89.
114. *Ibid.*, pp. xl-xliv.
115. *Ibid.*, p. xliv.
116. *Ibid.*, pp. xlvi-xlvii.
117. *Ibid.*, p. 95 (emphasis added). The phrase emphasised was inserted in the 1804 edition, to make a stinging comment on the revival of Catholicism. Cf. *Analyse* (1799), pp. 62-3.
118. *Analyse* (1804), pp. 113-115.
119. *Ibid.*, p. 29.
120. *Ibid.*, p. 13.
121. *Ibid.*, p. 145. In 1806, Tracy in turn was accused of servility to Condillac's philosophy by a reviewer in *la Revue philosophique*: cf. J. Kitchin, *Un journal 'philosophique'*, p. 135n.
122. "Quels sont les moyens de fonder la morale chez un peuple?", in *Commentaire*, pp. 456-460.
123. *Analyse* (1804), pp. 145-6.
124. *Ibid.*, p. 147; "Quels sont les moyens ...", p. 459; *Traité de la Volonté* (Paris, 1818), pp. 499-503.
125. *Commentaire*, pp. 39, 389; *Analyse* (1804), pp. 146-7.
126. *Analyse* (1804), p. 158.
127. "Dissertation sur quelques questions d'idéologie", p. 514. Cf. the common contrast between science, on the one hand, and ignorant superstition on the other, e.g. J.-B. Say, *A Treatise on Political Economy* (1803) (New York, 1880), p. 81n.
128. "Quels sont les moyens ...", p. 460n.
129. Tracy to Mme de Stael, 23 February 1805, reprinted in R. de Luppé, *Les idées littéraires de Madame de Stael* . . . (Paris, 1969), pp. 163-4.
130. *Commentaire*, p. 98, repeated in *Traité de la Volonté* (1818), p. 367.

4. INDIVIDUALS AND SOCIAL RELATIONS

We have seen that, for Tracy, all our ideas come from the perceptions furnished by our senses; simple ideas are those given immediately by the senses, and other ideas are formed by separating and recombining simple ideas in complex ways. Our multitude of ideas have been generated by a small number of mental processes. The faculty of thinking, upon closer inspection, is seen to be composed of four or more specialised faculties, all of which are modes of sensing or perceiving, and they account for all the activity of the mind.[1]

1. Sensibility is our faculty of perceiving sensations, which are felt as simple pleasures or pains.
2. Memory is the faculty of being affected again by a past sensation.
3. Judgement is the faculty of perceiving relations, comparing and distinguishing between sensations, memories, simple and complex ideas, or any combination of these. If we suppose a perception of the relation between a pleasurable and a painful sensation, "there follows at once the desire to experience the one rather than the other."[2]
4. The will, or faculty of desiring, arises on the basis of our faculty of judgement, which in turn depends on our capacity to have simultaneous but distinguishable sensations.

Tracy regarded the individual self (*le moi*) as the ensemble of its sensibilities. The self is constituted by its flow of impressions, judgements and desires. More specifically, the self, said Tracy, is generally identified with the will, for this is the source of the individual's happiness.[3] The individual is a creature of needs and has certain means for satisfying those needs. His needs and his means exist by virtue of his constitution as a *desiring* being, susceptible to pleasure and pain, happiness and misery, and as an *acting* being, capable of power and influence.[4] There are two main problematical features of this doctrine of the self as a bundle of desires and consequent actions to satisfy these desires.

One problem is whether a genuine conception of individuality and personality can emerge from such a theory, a question which depends on whether individual desires and actions are seen as determined externally or as significantly controlled by the self. Tracy tackled these questions through his reconsideration of the old debate concerning free will and determinism, and through his hesitant attempts to elaborate a theory of the active subject exploring the external world. These are the themes discussed in the first section of this chapter. The second problem with Tracy's view of the self as an ensemble of sensibilities, is his implicitly atomistic conception of individuality. How can Tracy account for social affections, social co-operation and social conventions and institutions on the basis of his view of the self as pursuing the satisfaction of desires springing from its senses? Tracy's conception of the sources of social integration are considered in the second section of this chapter, while the following chapter examines some of his views on the role of law, education and social morality in producing a secure and enlightened form of social existence.

INDIVIDUAL WILL AS DESIRE AND ACTION

In his early "Mémoire sur la faculté de penser" in 1796, Tracy ascribed a crucial role to what he called the faculty of *motilité*, or faculty of perceiving our own movement and resistance to this movement by external objects. *Motilité* allowed us to distinguish between ourself and externality, and between various objects. Without the comparative judgements made possible by *motilité*, we could not attain knowledge of the existence of external bodies, nor develop our faculties of judgement and will.[5] *Motilité*, said Tracy, involved experience of the sensation of effort.[6] Here, Tracy came close to locating the generation of knowledge in the active subject, rather than simply in human sensibility.

Tracy's emphasis on the *motilité* of the willing and acting subject was continued in another paper read to the Institut in 1799.[7] Here Tracy showed that there was an important difference between Condillac's doctrine in the original edition of the *Traité des sensations* (1754), where knowledge of external objects was attributed to our sense of touch, and Condillac's revisions of that work, published posthumously in the *Oeuvres* of 1798, where he recognised the importance of bodily movement and the sensation of resistance to this movement by external objects. Tracy's doctrine of *motilité*, with its potential for further development towards a philosophy of effort or active willing, raised the possibility that Tracy's formula *je sens donc j'existe* might have been modified to accommodate the active subject: e.g., *je veux donc j'existe*, or perhaps, *j'agis donc j'existe*. It was left to Maine de Biran[8] to develop this potentiality in Tracy's doctrine of *motilité*, because the first volume of Tracy's *Eléments* in 1801 specifically withdrew the activist or voluntarist implications of the doctrine and insisted that every act of the will had to be understood in terms of a sequence of "prior facts".[9] It is necessary to examine these two doctrines in Tracy's writings on the will, showing the difficulties Tracy faced in outlining a consistent sensationalism, and leading us to a critical consideration of his conception of liberty as the power of the individual to satisfy his desires.

One of the interesting questions posed by Tracy in 1796 concerned the extent to which the will might be regarded as "free" and "active". Tracy suggested that all our faculties "are in part determined and in part voluntary, that is, they sometimes act without our will and sometimes in accordance with our will''.[10] He dismissed the notions of complete free will and complete determinism as equally false extremes. He illustrated the notion of a balance between voluntary and involuntary aspects of action in relation to each of the faculties described above. We cannot shut off our reception of simple sensations; we receive them whether we are seeking or avoiding them. However, we are able to concentrate our attention upon certain sensations to such an extent that others go unnoticed. In the same way, we cannot prevent memories from entering our consciousness, but we are able to recall ideas at will and can train our mind to become highly proficient at doing so. Our judgement may also be seen as partly independent, in the sense that we are obliged ''by our organisation'' or constitution to perceive a relation which clearly exists between two ideas; without this inner ''necessity'' we could never achieve certain knowledge. On the other hand, we can control our judgements insofar as we examine certain relationships rather than others, and focus our attention on certain perceptions and memories rather than others.[11]

Motilité is also partly independent, at least in the beginning. In new-born infants, for example, any sharp disagreeable sensations will cause involuntary movements and sounds. Agreeable sensations, Tracy speculated, were more likely to cause a contented passivity, rather than action, at least until the infant learned to communicate expressions of pleasure. The movements of new-born infants, before they acquire any ''knowledge'', may be regarded as independent of the will, however intentional these movements appear, as in suckling. Instinct is more highly developed in other animal species but plays some part in human behaviour. However, until the notion of instinct is further clarified by the physiologists, said Tracy, only movements which are the product of prior knowledge and judgement of relations should be taken as voluntary. There are many cases of such voluntary action, where a certain effect is intended. On the other hand, there are certain movements which remain independent of our will no matter what our age and experience, such as those involved in our organic growth and conservation.[12]

Finally, Tracy showed the simultaneous existence of both willed and unwilled aspects of the will or desire itself. The determined or passive aspect is that we cannot prevent ourselves from desiring agreeable perceptions or the absence of disagreeable perceptions.

> But it is only our first desires which are the necessary (determined) effects of our organisation; the more complex desires formed on their foundation depend more or less on the influence our will has established over the action of our judgement and other faculties; we have the capacity to examine these complex desires, to formulate them only after a reflective act of our judgement, and to correct or change them if our earlier judgement was hasty or false. Our will is, then, involved in the formation not only of our knowledge but of our passions.[13]

Having outlined the operation of the faculties, Tracy returned to the question of whether our sensibility is an active or passive faculty. The answer, he said, depends greatly on the meaning of the term "active". Perceiving a sensation is certainly an action of our faculty of perception; in that sense it is true that we are active when perceiving. But if "active" means performing an action freely and voluntarily, while "passive" means doing it by necessity or forcibly, then we are passive when we perceive a sensation without having desired it, and active when we experience it only after an express act of will.

The notion of being "free", according to Tracy, consists in being able to act in consequence of one's will: freedom, then, means the capacity to satisfy one's desires.[14] Can it be said that our will is free in this sense? In the absence of prior experience and judgements, our first desires must be "forced and necessary, deriving inevitably from the nature of things and their relation to our organisation. In this case, our will is only a rigorous consequence of our sensibility: it is not free".[15] But such cases are not typical of most human experience. Tracy therefore reasserts at length the difference between simple and complex desires:

> But if by the question 'Is our will free?' we mean to ask if our most complex desires are forced and necessary consequences of our organisation and of our simplest desires, without the intermediary of our will, we can reply ... that we can very often summon at will the perception of a sensation or a memory, and of specific relations among them; that we thereby draw new habits, ... new signs, ... and new knowledge, the basis of desires which did not exist in all these elements. So, these desires, based on elements produced by continual acts of our will, cannot be regarded as necessary and forced consequences of our first desires. Thus it cannot be said that our most complex desires are mechanical results of our organisation, as are the simplest desires; moreover the former are as different among individuals as the latter are similar. Our will has influenced their formation; the will is thus free in that sense.[16]

Tracy seems to have established a continuum between relative degrees of voluntary intervention. A simple perception implies automatic attraction or aversion to the receiver; the desire which follows it is thus necessary and forced. But whenever our will helps to select and arrange our perceptions (which is virtually always), the desire which follows these perceptions is not completely forced.[17]

Tracy appeared to be alarmed that this doctrine might imply a dualism between the organic and the intellectual aspects of human behaviour, and he sought to re-impose a theoretical unification through the doctrine that every action, strictly speaking, has a *cause* in a previous perception. Tracy's notion of scientific explanation assumed that every "effect" must have, at least in principle, a causal chain of prior effects. Thus he claimed, in a highly determinist and reductionist manner, that even the most "complex" desire is also a "necessary" result of the simple and intermediate desires which preceded it. Tracy agreed with Condillac's belief: "if we knew the chain of all the causes and all the effects, we would find that everything in existence is so necessarily: otherwise, why would it exist?"[18] Tracy believed that without such an insistence on causality, one would relapse into idealist metaphysics. In the physical realm, he said, we commonly attribute to chance whatever escapes our limited understanding of causes; likewise in the mental realm, we wrongly attribute to a free and independent will all our acts of desiring, even though all these acts are the effects of a prior chain of causes and effects.[19] However, said Tracy, the question of whether our desires are really the necessary results of prior perceptions is of little consequence. The important facts for the idéologiste are that the exercise of our faculties depends in most cases on our will; that we are free and happy when we are able to act in accordance with our will, but unhappy and forced when our will is frustrated; that we have the capacity to regulate our will, and indeed it is in our interest to do so.[20]

In the "Mémoire" of 1796, the doctrine of *motilité* held that our faculties of judgement and the will cannot develop before we have obtained a knowledge of external bodies, through their resistance to our movements. Initially our bodily movements and our perception of resistance were an involuntary result of our sensibility for we were not at birth capable of perceiving relationships and having desires. This doctrine, however, was fundamentally modified in the first volume of the *Eléments* in 1801, and further in the second edition in 1804. Tracy now argued that knowledge of external objects is gained only because we perceive their inertia or resistance to our *willed* actions.

This revised doctrine was made possible by collapsing the conception of will into the general faculty of sensibility. Tracy now finds that the will operates before, or simultaneously with, our first sensible perceptions.[21]

> ... everyone knows that many sensations have the inherent property of being agreeable or disagreeable to us. Now, what is finding a sensation agreeable or disagreeable, if it is not to make a judgement about it, to perceive a relation between it and our faculty of feeling? And ... is not this to feel at the same time the desire to experience this sensation or to avoid it? All these operations, then, can be and actually are united in a single fact, in the perception of any single sensation. I was wrong to deny it, and to have asserted that our faculties of judging and willing cannot begin to act until we have experienced the sensation of movement and that of resistance ... Indeed there is no sensation of resistance, properly speaking, unless there is a previous sentiment of will.[22]

Tracy provided an example: we are all aware, he said, that a sharp pain makes us feel the "need" (*besoin*) to move away, quite independently of whether we know we are being harmed. This need is itself a "desire", albeit an unreflective desire. It is therefore possible, he concluded, that "the first of all the movements made by each of us was accompanied by our will".[23] The outcome of such a doctrine, in my view, is to undermine the distinction he had earlier drawn between instinctive or determined behaviour, and more or less voluntary behaviour. "Instinctive" actions, he noted in the new doctrine, "include judgement and desire".[24] Congratulating himself that his "new theory is founded on positive facts",[25] Tracy doubtless believed that the physiological theories of Cabanis would be consistent with his revised doctrine. In fact, Cabanis was never so bold as to claim that human instinct includes judgement and desire.[26] Tracy, in expanding the sphere of the will into areas such as instinctive behaviour and actions of new-born children, virtually obliterated the distinction between voluntary and involuntary actions.

A related difference between Tracy's two positions is that the distinction drawn in his early writings between "needs" (*besoins*) and "desires" (*désirs*) is eliminated. Tracy in 1796 had agreed with Condillac that "all our faculties arise from a single origin, sensation; they are developed by a single principle, need (*besoin*); and they are exercised by a single means, the connection of ideas".[27] Tracy also agreed with Condillac that needs are based on pleasures and pains, and that needs give rise to desires. However, he criticised Condillac for subsequently extending the term "need" to include certain ideas involving judgements or comparisons between various pleasures and pains.[28] According to Tracy's early writings, need is thus the simple sensation of pleasure or pain, and desire is the more complex idea based on comparison or judgement.[29] In this view, our first needs, resulting directly from our organisation, are simple perceptions, immediate products of our sensibility, and precede all knowledge of relations. Comparative judgement about the relations of these sensations subsequently leads to the desire to experience one or avoid others. Every pleasure and pain is in itself a need; but need becomes desire only when our judgement introduces ideas of relation and comparison.[30] These distinctions were quite compatible with the involuntary *vs.* voluntary distinction.

In the revised theory, however, "needs" and "desires" are indistinguishable; indeed they are portrayed as synonyms[31] just as "sensations" and "ideas" had earlier been identified with one another. "Desires" now extend from the most "instinctive" to the most "reflective" actions.[32] Tracy's main reason for this all-embracing or monist conception of the will is his view that many sensations are immediately experienced as either pleasurable or painful. Tracy tried to justify this position in the essay he wrote in 1806 for the Academy of Berlin's competition on the topic "Are there immediate internal perceptions?" He began by repeating his fundamental view that all ideas are the product of our sensations transformed in various ways and that our intellectual operations consist entirely of perceiving, remembering, judging and desiring.[33] One might object, he noted, that by this simple classification one is forcing into the same category phenomena which are often distinguished. For example, it is common to distinguish between instinctive and reflective wants, those which are more obscure or more precise, stronger or weaker, and all kinds of wishes, dispositions and inclinations which are not *volitions* in any settled and positive way. Moreover, there are cases where we change our mind, and give way to a stronger will. However, these diverse mental phenomena are only variations on a common theme, all arising from the fact that

> we are so constituted that certain affections, certain modifications of our being please us and others displease us, some appear more agreeable to us than the others, and so we are capable of the sentiment of preference. This sentiment is the common basis of all these intellectual acts (of will). Without it, none of them would exist ... Thus I was justified in collecting under the general faculty of the will all those acts whose basis lies in some kind of preference.[34]

All acts of the will, according to Tracy, are based on the inherent tendency of animate beings to feel pleasure or pain in certain sensations; the acts of will consist in furthering one's pleasurable perceptions and minimising the unpleasant ones.[35] The ultimate reason why we experience some as desirable and others as undesirable is unknown.[36] (This was an area where Tracy expected the physiological idéologistes might eventually throw some light.) What is known by experience is that the faculty of desiring determines our well-being. "Desire ... is inherently an enjoyment if it is fulfilled and a suffering if it is not. Hence our happiness or misfortune depend on it. And if by error we venture to desire things which are essentially harmful ... we are inevitably unhappy".[37]

Tracy ultimately reaches a contradictory and confused position. On the one hand, he wants to claim that the will is the faculty which transforms into actions all the results of our other faculties, that it "directs the movements of our limbs" as well as "the operations of our intelligence": the will controls the ways we use our "mechanical" and our "intellectual" forces.[38] However, the causal links, he admits, are too complex and hidden to demonstrate: it would never be possible by scientific observation to prove that a given desire is the "cause" of action taken to satisfy that desire.[39] All we can say with confidence is that there is a "correspondence" or a "parallel" between our intellectual phenomena of desiring and our "mechanical, chemical and physiological acts".[40] Ordinary language holds that the will is the cause of voluntary actions which follow it. Tracy concedes there is little harm in admitting such usage, so long as the causal desires are understood as merely a shorthand expression for the complex chain of causality, including all those organic "internal movements" which are the immediate causes of our actions.[41]

On the other hand, Tracy asserts that the will is not "free" because we are unable to control whether or not we experience a desire.[42] There is an ultimate "necessity" underlying all our actions, in the sense that there is no action without a sequence of prior causal facts.[43] Properly posed, he claims, the question of free will may be reduced to whether our will is "dependent solely on itself". The answer is that it cannot be independent of prior judgements and sensations, and therefore the will is not really "free".[44] The very question of "free will", wrote Tracy in the *Commentaire*, is misleading. The question tends to arise only because in some situations we appear to have alternative choices available, whereas in other situations our conduct is virtually forced upon us. In the first case, our "free" choice is really an "illusion", claimed Tracy, because every act of will is caused by whatever determinations (however weak) led to its taking one direction rather than another.[45]

Tracy's strict insistence that every phenomenon is determined (because every phenomenon has a cause) is a good illustration of his scientism, and of his refusal to concede ground to any spiritualist interpretation of man's faculties or of man's place in the universe. Tracy assumes that "facts" are causally inter-related in a complex web, and the task of science is to find the causal sequences underlying each given "effect". If a causal chain remains hidden, it is only a matter of time before the sequence is revealed: a matter of making further observations, asking the correct questions. In principle, the unknown is "not yet known" rather than "unknowable", providing of course that the enquiry is directed at understanding processes (effects) rather than ultimate causes of reality.

Tracy's scientistic view of causality also has significant consequences for his approach to the moral and political sciences. Firstly, it implies the possibility of a social technology. If every idea (perception) and every need (desire) has a determinate cause, it is possible in principle to alter the causal sequence by re-education or re-direction to produce different ideas and desires. (This implication will be examined more closely in the following chapters.) Secondly, his behaviouralist approach leads to a particular view of the content of the moral and political sciences. *La morale* is no longer to be seen as a code of moral precepts (derived from tradition or revelation), but a study of the character and consequences of our actions in terms of their effects on our happiness. An expression of intention is no longer a sufficient explanation for an action, nor is it an adequate measure of the moral qualities of that action. Virtue, wrote Tracy, is to be judged by the *effects* of our actions upon the happiness and well-being of humanity.[46] *L'économie* is to be understood, again in behavioural terms, as the study of the actions we take to satisfy our needs (desires), and their consequences for our happiness. And finally, *la législation* is a utilitarian science which examines the policies available to public authorities to "direct" the actions of the citizens so as to increase their happiness.[47] It is clear that the scientific study of the will leads directly, in Tracy's approach, to a search for institutional methods for securing the welfare and liberty of the citizens, just as we saw earlier that the study of the formation of ideas leads directly to a search for ways of perfecting our faculty of judgement. How is Tracy's doctrine of the will related to his conception of liberty and happiness?

We saw in chapter one that in 1794 Tracy had seen an identity between liberty and happiness. This conception was elaborated in his early mémoires at the Institut, where he asserted a fundamental interdependence of the concepts of liberty, power and happiness.

> The more I have considered it, the more I am persuaded that being free consists in being able to act in consequence of one's will, and that the word *liber-*

> *ty*, however it is used, signifies nothing but the power to satisfy one's desires. Now, since it is clear that the well-being, the happiness of a sentient being, of a being susceptible of desires, consists in the accomplishment of these desires, it follows that liberty and happiness are two ideas essentially inseparable for it, or rather that it is absolutely the same idea considered under two different aspects, that of its means and that of its goal. Thus, to mention in passing, the truths of morals, ... politics, ... and physics and mathematics, ... are at the same time means of our happiness and liberty, well-being and power.[48]

Several years later, Tracy repeated that

> the idea of *liberty* arises from the faculty of willing; for, with Locke, I understand by liberty the power to execute one's will, to act according to one's desires ... Thus there would be no liberty if there were no will; and liberty cannot exist before the birth of the will.[49]

The will has the capacity to regulate most of our movements, to direct the use of almost all our faculties, and thereby to create all our means of enjoyment and power. For Tracy, our liberty or the power to execute our will

> ... is thus the remedy of all our ills, the accomplishment of all our desires, the satisfaction of all our needs, and consequently the foremost of all our goods, that which produces them all and includes them all. It is the same thing as our *happiness*; it has the same limits, or rather, our happiness cannot be of greater or lesser extent than our *liberty*, i.e. than our power to satisfy our desires.[50]

Tracy's conception of liberty is defined not only in terms of an absence of restraints upon action, but also in terms of the actual accomplishment of our desires (= happiness). It is not a strictly "negative" conception of freedom as absence of impediments (as in Hobbes); although this remains the most important strand of his liberalism.[51] The additional element is Tracy's concern that one criterion of freedom is the degree to which one has the capacity or power to satisfy one's desires, and thereby attain happiness. Tracy's concern with positive outcomes, as well as with an absence of restraints, was perhaps related to his experience of politics in the early years of the Revolution, when "liberty" was invoked to justify all kinds of illiberal measures jeopardising the welfare and happiness of many citizens. But his concern with happiness, as something more than absence of restraint, may also be seen as a characteristic of a social philosophy which assumed that certain kinds of actions should be *encouraged* and others *discouraged*. Tracy was not indifferent to the ways in which men used their freedom to act. He wanted to promote the sentiments of benevolence, modesty, frugality and civic-mindedness and to discourage behaviour which was anti-social, malevolent, prodigal or mean. He also wanted to promote scientific perspectives and to combat various sources of obscurantism and prejudice. He wanted to encourage talents and industry of all kinds, and to abolish traditional constraints upon such activities. It is not surprising, then, that Tracy sometimes wanted to suggest, or prescribe, what men should do with their freedom. Yet he remained unattracted to illiberal doctrines which sought to define, and enforce, a systematic view of how all men should behave.

Tracy gave some attention to the concept of "constraint" as the opposite of liberty. Constraints which prevent us from satisfying our desires thereby cause suffering rather than happiness. Constraints may take many different forms, and there are several ways of trying to overcome them. Some constraints, the effect of physical forces, are direct and immediate: other constraints, the effect of moral and intellectual considerations, are more indirect though no less "real" in their effect.[52] In some cases, the constraints might be insurmountable, imposed upon us by our natural capacities. It would be wise to abandon desires which are confronted by insuperable obstacles of this kind. Freedom commences only on the basis of our recognition of necessity, and a knowledge of our capacities.[53] In other cases, certain of our desires can be accomplished only at the cost of abandoning other desires, or by creating additional unwanted effects. Tracy here sees the need for a prudential calculation of relative advantages and disadvantages, in order to choose between alternative courses of action. Tracy claims that it is in our interest to study the nature of the obstacles or constraints upon the satisfaction of our desires, and to adopt the means which are most likely to advance our goals.[54] Our interest, in other words, is to increase our liberty or power, and to use it well, "that is, to use it so as not ultimately to impede or restrain it".[55] Such calculations of long term interests would require a highly developed faculty of judgement, to the improvement of which Tracy had devoted much of his writing on idéologie.

The above conceptions of liberty and constraint were drawn at the level of individual desires and their realisation or frustration. Tracy encountered certain difficulties in making the transition from this level of individuals, as bundles of desires, to the level of society and history. The individual self was defined as the composite of one's sensibilities, or as a collection of desires,[56] and not, as with Marx, in terms of the ensemble of one's social relations.[57] How could the desiring individual obtain his satisfactions when competing for scarce resources with other individuals? How is society possible in such a situation of endemic conflict? How do rules, duties and rights arise? How are they enforced? Is such enforcement a constraint upon the liberty of the individual, and if so, should it be resisted?

The gap between analysis at the level of individual will and that of social practices or institutions is very wide in Tracy's theory, as in most forms of utilitarian social theory. Tracy adopted two main strategies for bridging the gap. One, an extension of his analysis of individual will, attempted to show by an analytico-deductive method how diadic and wider social relations may be seen to evolve from interaction between desiring wills. Tracy "deduces" the origin of rights and duties, and the institutions of law and property, in such a manner. His second approach is more genuinely social in character. Here, he takes men's sociality as more or less inherent in their historical existence and as a precondition for a truly "human" existence. Language and sympathy, for example, are seen as intrinsic to the evolution of the species; and various forms of co-operation, as in the division of labour and commerce, add a further dimension to the strength and integration of society. These explanations of social existence are examined briefly in the following section.

THE BASES OF SOCIAL EXISTENCE

Tracy sought to deduce the bases of social practices and conventions from his naturalistic concept of the individual *qua* will. He claimed that the desiring self, or what he sometimes called the moral personality, attained an awareness of its separate identity through its faculty of *motilité*. One's personality or self-consciousness arose through a recognition of one's separation from other personalities and from external objects.[58] This self-awareness entailed an understanding that the self was the "exclusive proprietor" of its body and its actions.[59] The concept of property, he claimed, appertains only to a desiring and acting being, who *has* needs and means, and thereby *possesses* something.[60]

The notion of property as private and exclusive arose from the fact that the desiring and acting self had been endowed by nature with a "necessary and inalienable property, that of his individuality". This "natural and necessary" property was the analogue of all forms of property which had subsequently been established by conventional understandings among men in society. The very ideas of "mine" and "yours" were claimed to follow naturally from the elementary distinction between myself and any other self.[61] For Tracy, private property was an ontological fact of human existence. It was merely vain speculation, in his view, to enquire whether the institution of property was advantageous or not to men, as if it depended on our whim to change our mode of existence.[62] Private property, then, originated in our "inalienable possession" of our individuality and its faculties. Tracy claimed to have demonstrated "how the sentiment of personality or the idea of self, and that of property which necessarily stems from it, are derived from our faculty of willing".[63]

Tracy's "deduction" of private property from the concept of the desiring self is a clear example (albeit a faulty application) of the method of *analyse*. Taking the isolated individual as his secure and certain starting-point, Tracy claimed to discover a host of other concepts implied in the first, like a nest of boxes. Locke had also argued that private property was an inalienable or natural right of the individual, but his reasoning was based mainly on a right arising from labour upon and usage of land and resources, subsequently guaranteed by social conventions.[64] Tracy, who also adopted a labour theory of value,[65] did not apply it in this case to explain the origin of private property (though he later used the labour theory to suggest how to make best use of one's property). Tracy's approach is all the more surprising because even a physiocrat like Dupont de Nemours followed Locke's account of the origins of private property in terms of mixing one's labour with nature.[66] The main error in Tracy's deduction of private property from the concept of the desiring individual, stemmed from his failure to see a distinction between possession-as-use and possession-as-exclusive-entitlement or control. Tracy acknowledged that the individual, with exclusive control of his own faculties through his will, "needed" to appropriate from nature the materials to satisfy his wants. But Tracy was wrong to believe there was a logical derivation of private and legally-guaranteed private property from the fact that we must make use of external objects to satisfy our wants.

Just as personality and property were linked to Tracy's view of the desiring individual, so were the concepts of rights and duties. Rights, according to Tracy, come into existence only because a desiring and acting being is weak, vulnerable and subject to deprivations of various kinds; a being which did not experience pleasures, pains or deprivations would not require rights.[67] In acting upon one's general right to satisfy one's desires, one is only acting in accordance with the "laws of one's own nature" and obeying the "conditions of one's existence" as a sentient being.[68] Similarly, duties are attributable only to desiring and acting beings who are obliged to interact. A being incapable of action (a being with no "means") would have no duties towards others. Duties are modes of regulating the ways in which we use our powers or means.

According to Tracy, everyone has a general "duty" to satisfy his wants and "to employ his means as well as possible" for the satisfaction of his desires.[69] This general duty, upon further analysis, is found to contain the specific duties of "properly assessing" the desires which are to be satisfied, studying the means available, and "restraining" one's wants and "extending" one's means as much as possible. For one's unhappiness, said Tracy, is largely a consequence of one's wants outstripping the means to satisfy them.[70] It is clear that a number of prudential maxims, purporting to be derived from natural necessity, have been inserted here into Tracy's "scientific" analysis of desires, means, rights and duties, as if the maxims could be deduced from the nature of *l'homme sensible*. It is also clear that the concept of "duty" (especially in the form of a "duty to oneself") is identical with individual self-interest. This identification of duty and interest appeared in Tracy's early mémoires at the Institut, where he noted that we not only have the ability to regulate our will, but also "we have the duty, that is to say the interest, to do so."[71]

Rights and duties in society are held by Tracy to have an analogue in nature, or in the natural condition of man. Wishing to exclude all "metaphysical" conceptions of rights and duties, Tracy believed that a scientific analysis would locate them in man's "natural" constitution, i.e. in his needs and capacities. The task of analysis was to show the natural (or scientifically-based) analogue of social conventions. By following the "natural" rules arising from such an analysis, Tracy believed (in the manner of the physiocrats) that man would be following the only morality which was compatible with his human nature and thus his happiness.

One of the most striking examples of Tracy's deduction of interests, rights, duties and moral rules from an abstract consideration of the isolated individual, is presented in his "Mémoire sur la faculté de penser". Starting with the proposition that man is a sentient being with desires, Tracy rapidly deduced that man has the "interest to satisfy his desires", that man has the interest to possess the "power" to satisfy his desires, and thus that "man has the interest to be free".[72] Man's interest is seen to extend, upon further analysis, to the development of his faculties, his education, his respect for the similar interests of others (so that they in turn will respect his interest), and his recognition that social co-operation increases man's physical and intellectual abilities. It is finally seen that the "duties and utility" of social existence consist in these objectives. "All this is implicitly contained in this first truth, that man is sentient".[73] Tracy thus found no difficulty in moving rapidly from the level of brute facts of individual existence to the levels of social organisation and moral prescriptions. All were seen as outcomes of the concepts of need and interest, which Tracy saw as the basic mobiles of all human action.[74]

The natural right of the individual to seek to satisfy his desires is a right common to all animate creatures, in Tracy's view. Satisfaction of desires is also the interest (or duty) of the individual, for his survival. Tracy illustrates this by suggesting that nature itself is a system of absolute laws which man can ignore only at his own peril, for to infringe such laws is to break the laws of one's own nature.[75]

> ... every duty presupposes a *penalty* which follows its infraction, a *law* which pronounces this penalty, and a *tribunal* which applies that law. In the present example, the penalty for making poor use of his means is for the individual to see results less favourable to, or even destructive of, his satisfaction. The laws which pronounce this penalty are those of his organisation as a desiring and acting being; they are the conditions of his existence. The tribunal which applies these laws is that of necessity itself, against which he cannot protect himself.[76]

This metaphor of natural necessity as a legal system gives us several clues concerning Tracy's attitude to morals and legislation. It is apparent that "nature" penalises men owing to their lack of knowledge, or carelessness, towards the operation of necessity. It penalises ignorance, error or negligence, rather than immoral intentions. Moral behaviour is the accomplishment of one's duty, but we have already seen that duty is identified with interests. Tracy's "moral" prescriptions for human conduct, in the face of the necessities of men's organisation and their environment, are reducible to prudential and utilitarian maxims urging moderation, self-restraint and mutual respect for one another's interests.

Tracy finally examined the conception of rights and duties as applied to men in society. First, he took up Hobbes' discussion of the state of nature (a term not used by Tracy), where individuals could not properly communicate with their fellows nor make conventions with them. Such a situation would be similar to that of man's relations with animals,[77] but would not be a state of *war* where each man sought the destruction of the other as the only means of ensuring his own preservation. Rather than a state of complete mutual hostility, men would generally live in a state of mutual indifference or separation (*étrangeté*), each seeking his own satisfactions, and unable to attain mutual understanding or conventional modes of resolving differences.[78] Interaction would be humanised to some extent by the natural sympathy of men for their own kind, which would become quite strong in cases of sexual relations and sentiments of parenthood. But in the absence of mutual understandings and conventions, quarrels would be frequent for there would be no conception of justice or injustice and no limitations placed on one's right and duty to satisfy one's wants.

The ancient Greeks, continued Tracy, had located the origin of laws and justice in the period when men's relations became stabilised in agricultural pursuits, and hence they called Ceres the legislator.[79] But they should have gone even further back to the origin of the first conventions, and thus acknowledged the central importance of language.[80]

> Hobbes, then, was quite right in establishing the basis of all justice on conventions; but he was wrong in saying that the earlier condition is rigorously and absolutely a state of war, and that this is our true instinct and the desire of our nature. If this were so, we would never have escaped it ... It has always struck me as highly remarkable that this philosopher, who ... is perhaps the most to be commended for the rigorous concatenation and close connection of his ideas, should have reached this fine conception of the necessity of conventions, the source of all justice, despite having started from a false or at least imprecise principle (the condition of war as the natural state) ...[81]

Language, the basis of conventions, is for Tracy one of the necessary conditions of social existence.

Tracy also examined the claim made by some versions of the social contract theory that men sacrificed a portion of their liberty, in entering society, in order to secure the remainder. Tracy tends to agree with Rousseau rather than Locke in arguing that the individual's liberty can be increased by his social relationships. For Tracy, the individual who constantly strengthens his social interaction with his fellows and is linked to them through social conventions, does not expect to suffer a net loss of liberty, or to diminish his capacity to execute his will. If the individual renounces certain types of action, it is so he may be assisted, or at least not opposed, in other areas which he regards as more important to him.[82]

> He consents that his will should be restrained a little, in certain cases, by that of his fellows; but that is so it may be much more powerful over all other beings, and even over his fellows on other occasions; so that the total mass of power or liberty which he possesses should be increased.[83]

The object of "true society", based on justice, "is always to increase the power of each one, by making that of others concur with it, and by preventing them from mutually harming one another."[84]

Tracy generally avoided contractual explanations of social order, despite the utilitarian calculus alluded to above. He was aware that the desires of individuals were bound to conflict, and that society would be improbable if such conflict could not be regulated. But he resisted a contractual theory even though he sometimes used its rhetoric of natural rights and the purposes of political association. He was aware, with David Hume and Adam Smith, that there was no historical basis for a rationalistic contract between ruler and the ruled, or among the associated members of a society. Tracy believed that men were incapable, by their very organisation and needs, of living either an isolated and atomistic existence or in a condition of total hostility. Tracy acknowledged that a social order "does not commence ... on a particular day or by premeditated design. It is established imperceptibly and by degrees."[85] The human species had always lived in communities of various types. And yet, the achievement of a high degree of social co-operation and harmony among individuals with diverse wants and capacities had to be seen as the triumph of "art" over "nature".[86] Herein lay man's historical progress and further evidence of his superiority over the animals.

Tracy's historical appreciation of man's sociality is not entirely consistent with his psycho-physiological conception of man as a desiring creature seeking to maximise his satisfactions. The dualism became explicit in Tracy's later writings, where he distinguished between two major aspects of human existence.*La vie organique ou intérieure* denoted all those aspects of life concerned simply with the "conservation" of the individual's body, and included a preponderance of involuntary organic actions.[87] *La vie animale ou extérieure*, on the other hand, denoted those aspects of life in which the individual is placed in "relations" with others. The relational aspects of life, according to Tracy, consisted of

> the use of our various senses and the operation of our faculty of movement, of speech and of reproduction, functions which effectively place us in relations not only with our fellows and all the beings which surround us, but even with the diverse parts of ourselves which we learn to know separately and distinctly.[88]

This distinction between two modes or sides of our human existence corresponds with a distinction between two orders of sentiments, needs and interests. The one is essentially self-centred and the second is essentially other-centred. The sentiments of individual personality and private possessions are part of *la vie organique*: they are tied to our fundamental structure of existence and are the unalterable precondition of everything we do, whether as new-born infants or as fully socialised adults. All morality must come to terms with this aspect of our human existence. Each person necessarily has "a host of interests" peculiar to him; and since everyone else is in a similar position, it is inevitable that their interests will be in opposition. On the one hand, then, *la vie organique* or biological substructure ensures that men are often in conflict and are bound to suffer since their desires will be frustrated.[89]

On the other hand, *la vie animale* or relational activities lead us into forms of co-operation and association which are the source of our moral and material progress. The study of *économie* demonstrates that associated individuals are more intelligent, wealthy and powerful than isolated individuals, and that the help of our fellows is necessary even to meet our needs of conservation. Nature gives us "a great attraction to each other", which "strongly counter-balances the mutual opposition of our individual interests". We are naturally drawn together, but not only for the mutual satisfaction of our physical needs for survival. "Nature has given us real needs for (social) relationships and has even made them obligatory (*très-impérieux*). This is doubtless why men everywhere live in associations called societies".[90] For Tracy, then, the desiring individual undergoes a metamorphosis at the level of social relationships. This is because "the basis" of his social interaction is his natural "need to sympathise" (*besoin de sympathiser*), a sentiment which Tracy identifies in a Rousseauean fashion with an "original goodness".[91] Sympathy, and not any malevolent sentiment, is the basis of *la vie de relation*.

> I call the need to sympathise, or sympathy, that disposition which leads us to associate ourselves with the sentiments of our fellows and even with those of all animate nature; which makes the sight of grief a sorrow to us and that of joy a pleasure to us; which makes us in need of being pleased when we are unhappy and makes our happiness incomplete unless it is shared; and finally, which makes the sentiment of loving agreeable for us to experience and to inspire, and makes the sentiment of hating or being hated painful and sad for us.[92]

The importance of this principle for Tracy's science of human behaviour is that it is an observable and inherent part of human existence, and also that it tends to heal the breaches opened by individuals' conflicts of interest.

> ... the sentiment of sympathy derives as necessarily from our life of relation, as the sentiment of personality derives from our life of conservation. It is this powerful attraction which brings us close again to our fellows at times when our individuality draws us apart. It is what softens the hard and repelling aspects of individuality.[93]

Tracy acknowledges that the reconciliation of these twin principles is highly desirable but cannot be taken for granted. Owing to the clash of wants, personal interest is the "first cause of all our hateful passions", whereas sympathy is the "source of all our benevolent passions". Personal interest is not always a bad or harmful thing. It gives us the ability to increase our powers and overcome the problem of privation and scarcity; and, "properly understood", it can lead us into forms of co-operation. But we must beware lest it lead us to consequences which are ultimately harmful to our own interests.[93] Mutual benevolence remains the "great law of our happiness".[95]

The concept of sympathy had been widely discussed among the social and moral writers to whom Tracy's philosophy was indebted in various degrees. Rousseau, in his Second Discourse on the *Origin of Inequality*, had discussed men's natural sentiments in terms of two complementary and sometimes conflicting principles: *amour de soi*, which roughly corresponded to Tracy's egoistic drives, and *pitié*, which corresponded to Tracy's conception of sympathy and compassion.[96]

Hume and Smith had placed great importance on sympathy in explaining social conduct.[97] Their writings (especially those of Smith) had attracted widespread attention in France. Smith's *Theory of Moral Sentiments* (1759) had been translated into French in 1774, and a new translation of the seventh edition was published in 1798 by the widow of Condorcet. She appended a series of eight *Letters on Sympathy* (addressed to Cabanis), in which sympathy was defined as "the disposition we have to feel in the same manner as someone else".[98] Cabanis had included a discussion on sympathy in his *Rapports du physique et du moral de l'homme* in 1802.[99]

Tracy's first discussion of sympathy dates from 1796, in his "Mémoire sur la faculté de penser". He began by proposing the doctrine that in our relations with animate beings the part of them we want to possess is their will. This is because their will affects our own pleasures and pains, depending on whether it is in conflict or conformity with our own will.[100] Once we recognise another being as a creature of will, that being becomes precious or otherwise to us only by virtue of its will. The pleasure we gain from finding the will of another conforming with our own and our desire that it should be so "are necessary results of our sensibility".[101] This desire to influence and possess the will of others

> enters into all our moral sentiments, or those which relate to our fellows; and on close analysis, it is seen to be the principal cause of our desire for power, wealth, glory, honour and even the frivolous pleasures of vanity; accordingly, by more or less false judgements, we believe all these things suitable for reconciling other wills to ours.[102]

The same desire for a correspondence of wills underlies the charm of true friendship and true love. It gives us a need for the esteem of others, and even for self-esteem.

> There arises from this the pleasure of our moral sensibility, of philanthropy, of all that we properly call the good sentiments, i.e. those favourable to our fellows. In fact, we are quite sure of being in basic accord with them when we wish their good, though we might often wish them a good that they are not aware of, or even which they disregard.[103]

This same desire to possess the will of others, said Tracy, is also the reason we value their frankness and confidence and want them to count on our own truthfulness, so that there is a reliable understanding of each other. It also accounts for our shyness in the company of strangers, whose will towards us is unknown. Finally, it is the source of our hatred, envy, jealousy and distrust, insofar as the wills of others are seen to be in conflict with our own.[104] In short, for Tracy, "the need to possess the will of our fellows is the source of all our social and even our anti-social affections".[105]

At a later point in his "Mémoire", Tracy introduced the importance of sexual relationships and the reproduction of the species for the development of social bonds. Imagine, he writes, a meeting in the forest between two of the celebrated *enfants abandonnés*, a girl and a boy who had no experience of human society. Their natural need for sexual relations would draw them together and they would soon learn to communicate and give pleasure to each other.

> ... and there is the birth of the great social need, the need to possess the will of one's fellow. We have already seen that it is the source of all morality. From it also stems their mutual need to express their affections and to know those of their companion, in a word, to communicate.[106]

To the pleasures of sexuality and communication through language, are added the affections of parenthood whereby the mother, at least, is obliged to live in permanent society with another human being, her child. In this way, said Tracy, it can be seen how all aspects of our social and moral life may be derived from the simple physical needs of our organisation:

> ... from the need for reproduction there arise all our moral sentiments and all our means of developing our ideas, for, in giving us the need to possess the will of our fellows, it (reproduction) gives us the need to communicate with them.[107]

Tracy had intended to write a treatise on *morale*, or the social effects of moral sentiments, as the fifth part of his *Elémens d'idéologie*. It was never completed. The introductory chapter had established the general principles of two types of sentiments, discussed above, arising from *la vie de conservation* and *la vie de relation*. The desire for sympathy was just as naturally and firmly rooted in human life as the more narrow desire for egoistic satisfactions. In the subsequent chapter, Tracy had intended to analyse the various moral sentiments and their social consequences, beginning with a series on benevolent sentiments to be followed by a series on malevolent sentiments. But only the very first of such discussions was ever written, the chapter on *l'amour*. The French edition of his *Traité de la Volonté* included only a few pages of Tracy's discussion of love; in a final note, he had written that he no longer hoped to complete his volume on *morale*, and that "this fragment will be my last work".[108] In fact, however, Tracy had completed by 1813 an extended analysis of love and its social forms. He withheld this extended discussion from the French editions from 1815 onwards, claiming he did not want to publish his personal views on such sensitive matters.[109] But he allowed the full text of the chapter on *l'amour* to appear in an Italian translation[110] of the treatise on the will in 1819, and he also sent the complete manuscript to Jefferson[111] in 1821.

The fragment on love in the French edition presents only a general perspective, claiming that love is the most important of those benevolent sentiments which are conducive to sociality and happiness. Love, writes Tracy, has two main aspects, physical and sentimental. On the one hand, Tracy acknowledges the great influence of *le besoin de la reproduction* on our vitality and our temperament, and suggests it can be the most violent of all our passions when felt in all its force. But physical passion and the attraction of beauty is only a part of love. Love is also a sentiment of attachment between individuals, in which sexual enjoyment may be less important than the pleasure of loving and being loved.[112] Forced enjoyment is unsatisfying and even distressing, and enjoyment which is too easily obtained lacks the sentiment which provides its full savour. The consent of participants is "one of its charms", and *la sympathie* is "one of its greatest pleasures". The full development of love in the human species consists of "friendship enhanced by pleasure", or "the perfection of friendship". Such a sentiment is the pinnacle of our existence as beings of desire and action.[113]

In the more extended discussion, published in the Italian edition, Tracy was critical of various formal restrictions upon the relations between men and women, which were especially inhibiting for women, and he urged a liberalisation in such relationships. He gave a generally favourable account of marriage as the main institutional basis of love, though he urged that divorce should be made easier where a particular marriage had broken down. The details of these remarks on institutionalised relations between the sexes are of some interest, but are only of marginal relevance to the present study. It may suffice to cite his remarks at the conclusion of the chapter on love:

> In resumé, I say that the need of reproduction attracts and brings together the two sexes; to this need is joined that of sympathy, which enlivens it even more. This is the most important of all our inclinations; through it, the human race is perpetuated and society is established, for society is not composed of isolated individuals, and a man or woman taken separately do not constitute a complete and perfect whole: they are only simple fractions. The family is the true social unit, rather as we have seen in my *Grammar* that propositions are the true elements of discourse and that words taken in isolation have no value by themselves.[114]

We have seen that Tracy posits a view of man as a desiring individual who seeks to maximise his satisfactions. At the same time, he posits the view that man is an essentially social being, who is initially drawn to his fellows by his sexual and communicative needs. This latter view is associated with the doctrine that men are inherently sympathetic towards the feelings and needs of their fellows, seeking their approval and esteem, and extending their sphere of shared meanings through gestural and verbal communication. Both these pictures of "natural man" are true, according to Tracy, for they are both aspects of man's natural capacities and inclinations. The clash between individual and social sentiments (arising from the natural opposition of personal interests) is recognised by Tracy as inherent in man's social life, as a dualism rooted in human nature itself. The resolution he proposes depends largely on the use of reason to formulate rules ensuring that the interests and liberty of each are protected as much as possible from others' unregulated selfish pursuit of wealth and power.[115] (This is the realm of legislation and public morality which will be examined in the following chapter.) At the same time, Tracy expects that men's natural sympathy, love and communication will draw them together in relations of mutual trust and co-operation. But there is another dimension of sociality outlined by Tracy, the concept of society as "a series of exchanges".

In the first chapter of his study of *économie*, society is examined purely in relation to "our most direct needs and our means of satisfying them", rather than in relation to moral sentiments and moral duties. From the economic aspect, "society is purely and solely a continual series of exchanges".[116] This is true of the most primitive and the most advanced societies. Exchange, claims Tracy, is "an admirable transaction in which the two contracting parties always both gain; consequently, society is an uninterrupted succession of advantages springing up ceaselessly for all its members".[117] Reverting to the contractual metaphor, Tracy claims that exchange is evident in the very first convention or agreement among men, wherein they promise mutual security, without which society cannot exist. This convention is a real exchange: "each renounces a certain way of using his powers, and receives in return the same sacrifice on the part of all the others". On the basis of this security, men enter into a multitude of economic relationships which consist in rendering a service to receive a salary, or bartering some merchandise for other goods, or taking part in some work in common. In each case, there is an exchange, in which one mode of activity is pursued as being more advantageous than another.[118]

Tracy insists that exchanges undertaken "freely and without constraint" are always to the benefit of both parties, because each prefers what he obtains over what he gives. The fact that some individuals miscalculate their relative advantages and suffer a loss does not impinge on the essence of free exchange, which is to be advantageous to both parties. And so Tracy concludes, that, from the economic aspect, "the true utility of society is to make possible among us a multitude of such arrangements".[119] Over a period of time, this host of small particular benefits produces the wonders of perfected society, far distant from the conditions of primitive societies. The accumulated material riches and intellectual skills of a civilised society constitute "the general good" in which everyone shares.[120] Only the human species is able to make exchanges based on such conventions; hence, only man has a true society, "for commerce is the whole of society, just as labour is the whole of wealth".[121]

The great effects of civilised society are entirely a product of "the reciprocity of services and multiplicity of exchanges".[122] Relations of exchange, says Tracy, have three remarkable effects. In the first place, social or collective labour is far more productive than that of men acting independently;

co-operation allows many tasks to be accomplished which could not have been undertaken successfully by individuals acting alone. Secondly, the same is true of the generation, preservation and diffusion of knowledge and skills, through communication and language. Intelligence increases rapidly when many contribute to resolving problems, and the results of invention become the general property of all. Thirdly, where several men labour reciprocally for one another, each may devote himself in a division of labour to the occupation in which he is most skilled and thus be more efficient and successful. These "three great benefits of society"—namely, "concurrence of force, increase and preservation of knowledge, and the division of labour"—are the result of reciprocity and exchange, and are responsible for all the advances of civilised society.[123]

Tracy's emphasis on individuality as the irreducible basis of human existence is complemented, then, by his theory that sympathy, co-operation and exchange are the basis of man's social existence. These factors, mediated through the development of language,[124] broaden the limits of men's experience and "socialise" them in the values and expectations of their fellows. The process of socialisation and civilisation has a "natural" basis in the sense that reproductive and communicative desires are inherent in man's constitution, but the institutional forms and conventions of society are the historical work of many generations. They represent what Tracy called the triumph of "art" over "nature"; though he also insists rhetorically, in the style of the physiocrats, that social institutions have an analogue in natural relationships[125] so that the disjunction between nature and "true" society is not complete.

We have seen in this chapter that Tracy's conception of the individual as a creature governed by pleasures and pains posed several problems for developing a theory of society or of the social basis of individuality. Tracy's derivation of social institutions from analysis of the faculties of the individual is implausible and leads him into contractual explanations which he elsewhere rejects as unhistorical. His second strategy, positing man's "natural" need for social interaction and the esteem of others, provides some basis for a theory of sympathy and language as the foundations of social existence, and leads to an economic analysis of society as a system of utilitarian exchanges for mutual benefit. The contradiction arising between man's egoistic impulses and his civilised benevolence is not automatically resolved. The institutions of government, public morality and public instruction were seen by Tracy as instruments of an on-going reconciliation between these two sides of human behaviour. The reconciliation of private and social interests will be examined in the following chapter.

Notes

1. "Mémoire sur la faculté de penser", pp. 336, 343, 327ff.
2. *Ibid.*, p. 332.
3. *Elémens*, Vol. I, p. 248; *Traité de la Volonté* (1815), pp. 65-71; "Mémoire sur la faculté de penser", p. 311n.
4. *Logique*, p. 433; *Traité de la Volonté* (1815), pp. 83-92.
5. "Mémoire sur la faculté de penser", pp. 302, 313, 335, 338, 343.
6. *Ibid.*, p. 333; also p. 338. These are the only occasions in his published writings where Tracy described action in terms of "effort": it was a word which appealed greatly to Maine de Biran in his attempt to elaborate a more activist conception of the self.
7. "Dissertation sur quelques questions d'idéologie", in *Mémoires de l'Institut*, Vol. III (1801), pp. 491-514.
8. Regrettably there is no space to discuss Maine de Biran's revisions of Tracy's viewpoint. Their widening disagreements are documented in their detailed correspondence from the years 1804-1814 published by Pierre Tisserand in Vol. VII of Maine de Biran, *Oeuvres philosophiques* (Paris, 1930), pp. 227-366; see also Cabanis' letters to Biran in *Ibid.*, pp. 209-225. Biran's gradual rejection of the philosophy of sensations, as propounded by Tracy and Cabanis, has been ably discussed in H. Gouhier, *Les Conversions de Maine de Biran* (Paris, 1947), esp. Ch.3; and P. Tisserand, "Introduction", pp. vii-lxiv, to Maine de Biran, *L'Influence de l'habitude sur la faculté de penser* (Paris, 1954); and by S. Moravia, *Il pensiero degli idéologues* (Firenze, 1974), pp. 457-529.
9. *Elémens*, Vol. I, p. 247.
10. "Mémoire sur la faculté de penser", p. 346.
11. *Ibid.*, pp. 347-8.
12. *Ibid.*, pp. 349-350.
13. *Ibid.*, pp. 350-1.
14. *Ibid.*, pp. 362-3. (Cf. *Elémens*, Vol. I, p. 252.)
15. *Ibid.*, p. 364.
16. *Ibid.*, pp. 364-5.
17. *Ibid.*, p. 365.
18. *Ibid.*, p. 366.
19. *Ibidem.*
20. *Ibid.*, p. 368.
21. *Elémens*, Vol. I (3rd ed. 1817) ed. Gouhier (Paris, 1970), pp. 115, 141-2, 153, 239-251 (cf. also p. 433).
22. *Ibid.*, pp. 149-150.
23. *Ibid.*, pp. 150-1.
24. *Ibid.*, p. 151n.
25. *Ibid.*, p. 152.
26. For Cabanis' remarks on instinct, see *Rapports*, in *Oeuvres philosophiques*, Vol. I, pp. 558-562. There is no space to develop the differences of emphasis between Cabanis and Tracy. In his summary of Cabanis' physiological doctrines in the 1805 edition of the *Rapports*, Tracy showed a tendency to adopt an even more uncompromising materialism than his mentor: cf. Tracy, "Table Analytique", in Cabanis, *Rapports* (1830 ed.), Vol. I, pp. 23-65. On instinct, see pp. 56-7 of the "Table analytique". See also M.S. Staum, *Cabanis* (Princeton, 1980).
27. Condillac, *Traité des animaux*, in *Oeuvres philosophiques*, Vol. I, p. 379.
28. Condillac, *Traité des sensations*, in *Ibid.*, Vol. I, p. 228.
29. Tracy, "Mémoire sur la faculté de penser", p. 354.
30. *Ibid.*, pp. 356-7.
31. *Traité de la Volonté* (1815 ed.), "Introduction", pp. 84, 86, 88, 96.
32. *Ibid.*, p. 83.
33. Tracy, "Mémoire de Berlin", published by P. Tisserand in *Revue philosophique de la*

France et de l'étranger, Vol. 116 (1933), at pp. 170-2.
34. *Ibid.*, p. 173.
35. *Traité de la Volonté* (1818 ed.), pp. 476-7; *Elémens*, Vol. I, p. 245.
36. *Elémens*, Vol. I, p. 130 (cf. also p. 429); *Traité de la Volonté* (1818), pp. 502, 504.
37. *Elémens*, Vol. I, p. 68.
38. *Ibid.*, p. 69; *Traité de la Volonté* (1815), p. 110.
39. *Traité de la Volonté* (1818), pp. 478, 494-6 (cf. *Elémens*, Vol. I, p. 234).
40. *Ibid.*, p. 480.
41. *Ibid.*, p. 505.
42. *Elémens*, Vol. I, p. 70.
43. *Traité de la Volonté* (1815), pp. 109-110; *Traité* (1818), pp. 501-2.
44. *Elémens*, Vol. I, pp. 246-7.
45. *Commentaire*, pp. 142-3.
46. *Traité de la Volonté* (1818), p. 503; *Elémens*, Vol. I, p. 249; *Logique*, p. 436. An anonymous critic of Tracy's first volume on idéologie drew attention to Tracy's recommendation that intentionality be abandoned as unscientific and his view that every desire is the result of a prior sequence of causes. This doctrine "would soon dispense with (our need for) a civil and criminal code." (*Mercure de France*, 16 nivôse an X (6 January 1802), p. 100.)
47. *Logique*, pp. 437-9 (see also pp. 391-5).
48. "Mémoire sur la faculté de penser", p. 363.
49. *Traité de la Volonté* (1815), pp. 108-9. The same point is made in *Elémens*, vol. I, p. 252; *Commentaire*, pp. 141-2, 227-8.
50. *Traité de la Volonté* (1815), pp. 110-111; cf. *Commentaire*, p. 144.
51. Cf. Tracy's defence of the liberty of the King's aunts to emigrate in February 1791, on the grounds that what the law does not forbid is the area of free action: *Archives parlementaires*, XXIII, p. 497.
52. *Traité de la Volonté* (1815), p. 111.
53. *Ibid.*, p. 113; also *Traité* (1818), p. 262.
54. *Traité* (1815), p. 112.
55. *Ibid.*, p. 113.
56. Cf. "Mémoire sur la faculté de penser", p. 311n-312: here, Tracy uses the metaphor of a ball (as in dancing) to describe the self as an ensemble of elements, subject to change, yet unified.
57. Cf. K. Marx, "Theses on Feuerbach", No. 6 (1845).
58. *Traité de la Volonté* (1815), pp. 65-71.
59. *Ibid.*, p. 73.
60. *Ibid.*, pp. 56-7.
61. *Ibid.*, pp. 74-6.
62. "Quels sont les moyens...", in *Commentaire*, pp. 448-450; *Traité de la Volonté* (1818), pp. 263-4. Cf. Proudhon's criticism of Tracy's doctrine in *Qu'est-ce que la propriété?* (1840), ed. E. James (Paris, 1966), pp. 100-3. Marx made similar criticisms.
63. *Traité de la Volonté* (1815), p. 82.
64. J. Locke, *Second Treatise*, section 25 ff: cf. *Two Treatises of Government*, ed. Laslett (New York, 1965), pp. 327 ff.
65. *Traité de la Volonté* (1815), pp. 92-102.
66. Cf. Dupont de Nemours, *De l'origine et des progrès d'une science nouvelle* (1768), ed. A. Dubois (Paris, 1910), p. 11.
67. *Logique*, p. 433.
68. *Traité de la Volonté* (1815), pp. 117, 119, 135.
69. *Ibid.*, pp. 128, 135. The physiocrats also claimed that one's natural *duty* is to care for one's own needs (and to respect the liberty, person and property of others).
70. *Ibid.*, pp. 120-1, and 112-3.
71. "Mémoire sur la faculté de penser", p. 368.
72. *Ibid.*, pp. 380-1.
73. *Ibid.*, pp. 381, 383.

74. *Commentaire*, pp. 16-17. Tracy adds, however, that while need and interest are correctly seen as general explanations of human action, they tell us too little about any particular action to be truly explanatory. However, this qualification remained undeveloped elsewhere.
75. *Commentaire*, pp. 2-5; *Traité de la Volonté* (1815), pp. 118-121.
76. *Traité*, (1815), p. 120.
77. Tracy includes a curious discussion of the proper relationship between men and animals, in the light of their conflicting rights and lack of mutual communication (*Ibid.*, pp. 123-6). His "conclusion" is that we should avoid extremes both of violent destruction and of exaggerated sentimentality in our dealings with animals, and regulate our behaviour in accordance with the extent to which reciprocal relations of benevolence and habit can be established between man and beast.
78. *Ibid.*, pp. 128-9.
79. This was also the view of the physiocrats. Cf. also the "four-stages" theory of social evolution, mentioned in chapter seven.
80. *Traité de la Volonté* (1815), pp. 130-1.
81. *Ibid.*, pp. 131-3.
82. *Ibid.*, p. 115; *Commentaire*, pp. 161, 219.
83. *Traité* (1815), p. 116.
84. *Ibid.*, p. 137.
85. *Ibid.*, p. 115.
86. *Ibid.*, p. 132 n.
87. *Traité de la Volonté* (1818), pp. 507-8.
88. *Ibid.*, p. 508.
89. *Ibid.*, pp. 512-513.
90. *Ibid.*, p. 514.
91. *Ibid.*, p. 515.
92. *Ibidem.*
93. *Ibid.*, p. 516.
94. *Ibid.*, p. 517.
95. *Traité de la Volonté* (1815), p. 79.
96. Cf. J.-J. Rousseau, "Discourse on the Origin of Inequality" (1754), in *The Social Contract and Discourses*, trans. G.D.H. Cole (London, 1973), esp. pp. 64 ff.
97. For discussion of these writers' views on sympathy, cf. G. Bryson, *Man and Society: The Scottish Inquiry in the Eighteenth Century* (Princeton, 1945), esp. chapter 6; G. Morrow, "The significance of the doctrine of sympathy in Hume and A. Smith", *The Philosophical Review*, vol. 32 (1923), pp. 60-78; R. Lamb, "A. Smith's System: Sympathy not self-interest", *Journal of the History of Ideas*, vol. 35 (1974), pp. 671-682.
98. Cf. A. Smith, *Théorie des Sentimens Moraux ...*, traduit de l'Anglais ... par S. Grouchy, Veuve Condorcet (Suivie de huit lettres sur la sympathie) (Paris, 1798), vol. II, p. 357.
99. Cf. Cabanis, *Oeuvres philosophiques*, vol. I, pp. 158-9, 563-578.
100. "Mémoire sur la faculté de penser", p. 359; cf. *Principes logiques* (1817), in *Elémens d'idéologie*, 5 vols. (Bruxelles, 1826-27), IV, p. 220.
101. "Mémoire sur la faculté de penser", p. 360.
102. *Ibidem.*
103. *Ibid.*, p. 361.
104. *Ibidem.*
105. *Ibid.*, p. 385.
106. *Ibid.*, p. 404. The implications of sexual desire for the growth of population was discussed by Tracy in *Traité de la Volonté*, ch. 9.
107. "Mémoire sur la faculté de penser", p. 405.
108. *Traité de la Volonté* (1818), p. 523 (or 1815 ed. p. 576). The fragment on *l'amour* occupies pp. 518-521 (1818 ed.) and pp. 568-573 (1815 ed.).
109. Cf. G. Chinard, *Jefferson et les idéologues*, p. 209 (letter of Tracy to Jefferson, 22 February 1821).

110.Destutt de Tracy, *De l'amour*, trans. & ed. G. Chinard (Paris 1926): for the date of composition, see p. 33n.
111.Chinard, *Jefferson et les Idéologues*, pp. 208ff.
112.*Traité de la Volonté* (1818), pp. 519-520.
113.*Ibid.*, p. 521.
114.*De l'amour*, pp. 59-60. One might be forgiven some surprise that Tracy suddenly finds in his last writing that "the family" is the "true social unit". Had he started from such a "basis", his social theory might surely have taken a different direction.
115.Cf. *Traité de la Volonté* (1818), pp. 517-518; cf. *Traité* (1815), p. 137.
116.*Traité* (1818), p. 131.
117.*Ibid.*, pp. 131-2.
118.*Ibid.*, pp. 132-3.
119.*Ibid.*, pp. 134, 135.
120.*Ibid.*, p. 136.
121.*Ibid.*, p. 143.
122.*Ibidem*.
123.*Ibid.*, pp. 144-6. A generation before Smith's notable discussion, the physiocrats had discussed the importance of "exchange" as a principle of social progress: cf. R. Meek, *Precursors of Adam Smith* (London 1975), p. 111 (Quesnay and Mirabeau).
124.Cf. *Elémens*, Vol. I, pp. 377-8; "Mémoire sur la faculté de penser", p. 420.
125.Cf. *Traité de la Volonté* (1815), pp. 74-5.

5. SOCIAL MORALITY AND CIVIL SOCIETY

Tracy's identification of a kind of social instinct in man plays a large part in his account of how society and social progress are possible. But there remained critical problems, for both social theory and political practice, concerning how to reconcile individual and social interests. How was it possible to identify and counteract those desires and actions which are anti-social, or destructive of the liberty and happiness of one's fellow citizens? To what extent could education, in the broadest sense, encourage certain kinds of desires and weaken or repress others?

MORAL EDUCATION AND POLICING

The reconciliation of private and general interests, according to Tracy and the idéologues, must be the work of reason and experience. The most powerful influence upon the social conduct of the citizen is his education, taken in the broadest sense. A distinction was drawn between the terms instruction and education.[1] *Instruction* denoted formal schooling and the teaching of specified curricula. *Education*, on the other hand, was a term of much wider scope, commonly taken to include the moral education of the citizen, imparted often by the family or the Church; the values and restraints embodied in the criminal and civil law; and the ideas engendered by social institutions as a whole. Liberal writers were concerned that all citizens should be sufficiently instructed in their rights and duties as citizens (as well as in their occupationally-related skills) in order that a free society could be maintained. But they were opposed to the suggestion that governments should become involved in prescribing moral rules or defining an exclusive doctrine for inculcation in schools.[2]

Utilitarian and liberal social theorists, such as Helvétius and Beccaria,[3] had claimed that men's ideas and values were products of their environment, their education and their habitual modes of acting and thinking. To change those ideas and values, it was necessary to change their environment, education and habits. Tracy and the idéologues became deeply involved in attempts to reform the curricula taught in the system of public instruction under the Directory. Our focus here, however, is more limited, taking up Tracy's views on educating citizens in matters affecting the public interest. He believed that the two great instruments of enlightened reform and social harmony were legislation and public instruction. Tracy supported a programme of "civic education" in the broad sense, as did all the French writers on social and moral questions in the 1790s.[4] He had several reservations, however, concerning the effectiveness of direct moral and civic instruction, and called attention to the importance of such indirect influences as the probity of government, the rigorous enforcement of legal codes, and the effects of legislation in creating various kinds of incentives for citizens to act in ways which contributed to public order and social co-operation.

Tracy's writings on *la morale* attempted to avoid moral preaching and exhortation. He claimed only to demonstrate the social effects of various sentiments and actions, leaving to legislators the task of defining the laws appropriate to a "sound" and "rational" morality. *La morale*, he said, is a "science" based upon "experience and reflection". It is "the knowledge of how our various inclinations and sentiments affect our happiness".[5] The scientific study of moral sentiments, he wrote, does not consist in deriving precepts of virtue, but in examining

> those of our perceptions which include a desire, the way they are produced in us, their conformity or opposition to the real conditions of our existence, the solidity or futility of their motives, and the advantages or disadvantages of their effects.[6]
>
> I do not claim to give any rules for conduct. I do not aspire to state principles or establish maxims (of moral action) ... I simply wish to write the history of our affections, sentiments or passions and show their consequences. May each person then make his own laws for himself or even for other people if he thinks he is able.[7]

Tracy's wish to maintain a distinction between an objective science of moral sentiments (studying origins and consequences, rather than motives and injunctions) and a more practical guide for the creation of virtue, sometimes became blurred. Part of his scientific enterprise was to examine how certain kinds of sentiments and actions affected human happiness, and he clearly believed that those which led to misery and hostility were contrary to individual and public interests. Tracy's thoughts were never far removed from the practical problems of "regulating our desires and actions in the manner best fitted to make us happy".[8] A complete knowledge of our intellectual faculties, he wrote, was the precondition for such strategies: the alternative was "a blind routine devoid of principles". The "art" of finding individual happiness, he continued, "consists almost entirely in the avoidance of holding contradictory desires ..., in guarding ourselves as much as possible from physical harm ..., and in obtaining the goodwill of our fellows and our own self-esteem ..."[9]

The question of *la morale publique*, or what I have chosen to call social morality, was discussed directly in Tracy's pamphlet of 1798: *Quels sont les moyens de fonder la morale chez un peuple?* The question had originally been proposed in that form as a subject for a prize essay competition by the Institut in 1797, but had later been withdrawn because no entry was deemed worthy of the prize. Tracy then decided to write a reply to the original question and his essay appeared in the *Mercure français* in February-March 1798 and as a pamphlet later that year. Tracy again republished the text as an appendix to his *Commentaire* on Montesquieu in 1819. The essay question was of great interest to the idéologues; Roederer[10] and J.-B. Say as well as Tracy discussed this topic. J.-B. Say wrote an essay sketching the moral and social organisation of a utopian republic (*Olbie*) where legislators and educators made civic virtue profitable for the citizens.[11]

In his essay of 1798, written in the midst of the relative turbulence and social unrest of the Directory period, Tracy's main concern for a social morality lay in creating stability and security, rather than the more "ideological" values of liberty and individual rights. Tracy was emphatic that the most effective way to prevent major crimes from being committed was to ensure that all offenders were arrested and punished. The important thing, he wrote, is not that the penalties be severe, but that they are known to be inevitable. "The most useful principle of *la morale* ... is that every crime is a certain cause of suffering for he who commits it." The enforcement of the law is the essential base of *la morale publique*, and the public officials engaged in this task are "the true supports of society".[12] Tracy adopts a deterrent theory of punishment, rather than notions of vengeance or rehabilitation. (This emphasis on the repression of crime has led some commentators to speculate on the influence of his military background[13].)

Tracy made some specific recommendations concerning the organisation of the various branches of law enforcement. The police or constabulary (*la gendarmerie nationale*) undertake the dangerous task of arresting criminals, a task where their gentler sensibilities are likely to be undermined and they are thus more exposed to moral corruption than other citizens. Their self-esteem and devotion must be encouraged by their superior officers and their promotion should be in accordance with fixed regulations. Tracy recommends that payment be proportional to the number of arrests, in order that the gendarme finds it in his interest to perform his duties well. The efficiency and stability of the gendarmerie would be improved by being controlled by a single permanent head, rather than by a succession of short-term appointees who are bound to create uncertainties and confusions.[14] Jailers or prison officers have one major responsibility: to prevent the escape of prisoners. The jailers should be punished in some way if they neglect this supreme duty. The prisons and the gendarmerie should be brought under the same system of authority, for they share the same principle: namely, that it is in the greatest interest of society that no criminal should escape punishment.[15]

The jury system, wrote Tracy, is a fine institution insofar as the jurors are independent of authority and not prejudiced for or against the accused; the liberty of the subject is thereby protected. But the minds of the jurymen are often influenced by the period in which they live: in times of turbulence and factional dispute, they may behave like "party" men, whereas in times of peaceful calm they may become too sympathetic and lenient towards the accused. In either case, they would have lost a proper degree of objectivity and concern for the public interest. Judges ought to be as independent as possible both of governments and of those who come before the courts. For this reason, Tracy said, they should be well-paid, appointed for long terms of office, and itinerant. Public prosecutors, on the other hand, should be dependent on the government and more easily dismissed for simple negligence.[16]

The laws should recognise that the severity of punishment should be proportional to the crime and to the temptation of committing it. Criminal procedure should enable the accused to conduct a proper defence; but it should also be sufficiently rigorous to ensure that guilty people are punished. Our understandable concern lest a single innocent person be convicted in error may sometimes lead us to let guilty people escape their just punishment. But cases of mistaken conviction are fairly rare, in Tracy's view. It is better to err on the side of strictness, because mistaken convictions do not lead to a general decline in moral behaviour whereas the continued freedom of criminals is a threat to social morality and security.[17]

In summary, Tracy's first principle for the establishment of *la saine morale* is to make the punishment of crimes virtually inevitable. But the legislator or political leader will also be concerned with suppressing all other kinds of roguish and dishonest behaviour. While he cannot punish all such actions directly, he can influence matters so that the culprits suffer financially or suffer the loss of their reputation if public opinion has been suitably influenced by sound institutions. Dishonest behaviour can be further discouraged by well-organised civil tribunals; by costs being granted against those who bring a civil suit in bad faith; strong measures against fraudulent bankruptcy; exclusion from government offices of all men whose "reputation" is unsavoury; and by the practice of employing men in the province of their birth, where they are judged by those who are familiar with their past conduct.[18] (Officials who are *dépaysés* can be dangerous, said Tracy, and he added in the 1819 text that there were quite a number of distressing examples in contemporary France.)

The friends of liberty should not be too quick to condemn the activities of the police, even though its powers could potentially be used in an oppressive way. Providing that the accused are brought speedily before the courts, little harm can be done, especially if the governmental authority as a whole is soundly based. A system operating with small imperfections is preferable to a system paralysed by restrictions, all the more so "because the second basic principle of *la morale* is certainly to make the success of dishonesty as difficult as possible."[19]

If all crimes and dishonesty were punished, men would be led towards the good and happy life, but the law cannot be so efficient or all-encompassing. Laws are subject to human weaknesses in their formulation and execution. There is a world of difference between the certainty and power of the laws of nature and the laws established by men to regulate their societies, which are mere conventions.[20] Some ancient philosophers, seeking to eliminate the possibility of men harming each other, had identified the root of immoral behaviour as anchored in private property. This erroneous view, wrote Tracy, is rebutted by the fact that individuality could not be suppressed even where the product of one's labour became communal property: there would still be conflict over the division of such communal goods. Each man always has property in his ideas, his labour and the products of his labour. Rousseau had been wrong in declaring that private property was the cause of all crime: but at least he was more consistent than the ancients in concluding that society was the source of all vices and that a condition of isolation would be required for individual integrity.[21]

For Tracy, individuals necessarily have distinct and sometimes opposing interests. Since these cannot be eliminated, the task is to "reconcile and contain" them.[22]

> The nature of men is such that they cannot be associated without having distinct and opposed interests and yet they are obliged to draw closer in order to help one another and even to exist. What, then, can they do? ... They set up common rules to prevent themselves from using their frequent opportunities to harm one another. These rules are the laws which we have mentioned, those which punish crimes and restrain misdemeanours. They are the true supports of *la morale*; they cannot prevent opportunities for evil, but they can forestall the harmful effects; they are good laws.[23]

But in our present societies, "established before an understanding of the true interests of men",[24] not all laws have these beneficial effects. There are some "obscure", "useless" and "impractical" laws which may even create new sources of evil and harm and bring public authority into disrespect. Tracy lists a number of examples: laws which create opposing interests in different classes; laws which prohibit actions which are innocent in themselves; negligent administration or disorder in public finances; institutions which promote errors, prejudices or superstitions; and laws which seek to upset the "eternal nature of things", such as that which substitutes paper money for gold.[25] On the other hand, the opportunities for harm are reduced by those legislative and administrative actions which

> tend to base all interests upon the general interest, to draw all opinions towards reason, their common centre, ... to restore to all citizens the full exercise of individual liberty which is not harmful; and ... simplicity, clarity, regularity and constancy in the actions of government ...[26]

All legislative and administrative activities, wrote Tracy, have an important influence on *la morale*, insofar as they increase or diminish the occasions for bad conduct. Our efforts should be directed towards reducing the opportunities for new offences, and in this task "the most powerful of all our moral means ... are repressive laws and their full and complete execution".[27]

Tracy believed it was merely illusory (*chimèrique*) to hope that all occasions for mutual harm could be removed; the essential thing was to reduce men's desire to commit harmful actions. Legislation and the execution of the law were not sufficient in this regard. It was also necessary to use "all the indirect manners of influencing the inclinations" of the citizens. Of course, everything in the world has *some* degree of influence on our dispositions and feelings. However, claimed Tracy, the essential thing to grasp is that since our acts of will are consequences of our acts of judgement (a proposition he takes as "proven"),

> it follows that to guide the one, it is necessary only to direct the other; and that the only way to make something wanted, is to have it judged as preferable. Thus, all these diverse means of acting for good or bad upon the inclinations of men are ultimately reduced to *indoctrinating* them well or badly.[28]

This proposition, implying the possibility of educative control of men's beliefs and values, was inconsistent both with Tracy's later theory of the will and with his liberal approach to educational issues. A brief explanation is necessary.

Tracy's early theory of the will held that our "desires" are a product of "judgements" we make, using the raw material supplied by our immediately perceived "needs". Desires, on this rationalistic view, were directly related to "our true or false knowledge". Hence, concluded Tracy, "in order to direct and regulate our desires, it is only a question of correcting our judgements, and here we find the only solid foundation for all morality".[29] Proceeding on this assumption, Tracy had concluded that the problems of education and of morality would be resolved if men's capacity for making "good judgements" was improved to the extent that it became "habitual".[30] However, Tracy does not seem to have noticed that his later doctrine of the will, in which "desires" may be immediately given without the mediation of judgement and comparison,[31] undermines the likelihood that a rationalist educative process, aimed at improving logical inferences, could control undesirable passions.

Secondly, Tracy's use of the term "indoctrinating" the people appears to be an instance of illiberal enthusiasm for the correctness of his own "rational" morality. However, we cannot take his term "indoctrinating" too literally, since he immediately goes on to say that direct instruction in matters of *la morale* is ineffective. Moral education, on the contrary, is acquired mainly by experience and example. If our environment was so perversely arranged that virtue was punished and vice rewarded, direct moral instruction could do nothing to change that unfortunate system. But if, by wise laws and their enforcement, men could see that vice was punished and rational co-operation rewarded, there would be a close link established between virtue, reason and happiness.

Moral notions and responses are learned, insists Tracy: they are not innate in our minds from birth, nor are they identical in all individuals or in all cultures. Tracy expresses astonishment that his hero Voltaire, who had attacked "so many metaphysical prejudices" and shown that religion was a "human creation" of many cultural and historical varieties, should have also believed that *la morale* is divinely implanted in us and that this explains why its essential principles are similar everywhere.[32] That murder and theft are regarded as crimes in all societies did not convince Tracy of the uniformity or the divinity of moral notions. Men living in association understand rapidly that killing or harming one another undermines the advantages of their social existence, and that if they break their conventions, their security and happiness are jeopardised. Such truths are so obvious that everyone can understand them. But beyond these simple truths, there is great scope for disagreement, misunderstanding and ignorance about moral notions.[33]

Knowledge of *la morale*, the science of our sentiments and their effects on our happiness, is dependent on our understanding of *idéologie* and *la physique*. According to Tracy, that is why "*la morale* is always the last of the sciences to be perfected, always the least advanced, always that on which opinions must be the most divided".[34] It was almost as if there were as many ways of seeing and feeling as there were individuals: a far cry from any uniformity of moral notions.

LEGISLATION AND INSTRUCTION

Tracy believed that it was laudable to wish to improve the social morality of the adult citizens, but it was inappropriate to make such an attempt through the direct teaching of moral doctrines. Very few adults had the time or the desire to follow a long course of instruction, and even fewer had the ability to grasp a closely reasoned system of ideas. In an élitist fashion, Tracy claimed that only the legislators were really obliged to have a comprehensive and rigorous understanding of *la morale*; other citizens need only to know some of the most important principles, rather as craftsmen practising their art make do with a few proven rules and ignore the learned theories on which they are based.[35] Tracy made the same point a few years later in his *Analyse* of Dupuis: it is unnecessary to make the common man understand the finer points of philosophy, providing that he is clearly presented with the distilled results.[36] A similar dichotomy was to pervade Tracy's detailed discussions of public instruction (discussed in chapter ten).

The general thrust of Tracy's notion of moral socialisation is that we are much more strongly influenced by "the truths we have ourselves deduced from observation of our surroundings" and which are constantly drawn to our attention by experience, than by those truths we have been taught directly.[37] Thus, the public festivals established by the education law of October 1795, and the moral catechisms written by Volney, Lachabeaussière and Saint-Lambert, would be of little consequence. Moral instruction of citizens could only "impart in a few minds the abstract truths of sound morality", and help to advance the scientific theory, but could do nothing to spread the practice of a rational morality. The teaching of adult citizens could result in "a few more enlightened speculative moralists", but could never make the bulk of the citizens suddenly more virtuous.[38]

The individual has three kinds of needs relative to *la morale* which have to be satisfied, said Tracy: physical needs, the need to gain the goodwill of his fellows, and the need for his own self-respect. To satisfy these needs, he has correspondingly to avoid punishment, blame and remorse. These motivations supply the basis for acting in a morally sound or "virtuous" manner, that is, being "useful to his fellows and to himself".[39] Direct moral instruction influences mainly the third motivation (which is the least influential in most men). The other two motivations are developed and shaped by the various institutions of society. Hence the irrelevance of direct instruction, and the central importance of social experience and practices, for the moral education of the citizens.

> Legislators and rulers: these are the true teachers of the mass of humanity, the only ones whose lessons have any efficacy. Moral instruction ... is completely in the acts of legislation and administration.[40]

Public authorities thus do not have to rely solely upon repression and punishment: they are also able to discourage dishonest and anti-social impulses through their legislative and administrative activities. These public officials can accomplish a great deal in encouraging and maintaining a social morality, guided by a reasoned understanding of

> political truths, which teach us so to arrange our relations with our fellows that their desires are the least harmful and the most helpful in the accomplishment of our own.[41]

Tracy gave a number of examples contrasting the influence of the teacher and the legislator. A moral theorist may logically demonstrate that allowing pecuniary interests to reach into family affairs is destructive of inner happiness. On the other hand, the legislator who establishes equal inheritance can virtually eliminate at a stroke all sentiment of rivalry and all suspicion of dissembling affection. In the same way, the legislator who establishes a divorce law abolishes most marriages of interest and maintains all other marriages by the possibility of their being dissolved.[42] A teacher may urge that we should take reason as our guide and claim that reason alone suffices to demonstrate that we have a real interest in being just; but he will urge in vain. The legislator, however, can terminate the payment of priests and stop their involvement in civil affairs and in teaching, with the result that after ten years, everyone implicitly will agree with the teacher without his having said a word.[43] A teacher may strive to show that virtues and talents are the only precious qualities; but public opinion on such a matter will be determined by "whether the law recognises or forbids equality of conditions". It would be a waste of effort to demonstrate that success in the sciences was the most meritorious way of serving one's country, if it were seen that a clever scoundrel could acquire more consideration and credit in one year than a great man by a life's work. A theorist might demonstrate that a man who earns a comfortable living by honest and useful industry gains more inner satisfaction than one who lives by shameful deceit or who languishes in idleness. But, Tracy noted,

> if a thousand roads are open to get rich by plunder and fraud, or to receive great benefits from the state without deserving them, everyone will rush in; whilst, if all the means of gaining a too hasty fortune are prevented by an economical administration of state finances, by a great security and great facility for loans ..., by a great liberty to undertake all forms of industry ...; if, finally, the prompt dispersal of acquired wealth is promoted by equality of inheritance ..., you will soon see everyone devoting themselves to useful work and adopting the values of an active life and a modest existence.[44]

In the same way, it would be in vain to preach loyalty to friends and respect for the innocent, if the law facilitates denunciations and allows confiscations, leading to a multiplication of betrayals and unjust condemnations. A large number of sequestrations would do more to make administrators into scoundrels, and vice versa, than all the instruction in the world could ever do to prevent this happening. And if public officials were suddenly involved in buying and selling property on a large scale, three quarters of them would become speculators, receiving bribes and violating their duties, despite all the philosophical and religious sermons and even despite the surveillance of the law. Public opinion cannot in itself be an effective check on such activities if so many people are involved.[45]

Tracy summed up his position on how to provide a moral education for adult citizens: first, and most important, "the complete, rapid and inevitable execution of the repressive laws". Second, "an exact balance between the income and the expenditure of the state". When the state is heavily indebted, warned Tracy, the way is open for fortune-hunting and discontent, the weakening of justice and the impoverishment of the people as a whole. The state should never raise the interest rate and increase the number of idle *rentiers* by its loan-raising activities. Tracy also recommended several other measures which he believed would promote a sound social morality: civil equality and the abolition of privilege and hereditary power; the non-payment of priests and their exclusion from educational and other public offices; the uniformity of laws and administration; divorce; equal inheritance; and freedom of industry, commerce and credit-finance.[46]

If these measures were implemented,

> crime would be punished, reason strengthened, domestic happiness assured, equality maintained to the extent it is possible and useful, economy made necessary, and work made honourable. I can scarcely imagine what else would be desirable to lead men to virtue and I have not yet said anything about public instruction in the strict sense.[47]

Tracy regarded these institutional devices for forming social and private morality as a necessary background to any direct moral instruction provided by the schools and public festivals. In cases where there is a breakdown in public finance and government functions, costly remedies such as public instruction are widely seen as irrelevant. Moreover, the mere multiplication of teachers and of moral catechisms does not give citizens the necessary incentive and time to study. Recalling, no doubt, the turmoil of the recent past, Tracy pointed to the dependence of public instruction on rational and stable social institutions.

> Suppose a nation excited by lively passions, upturned by violent movements, where greedy men are unrestrained, where almost everyone is impoverished, where all fortunes are made or destroyed overnight, where no existence is assured, no reputation intact and no-one lives in his usual dwelling; and imagine if you can the profound indifference for your schools and festivals and their complete uselessness.
>
> Suppose, on the contrary, a people in the cirumstances described earlier, who have been made hard-working, modest, sensible, happy and prosperous; do you doubt that the desire for instruction and common enjoyments would be quick to develop? Public festivals would be established, schools would be desired.[48]

Tracy concluded his essay of 1798 with a few remarks on the moral education of children. The child's moral education is readily formed in the family circle if the parents have acquired good habits and have been "formed, so to speak, by wise institutions". But if society is given over to prejudices, vice and disorder, the satisfactory moral education of children is not possible. Tracy insisted again on the superiority of experience and example over direct instruction in moral education. Our early sentiments and inclinations are formed not so much by "classes, sermons and public exhortations", but by our surroundings, by what we experience in those moments we are not being "indoctrinated".[49] The corrupting influence of parents and institutions imbued with bad principles would completely negate the benefits of sound moral principles imparted in formal instruction. The essential point was that direct attempts to inculcate certain modes of conduct were always unsuccessful. But "arrange the circumstances in a favourable way and what you desire will happen without you appearing to have been involved". This was true, concluded Tracy, in regard to "the project of making men rational and virtuous".[50]

In the pamphlet edition of *Quels sont les moyens* ... (1798) Tracy had added a brief Supplement (wisely omitted from the 1819 edition) where he attempted to "apply" these principles to contemporary events in France. How could one explain the increased crime rate, the exasperated passions and the general level of disorder, in which "the best citizens are those who suffer most"?[51] The common answer, he noted, was that the Revolution had undermined the moral order.[52] But what could be the meaning of this alleged *démoralisation*? If it simply drew attention to the increase in crime and dishonesty, it would not constitute a causal explanation but only a restatement of the facts. If it meant that the republican government had corrupted our morals, this was surely to exaggerate how fast our moral sentiments actually change.

> ... the present is always, so to speak, the disciple of the past, and we are motivated today by the habits, passions and ideas contracted or acquired under the old social order. If these were the causes of our present evils, it would be necessary to attribute them all to the *ancien régime*, so foolishly lamented. But let us yet be just; that would overstate the reproaches it deserves, since in that society these same habits, passions and ideas did not lead to the same consequences.[53]

Could it be, then, that the so-called de-moralisation arose because the principles of the new social order were destructive of *la morale*? This was to call into question Tracy's fundamental belief in the rational superiority of the new system over the old. The new system "professes more respect for men's natural and original rights" than for later "usurpations", it places reason above prejudice and habit, it consults the interests of the majority rather than the minority.[54] Such a system was directed towards justice, not corruption. Moreover, he claimed, the critics of the new order had mainly attacked its alleged impracticality rather than its sublime principles of reason and justice.

Why, then, was there more corruption under the new system, devoted to reason, than under the old system, founded on errors?

> It is because the domestic and external troubles which have accompanied this great and sudden reformation, have further increased the needs of the state and consequently the disorders of the administration, and have reduced the effectiveness of repressive laws at the very time they were most necessary. Owing to these two circumstances, the practice of *la morale* has deteriorated, though its theory has been advanced.[55]

Refusing to admit that his principles were in any way threatened by the defects of social practice, Tracy consoled his readers that the decline was only "temporary". It was caused by the difficulty of establishing the new order, rather than inherent in its essential character. The new political institutions, wrote Tracy optimistically, have deep roots and are likely to overcome the problems of *la morale* in the near future.[56] Less than two years after these words were written, the Directory collapsed; Bonaparte pledged himself to restore law and order, and to this end encouraged the revival of traditional moral bonds in the place of the morality of reason advocated by the idéologues.

Tracy's successor at the Academy of Moral and Political Sciences, J.-P. Damiron, claimed that the corruption and materialism of the Directory period had been directly attributable to the official adoption of sensationalist philosophy by the intellectual and political élite. Utility, according to Damiron, was not an adequate criterion for a moral philosophy. It led to an emphasis on the satisfaction of material needs above all else and offered little resistance to a despotism which promised to provide for such needs. Its ethic was that of *l'industrialisme*, which saw government only in terms of physical and material objectives.[57] The utilitarian ethic was widely criticised by contemporary opponents of the idéologues. Bentham's doctrine of pleasures and pains, and Helvétius' sensual concept of happiness, were attacked in the pages of the *Mercure* and other journals.[58]

Tracy certainly believed that material satisfactions were important to well-being and happiness, but he was far from believing that they were the essential element of social and private morality. Nor did he hold that criminal actions by the poor should be excused owing to their imperative material needs: he did not lapse into an environmental determinism that eliminated the concept of moral responsibility.[59] He might well have agreed with Burke and Durkheim that it is essential for men to put moral chains upon their own appetites.

A more serious objection against Tracy's "project of making men rational and virtuous",[60] is the élitism of his claim to know how individual and social interests may be reconciled and how social virtue may be recognised and promoted. One commentator has described Tracy's conception of morality as "the hygiene of desires",[61] while another has likened the idéologues' programme to an "educational totalitarianism attempting to shape minds and hearts".[62] The thrust of these criticisms is that Tracy's doctrine was ultimately manipulative: an educated élite, proficient in ideological analysis of ideas and desires, would determine what kinds of ideas and actions were compatible with reason and virtue. The ordinary people, unable to understand the grand design at a philosophical level, would be given practical precepts telling them how to conform with the higher truths.[63] These criticisms are exaggerated, as will be seen in later chapters. It is true, however, that Tracy left himself open to such charges by failing to provide, alongside his concern with institutional techniques of social integration and progress, a defence of a private sphere of individuality or a defence of intellectual and moral pluralism. His criticism of direct moral inculcation in 1798 had been cast in terms of its ineffectiveness, not in terms of its illiberalism.

Tracy's epistemological position implied that there was ultimately only one correct judgement on any given issue; the problem was to find that solution and to convince others of its rectitude. Upon examination, however, the content of the "virtuous" social conduct he advocated amounted to little more than honesty, benevolence, prudence and moderation. Such qualities of conduct had little connection with the Jacobin "reign of virtue", nor with any political programme in which loyalty to the current régime took precedence over other principles of conduct. Moreover, Tracy always refrained from any "solutions" based on coercion or indoctrination: he believed that the future lay with those whose case was most in accordance with science, reason and experience. Persuasion and demonstration would suffice in the long run to inaugurate a peaceful and prosperous society of individuals, each pursuing his own satisfactions as he saw fit, mindful of the consequences of his actions upon the interests of his fellows. In the short term, the educated élite were in a position to use their influence to steer social institutions in the general directions pointed out by analysis of human nature and human needs. Tracy and the idéologues grasped their opportunities under the Directory; yet they failed to have any lasting impact upon the lives of the ordinary people. By the time he wrote his *Commentaire* in 1806, Tracy was much more explicitly committed to a gradualist or evolutionary perspective regarding moral and political reform, though his faith in the ultimate triumph of reason continued unabated.

In order to understand the relations which Tracy posited between the behaviour of citizens and the policies of legislators, administrators and educators, it is necessary to examine more carefully his science of social organisation, or *la science sociale*. This is the subject of the following chapter.

Notes

1. Tracy, "Mémoire sur la faculté de penser", p. 287; Louis de Bonald, *Mélanges* (Paris, 1819), vol. II, pp. 311-319; B. Constant, *Mélanges* (Paris, 1829), pp. 240-254; Condorcet, *Selected Writings*, ed. K.M. Baker (New York, 1976), pp. xxvii-xxviii of "Introduction"; C.H. Van Duzer, *Contributions of the Idéologues*, p. 95.
2. B. Constant, *loc. cit.*; Condorcet, "The Nature and Purpose of Public Instruction" (1791), in *Selected Writings*, esp. pp. 122-134.
3. Cf. Helvétius, *De l'esprit* (1758), ed. F. Châtelet (Paris, 1973), pp. 492-501; I. Cumming, *Helvétius* (London, 1955); A. Keim, *Helvétius* (Paris, 1907). On Beccaria, cf. D.-J. Garat, *Mémoires historiques sur la vie de M. Suard* ... (Paris, 1820), vol. II, pp. 203-8. Tracy cited Beccaria's view that "the most certain means of rendering a people free and happy is to establish a perfect method of education": see title page of *Commentary* (Philadelphia, 1811).
4. Cf. *Dictionnaire de la Constitution française* (Paris, 1791), article "Instruction publique", pp. 257-9; A. Sicard, *L'éducation morale et civique avant et pendant la Révolution* (Paris, 1884).
5. "Quels sont les moyens..." (1798), in *Commentaire*, pp. 458-9.
6. *Logique*, pp. 436-7; cf. *ibid.*, pp. 392-3.
7. *Traité de la Volonté* (1818), pp. 475-6.
8. *Elémens*, vol. I, p. 72.
9. *Ibid.*, p. 73. Cf. "Quels sont les moyens", in *Commentaire*, p. 462, and "Mémoire sur la faculté de penser", p. 363.
10. P.-L. Roederer, *Oeuvres* (Paris, 1853-9), vol. V, pp. 151-2, 156-8; also pp. 107-129 on moral catechisms. For a completely different view see L.-C. Saint-Martin, *Réflexions d'un observateur* (Paris, 1798).
11. J.-B. Say, *Olbie, ou essai sur les moyens de réformer les moeurs d'une nation* (Paris, an VIII: 1800). A slightly abridged version was reprinted in Say's *Oeuvres diverses* (Paris, 1848), pp. 581-615. *Olbie* was favourably reviewed in *la Décade*, 20 ventose an VIII (11 March 1800), pp. 476-485.
12. "Quels sont les moyens", in *Commentaire*, p. 438. Cf. *Logique*, p. 395, on the meaning of the term "police".
13. Cf. R. Lote, "Histoire de la philosophie", in G. Hanotaux (ed.), *Histoire de la Nation française* (Paris, 1920-24), XV, p. 531 and 531 n.l: Destutt de Tracy was "a former colonel who had retained in his theories a little military rigidity", and who "recommended recourse to the gendarme in matters of morality". *La Grand Encyclopédie*, before 1850,

claimed that "Destutt de Tracy is one of those materialists who replace God with a gendarme": cited in J. Cruet, *La philosophie morale et sociale de Destutt de Tracy* (Tours, 1909), p. 156. Finally, E. Joyau claimed that Tracy "simply wanted recourse to gendarmes and squadrons of cavalry to fortify the teaching of morality": *La philosophie en France pendant la Révolution* (Paris, 1893), pp. 174-5.

14. "Quels sont les moyens", pp. 439-440.
15. *Ibid.*, pp. 440-1.
16. *Ibid.*, pp. 441-2.
17. *Ibid.*, pp. 443-4. Of course, Tracy adds, if a man is *deliberately* victimised by means of the legal system, this is an "atrocious" crime and likely to lead to others.
18. *Ibid.*, p. 446.
19. *Ibid.*, p. 447.
20. Cf. *Commentaire*, pp. 2-5.
21. "Quels sont les moyens", pp. 448-9.
22. *Ibid.*, p. 450.
23. *Ibid.*, p. 451.
24. *Ibidem.*
25. *Ibid.*, p. 452. The vehement opposition to paper money was in part a response to the amazing depreciation in value of government *assignats* during the 1790s.
26. *Ibid.*, p. 453.
27. *Ibid.*, p. 454.
28. *Ibid.*, p. 455 (emphasis added).
29. "Mémoire sur la faculté de penser", p. 356; cf. *Elémens*, vol. I, pp. 67, 73.
30. "Mémoire", pp. 442-3; *Elémens*, vol. I, pp. 273-4.
31. *Traité de la Volonté* (1815), pp. 83 ff; and also above, chapter 4.
32. "Quels sont les moyens", p. 457.
33. *Ibid.*, pp. 457-9.
34. *Ibid.*, p. 460.
35. *Ibid.*, p. 461.
36. *Analyse* (1804), p. 148.
37. "Quels sont les moyens", p. 462.
38. *Ibid.*, p. 463.
39. *Ibid.*, p. 462.
40. *Ibid.*, p. 463; cf. *Elémens*, vol. I, p. 213.
41. "Mémoire sur la faculté de penser", p. 363.
42. "Quels sont les moyens", p. 464.
43. *Ibid.*, p. 465.
44. *Ibid.*, p. 466.
45. *Ibid.*, p. 467.
46. *Ibid.*, pp. 468-70. (Cf. his summary of "Quels sont ..." in *De l'amour*, pp. 28-29.)
47. *Ibid.*, p. 470. In his later writings, Tracy also drew attention to the detrimental consequences for morality of luxury: cf. *Traité de la Volonté* (1818), pp. 350, 368-9; and *Commentaire*, pp. 79 ff.
48. "Quels sont les moyens", pp. 471-2.
49. *Ibid.*, pp. 474-5.
50. *Ibid.*, p. 477.
51. *Quels sont les moyens* ... (Paris, an VI), p. 33.
52. Cf. Lafayette, *Mémoires*, vol. III, p. 384, where Tracy's close friend attributed *la démoralisation* of the Revolution to the breakdown of law and order after the Jacobin victory in the Legislative Assembly in August 1792.
53. *Quels sont les moyens* ... (an VI), p. 34.
54. *Ibidem.*
55. *Ibid.*, p. 35.
56. *Ibidem.*
57. J.-P. Damiron, *Essai sur l'histoire de la philosophie* ..., pp. 11, 25.

58. Cf. review of Bentham's *Traités de législation* (1802), and of an anonymous work on Seneca and Helvétius, in *Mercure de France*, 3 vendémiaire an XI (25 September 1802), esp. pp. 21-23 and *ibid.*, 9 thermidor an XII (28 July 1804), esp. p. 263.
59. *Traité de la Volonté* (1818), pp. 296-7.
60. "Quels sont les moyens", in *Commentaire*, p. 477.
61. A. Canivez, "Les Idéologues", p. 109. The concept of "hygiene" comes from the writings of Cabanis: cf. *Oeuvres philosophiques*, vol. I, p. 109 and vol. II, pp. 221-5.
62. M. Régaldo, "Lumières, élite, démocratie: la difficile position des idéologues", *Dix-huitième siècle*, no. 6 (1974), p. 207.
63. For a different kind of élitism among the philosophes, in which only the masses were held to require the moral discipline of religion, cf. R.I. Boss, "The development of social religion", *Journal of the History of Ideas*, vol. 34 (1973), pp. 577-589.

6. SOCIAL SCIENCE AND PUBLIC POLICY

I have argued elsewhere that the idéologues' conception of a science of society is deeply indebted to the physiocratic conception of a "social art", by which legislation and education would lead men to a prosperous society conforming to the "laws of nature".[1] This argument concerning the intellectual background to Tracy's writings on social science will not be repeated here; I will focus rather on Tracy's particular conception of social science as the scientific basis for public policies aiming to increase the happiness of the citizens.

The desire to become a "Newton of the social sciences" moved many a writer to sketch the outlines of a science of society in the decades after 1750.[2] One major approach may be found in Montesquieu and in the Scottish Enlightenment (Ferguson, Millar, Hume, Smith, and others); another approach was adopted by the physiocrats or *économistes* (Quesnay, Mirabeau, Baudeau, Dupont de Nemours, and others).[3] The Scots and Montesquieu were more historical and empirical in their approach, developing a conception of a "social" level of reality whose qualities were distinguishable from the multitude of individual actions. The social could not be explained purely as the sum of its simple components. The French *économistes* also developed a conception of society as a system distinguishable from individual action, but their system was analytically based upon the satisfaction of individual needs. Their science of economics was less historical and empirical, and more concerned to posit a desirable ("natural") order of society, conceived as an abstract system of rights, duties, interests and exchanges. The purpose of such a science was to enable men to recognise their true interests, and thus to discard their ignorant desires and prejudices. The task of legislators and educators (the "social art") was to provide laws, institutions and knowledges which would make the social order conform to the "laws of nature", understood as those which promoted men's true interests.

Tracy and Cabanis, together with several other idéologues, were members of the short-lived *Société de 1789*, which had taken up the conception of a "social art" as a liberal science of public policy issues. Tracy and his colleagues were deeply imbued with a desire to contribute to what Cabanis called *la science de l'homme*[4] (comprising physiology, analysis of ideas, and morality) and to what Tracy after 1801 increasingly began to call *la science sociale*. In his first paper at the Institut in April 1796, Tracy claimed that ideological analysis of the formation of ideas was the proper basis for the "arts" of grammar, logic, instruction, education, morality, "and finally the basis of the greatest of the arts, for whose success all the others must co-operate, that of regulating society in such a way that man finds the most help and the least hindrance possible on the part of his fellows."[5] The same point was made five years later in similar terms: the applications of idéologie would include "grammar, logic, instruction, private morality, public morality (or the social art), education, and legislation ...".[6] Tracy was much clearer in 1801 that these were "sciences" rather than "arts", but the distinction between these terms tended often to be blurred in the thought of the idéologues. While fully aware of the analytical distinction between sciences and arts, theories and applications, they were so concerned with the practical consequences of their meliorist theories that they tended to use a variety of terms fairly indiscriminately.

The original usages of the term social science (*la science sociale*) date from the early years of the French Revolution,[7] and are closely related to the rationalist concern for an ordered and prosperous society of free and happy citizens. Of central importance was the educational law of October 1795 which, in establishing the Institut National, had created a section entitled *Sciences sociales et législation* in the Class of moral and political sciences. Thus, the term had a semi-official status in the classifications of the sciences and arts during the period 1795 to 1803, after which the Institut was thoroughly reorganised by Bonaparte to eliminate the "ideological" sciences.

Optimistic faith in the progressive role of social science and its professed concern to promote the happiness, liberty and security of the people, formed the climate of opinion in which Tracy developed his own ideas about the nature of a general science of man in society. The leaders of the *Société de 1789*, and later the *savants* of the Class of moral and political sciences, assumed that the science they wished to establish was "new". This was because the conception of the "rights of man", embodied in a "free constitution", was a recent development both in philosophy and in political practice: the ancients thus had not been able to conceive of a social art or social science in this modern sense. The idéologues agreed that social science was underdeveloped, and subject to strong resistance by the accumulated habits and prejudices of the past. They were also convinced that social science was a direct guide to public policy: it would establish principles which could direct legislators and educators concerning the best way to attain the happiness of a free people.

TRACY'S "SCIENCE SOCIALE"

In his first paper to the Institut in April 1796, Tracy urged upon his colleagues the need to "create the theory of the moral and political sciences, which have languished until now in a disastrous uncertainty". The sciences were ultimately justified, he claimed, by their "utility". But before such practical applications could be successfully made, it was necessary to have a correct theory on which to base them. The enlightened minds of Europe therefore looked to the Institut in the hope and expectation that it would "establish the moral sciences on a stable and certain foundation".[8] Tracy, however, defined in practical terms the underlying problem to be tackled by the human sciences: namely, "having understood the faculties of a species of animate creatures, to discover all the means of happiness of which these beings are capable".[9] Tracy thus affirmed the view that the objective of the social art or social science was *le bonheur social.*

Tracy drew several parallels between the history of the natural sciences and the agenda for the new sciences of man. The Académie des Sciences had been established in 1666 to develop the physical and mathematical sciences; 130 years later, the moral and political sciences were now granted similar recognition, which would greatly assist their progress and dissemination. In astronomy, Copernicus had changed men's conception of the physical universe, and his work had been extended by Galileo and Kepler. According to Tracy, Locke may be seen as the Copernicus of the human sciences, Dumarsais as the Galileo, and Condillac as the Kepler who did most to advance the new paradigm of knowledge.[10] Tracy looked forward to the appearance of a Newton of the human sciences, a man whose work would systematically incorporate existing knowledge in a few fundamental laws, and whose work would allow important applications for increasing human happiness.[11]

Tracy refrained from claiming for himself the title of a Newton of the moral sciences, though the image must have had a powerful attraction for system-builders such as Tracy and Sieyès. One of Adam Smith's students, John Millar, attributed this laurel to the author of the *Wealth of Nations.*[12] Mme de Stael in 1791 described Sieyès as the Newton of politics,[13] and at the turn of the century she still believed in the possibility and desirability of a science of politics, founded jointly upon notions of calculation and morality.[14] The desire for certainty in the moral and political sciences was a driving force behind Tracy's reduction of their methodology to a consideration of concept-formation, taking his cue from Condillac's view that the sciences could not be perfected "unless we endeavour to render their language more precise".[15] The truths composing the human sciences, he wrote, could reach

> the same degree of certainty as those of the mathematical sciences. Too often, it is true, the reality of their relations is difficult to perceive, owing to ignorance of the way these ideas are formed, the multitude of elements which compose each idea, and the imperfections of the signs by which we calculate them. But this is all the more reason for us to give their connections all the *évidence* which can stem from the good order of a methodical deduction. Let us then return carefully to the very origin of the whole system. Let us imitate the mathematicians, who do not fear to begin with a truth so obvious that it seems pointless to express. Let us follow them further in their procedures; let

> us advance, like them, from the known to the unknown, without being discouraged by the slow and lengthy journey. For it is above all the moral sciences which have suffered from the sway of prejudices ...[16]

Tracy's faith in the possibility of certain knowledge about man and society was unshakeable. The obstacles could be identified. Ignorance and illusions were the main problem; and these could be overcome by scientific education and wise legislation. The complexity of ideas and defects in the usage of signs could be tackled by a methodical ideological analysis. "This science (of ideas) is positive, useful, and capable of a rigorous exactness".[17] In these opinions, Tracy was only voicing the typical idéologue viewpoint.

Lakanal, in introducing the law establishing the *école normale* at the end of 1794, had claimed that the superiority of the principles of the new social order could be demonstrated in the same rigorous way as in the "most exact" sciences. "The more progress made by human reason, the more this demonstration will become clear".[18] By using analytical methods, which alone could renovate the human understanding, the moral sciences would be "submitted to demonstrations as rigorous as the physical and exact sciences". The principles of our moral "duties" would be widely diffused among the people, and inequality of knowledge would be remedied. "Analysis" was thus the "indispensable instrument of a great democracy".[19] Cabanis also expressed confidence in the rigorous character of the human sciences: it would be possible to obtain "results which increasingly approached the highest level of probability, the only type of certainty which the practical sciences allow, especially those whose object is the moral aspects of man".[20]

Tracy's conception of science assumed that there were general truths, principles and causes underlying the complex facts of experience. The observer must rely upon empirical enquiry, but the genius is the man who discovers those general truths which bind together the multitude of discrete facts. Some sciences, according to this criterion, were more developed than others. Botany, zoology and mineralogy, for example, had not yet reached their maturity, because they were still preoccupied with the collection, classification and cataloguing of facts. They had not yet discovered those general laws from which the properties of particular phenomena could be deduced. Astronomy, physics and chemistry were highly advanced, because general principles (such as the law of attraction) had been discovered, which could explain all the past, present and even future phenomena.[21] How did the science of man measure up to these standards?

The human sciences tended to lag behind the others, wrote Tracy, because of ignorance, habits of thought, vested interests, and our need to obtain first an adequate understanding of nature.[22] The consequence of the illusions which obstruct the understanding of human behaviour, was that the theoretical side of the human sciences was poorly developed, despite the abundance of facts about man and society accumulated throughout history.

> Social science (*la science sociale*), for example, is certainly very rich in data: ... for history has preserved an infinite number of details on the numerous

> changes which have occurred in different human societies ... However, despite this over-abundance of observations, it can be said that social science hardly merits the name of a science so long as it has no recognised and systematic principles with whose aid we can explain and even predict the happiness and misery of diverse societies and see them only as necessary and constant results of proven laws. It seems to me, in truth, that it is now possible to trace this code, in setting out from this first general truth: man is a sentient being. But this has not yet been done; and that is enough reason that unfortunately I take social science as an example of an emergent science.[23]

Tracy's notion of a fully developed science, as a set of systematic principles explaining the happiness of a people, is very close to the concept of the social art championed by Sieyès and Condorcet in meetings of the *Société de 1789*. And in locating the starting-point of social science in man as a sentient being, Tracy was in accord with Condorcet's formulation in his *Esquisse*.[24] For Tracy, the possibility of increasing the level of social happiness depended on our ability to formulate general scientific laws explaining individual and social behaviour. A science, he wrote, "is useful only for the light it sheds on all the arts which depend on it; and so long as that theory is incomplete, the rules it provides for these arts can only be groping approximations".[25] The governmental and educational "arts" of ordering the social environment so as to maximise welfare and happiness were dependent on a "social science" which explained the principles involved.

All the aspects of the human sciences had an underlying unity, in Tracy's view. And if the various branches of human knowledge seemed at present to be separate and distinct, that was only because their relationships had not yet been sufficiently elucidated. If all these sciences were fully developed, it would be clear that

> the totality of the science of man (*la science humaine*) would be contained in a small number of propositions and that, to unite all the branches to their common trunk, a fundamental proposition would have to be found, from which all the basic propositions of every particular science are derived. Then we would really have a complete knowledge of all that exists, and we would clearly see that all the subsidiary truths are only consequences of a primary truth, in which they are all implicitly contained, and of which they represent only partial developments.[26]

This optimistic faith in the unity and perfectibility of the sciences recalls not only the "tree of knowledge" conceptions of Bacon and d'Alembert, and a belief in uniform methods of observation and analysis in scientific research, but also a reductionist search for a fundamental and general truth from which all our knowledge can be shown to be deducible.

Tracy returned to the subject matter of social science in his educational writings of 1799 and 1801. After joining the Council of Public Instruction in February 1799 as an advisor to the Minister of the Interior, François de Neufchâteau, Tracy drafted a number of circulars to teachers in the new secondary schools (*écoles centrales*) in the months of August and September.[27] The courses on legislation and history were of direct concern to the development of Tracy's notion of a social science (though the term social science was not specifically used in secondary curricula). His circulars on these courses will be examined here, while those on other subjects will be noted in chapter ten along with his general ideas on public instruction.

In his circular to teachers of legislation in the *écoles centrales*, Tracy pointed out that there was some confusion about the content of the course and its relation to other studies; some teachers had asked for guidance.[28] The course on legislation, he advised, should not deal with areas which might later be taught in an *école spéciale* for professional training in jurisprudence, political economy, government or diplomacy. It should provide only the knowledge required by "all citizens who have the time and means to undertake a careful education" beyond the level of primary instruction. The course should give young people "sound principles of private and public morality, with the necessary developments to make them into virtuous citizens who understand both their own interests and those of their country".[29] The course on legislation was said to be closely linked to that on general grammar (one of the key areas of idéologie); the generation of our ideas and sentiments should thus be studied before commencing the course on legislation. This was because "the general principles of morality must necessarily be established at the beginning and they can be derived only from a knowledge of our intellectual faculties".[30]

The course on legislation should preferably be studied before that on history, since "it is necessary to have some well established principles in order to read history without danger". If one reads history without a prior grounding in rational morality, one might imbibe more false ideas than "useful" knowledge.[31]

The content of the course should include:

1. the elements of *morale*, drawn from an examination of the nature of man and his intellectual faculties, and based on his interest, properly understood, and on his invincible desire to be happy; that is what is called natural right;
2. the application of these principles to the organisation of the body politic, to the code of criminal, civil and commercial laws, and to its relation with foreign nations—i.e. public law, criminal and civil law, political economy and the rights of nations—always showing what *should be* alongside that which *is*, in order to accustom (students) to judge the one in terms of the other.[32]

The circular concluded by stating that most of these points should be regarded as useful advice rather than firm regulations, and suggested that teachers might like to add some additional, more specialised material owing to the present absence of any *écoles spéciales* for those professions depending on the moral and political sciences.[33] Despite the friendly tone of the circular, it actually wished to prescribe a particular kind of approach to moral and political questions.[34] The analysis should begin from an understanding of human nature: man's needs, interests, intellectual faculties, rights. Institutions and practices should then be judged in the light of these ideal principles. This is a clear example of Tracy's ideological and evaluative conception of social science.

The circular to professors of history in the *écoles centrales* was more detailed. It reported that the teachers' lesson plans reflected "a great variety in their manner of envisaging and treating their subject".[35] The circular noted that the government had initially been unwilling to provide detailed instructions to the teaching profession, preferring to draw on the "fruits of experience" rather than precise and centralised direction. (Daunou, indeed, had championed the freedom of teachers from state regulation in October 1795, a principle established earlier by Condorcet.[36]) But the time had now arrived when more detailed guidance seemed to be necessary.

Three major objectives of the history course were stated, in extremely general and vague terms.

(i) To provide a general knowledge of events in world history.

(ii) To understand the causes of progress and temporary regressions in the sciences, arts and social organisation, and the "constant relation between men's happiness and the extent and accuracy of their ideas". This was the genuinely "ideological" objective.

(iii) To enable students to further their researches should they so desire.

History lessons, then, "should present a summary picture of universal history", together with a guide to sources for deeper study in each area, and advice on how to use and interpret historical authors.[37] There was, however, the problem that the writing of history really demanded a good knowledge of all the sciences. This problem became especially acute when the historian dealt with

> metaphysics, morality, the social art, and political economy. These sciences, the most important of all for those who want to observe and judge the actions of men in society, still have no well established fundamentals: the metaphysics which serves as their basis is only just emerging from chaos, and it has hardly been generally recognised that it should consist simply in the examination of our intellectual faculties. History, in this respect, might then serve just as much to preserve ancient prejudices as to bring about the discovery of true principles. The latter are found more by meditation than by (empirical) example.[38]

This sums up in many respects the idéologue view of the human sciences. The search for true principles in history (presumably those which confirmed the moral and political perspectives evidenced in Condorcet's *Esquisse* and Volney's *Les Ruines*), was seen to be more important than the examination of facts. The accidental imbibing of "prejudices" engendered by the old metaphysics was to be prevented by reliance upon the sensationalist philosophy of idéologie. The history course in the schools should, then, be preceded by the courses on general grammar (idéologie) and legislation, to provide a suitable preparation for understanding the broad canvas of human history.[39]

The conception of history emerging from Tracy's document has been criticised as narrow and biased: the real objective was not to understand history, claimed Duruy, but to glorify the established moral and political order of the French republic. In support of this interpretation, Duruy cites a letter by Lagrange, president of the Council of Public Instruction, to the Minister of the Interior (6 May 1799): a circular to the professors of history was needed, said Lagrange, to show them "the real viewpoint from which the course should be considered, and the new benefits for republican morality and for philosophy which should be derived from this properly directed instruction".[40] There is no doubt that Tracy and the idéologues wished to impart their distinctive conception of the human sciences to the courses taught in the *écoles centrales*. However, they were never in a position to impose their views upon teachers; the organisational mechanisms did not exist even if they had wanted a strict régime. Any attempt at authoritarian control over public education would also have been inconsistent with Tracy's philosophical faith in the primacy of reason and persuasion, his willingness to accept a dual system of state and private schools, the absence of compulsory education, and Tracy's belief that direct moral instruction was ineffective.

For Tracy and the idéologues, historical writing should be leavened by sound moral principles. The authority of facts had to be countered by the authority of reasoned principles, the basis of social science. While Volney[41] and Daunou[42] in some of their work may be exempted from such criticism, it is generally true to say that Tracy and the idéologues treated history with grave suspicion. The past was the arena of prejudice and oppression, as Condorcet had demonstrated. The past should therefore have as little hold as possible over the present and future. Politics or social science was essentially concerned with what should be, not with what exists.[43] (This will be further confirmed in chapter nine, in considering Tracy's commentary on Montesquieu.)

Tracy's *Observations* (1801) on the educational system established under the Directory also raised the question of a social science. History and the moral sciences, wrote Tracy, are alike insofar as everyone knows some history and everyone has a little system of moral notions, even without being aware of it.[44] These habitual ideas and sentiments determine most of people's behaviour: should these ideas be left to chance? On the contrary, it is necessary that students are taught history and the moral sciences, but the first step is to learn "the sound principles of morality and the social art. The principles are the model against which it is always necessary to judge events".[45] Those parts of the course on legislation and moral sciences dealing with "public morality or social science", need to be taught by giving many practical examples; just as in the history course, it is necessary constantly to "relate the facts to the theory".[46] Tracy made similar remarks in regard to the study of the positive laws of a society. Such study, wrote Tracy, should be seen as "an application of the principles of morality and of social science". [47] The study of law, like that of history, tends to lead to the false identification of what is with what should be, unless the student has first received a proper training in principles.[48]

Tracy increasingly came to use the term social science, rather than social art, after 1801. He used the phrase "moral and social sciences" in his *Analyse raisonné* of Dupuis in 1804,[49] and substituted the term "social science" for Cabanis' term "science of man" in his *Table analytique* (1805) for the second edition of Cabanis' famous work on the physical and moral aspects of man.[50] The question of a science of social organisation was also raised at the end of Tracy's *Logique* (1805). The sciences of economy and morality, he said, gave rise to a third science, that of "directing" our sentiments and actions in order to "produce the happiness of the desiring being, for happiness is the goal of the will just as truth is the goal of the judgement".[51] Tracy regarded this policy science as a new type of scientific enterprise, in much the same way that idéologie, as the science of the formation and expression of ideas, was new.

> Could this science (of social happiness) be so new, then, that there is no appropriate name for it, and we do not yet even know how to designate it? I fear so. For that which we usually call the science of government rarely concerns itself with the objective we have just indicated, and that known under the name of social science only covers part of the subject, since it does not include education, nor even perhaps all the branches of legislation. Now, the system of principles needed to guide men to their highest degree of well-being must include the principles of behaviour and control of men of all ages, and in all circumstances. Thus here we have another science still to be named. However, with suitable precautions, we can use the common expressions ...[52]

These three sciences, dealing with the actions, desires and guidance of the will, formed a "natural" sequence. The first, economy, provided not only a knowledge of the ways in which we satisfied our physical needs and gained material wealth, but also a knowledge of the intellectual and moral consequences of our actions, and their influence on the happiness of the individual and society. Such a work would not provide us with "the theory of social science",[53] but it could indicate the elements which would have to be included. The second science, morality, "follows quite naturally, for it is very easy to evaluate our various sentiments and their different degrees of merit and demerit, when we well understand all the consequences of the actions to which we are led (by these sentiments)".[54] The new social science also follows readily from the previous knowledges:

> for as soon as one understands the generation of our sentiments, one knows the means of *cultivating* some and *uprooting* others. Thus the principles of education and legislation are discovered, and the science of man as a desiring and acting being is complete.[55]

Such a complete treatise on the operations and guidance of the will would be the "most important" work one could undertake, given the present state of knowledge: for it would be "the basis of a methodical and certain theory of all the moral sciences".[56]

Elsewhere in his *Logique*, Tracy gave a similar sketch of the content of that social science which rested on the foundations of the moral and economic sciences: on this occasion, he used the term "science of legislation" rather than "social science".

> Taken in its broadest meaning (legislation) denotes the knowledge of the laws which must govern man in all circumstances and in all the stages of his life. Thus it includes not only the science of the laws which govern the interests of individuals, the laws which determine social organisation, and those which establish the relations of the society with foreign nations: but also the science of the laws which must guide children. The science of legislation comprises that of government and that of education. For government is only the education of men, and education is the government of children. Except that, in the first case, the main attention is given to actions, because they have an immediate effect; while in the other case, the main concern is to guide sentiments ... (The) goal of the science of legislation is to guide (*diriger*) the sentiments and actions of man ...[57]

The study of positive laws should be related to the science of legislation in this broad sense. Otherwise, legal studies are only "knowledge of what is ordered", without consideration of "what should be". It would have "no theory and no principles", a "simple history of what is".[58]

Tracy never wrote the treatise on political and educational matters, or social science, which would have constituted volume six of the projected nine volumes of the *Elémens d'idéologie* (see chapter two). In abandoning the total project in 1813, after writing the beginnings of his volume on moral sentiments, Tracy wrote:

> I would have left it to the philosophers and legislators to draw consequences from these (foregoing volumes) and to propose the political, civil, moral and penal laws best suited for developing our talents and virtues, for stifling or repressing our bad inclinations, and for assuring our happiness. I would, however, have perhaps ventured to make known my opinions on three important points, in separate pamphlets: namely, religious ideas, the organisation of society, and the instruction of youth.[59] This is what would have gone into the third part of the Treatise on the Will, the sixth volume of my Elements of Ideology.[60]

The significant omission from this list of materials relevant to the sixth volume, on social science, was Tracy's *Commentaire sur l'Esprit des Lois*. As mentioned in chapter one, Tracy's *Commentaire* was written in 1806-7, but could not be published in Napoleonic France because it contained a critique of all forms of illiberal and unrepresentative government.[61] Tracy sent the manuscript to Thomas Jefferson in Virginia; he was sufficiently impressed to undertake an English translation, published anonymously under the title *A Commentary and Review of Montesquieu's Spirit of Laws*.[62] Tracy's authorship was heavily disguised; Jefferson respected Tracy's wish to be taken for a Frenchman who had fled to America to escape "the tyrannies of the monster Robespierre".[63] Similarly, a French edition of the *Commentaire* in 1817 remained anonymous. Tracy claimed not to have authorised that edition (printed in Liège and reprinted in Paris two years later). But despite his official disclaimers in his own authorised edition in July 1819, the text of the 1817 edition was so close to the original that it was obviously based on a manuscript copy, rather than a retranslation from the American edition.[64] Tracy's edition in July 1819 publicly acknowledged his own name as author. He included a few notes updating his opinions on some points, but curiously failed to remove from the text those passages which gave the impression that the author had been living in America since the Jacobin régime.[65]

Tracy noted in his preface of 1807 that he had begun to make critical remarks on the important subjects discussed by Montesquieu, and soon realised "that the collection of these opinions would form a complete treatise on politics, or social science" if it were correctly and systematically executed.[66] But Tracy had decided to retain the order of presentation of material in Montesquieu's classic treatise, in order to do justice to that great author and facilitate comparisons between Montesquieu's opinions and his own. So Tracy did not write a systematic work on politics or social science, though he hoped that the *Commentaire* would have

> contributed effectively to the advancement of social science, the most important of all the sciences for the happiness of men, and that which is necessarily the last to be perfected for it is the result and product of all the others.[67]

The argument in the *Commentaire* gives us further evidence about Tracy's conception of a social science, even though the work is not the systematic treatise he had once contemplated. Tracy's commentary is quite inadequate as a account of Montesquieu's thought; Montesquieu's division of material simply provided Tracy with a framework for presenting his own views, with little attention to the finer details of the work he criticised. Tracy wanted to extract the rational kernel of the *Esprit des Lois*, and to ignore the mass of historical detail irrelevant to this central concern. Very often, Tracy finds nothing of substance in Montesquieu's discussion of a subject; on other occasions, he asserts that Montesquieu's categories and explanations are defective, and replaces them with his own conceptions. A major example, discussed below in chapter nine, is Tracy's replacement of Montesquieu's tripartite typology of government (monarchy, republic, despotism) by his own two-fold division into governments which uphold the rights of man and those which are based on particularistic forms of privilege.

The *Commentaire* is in some ways the most historically informed of Tracy's writings, and yet it evidences a view of historical facts which seems to contradict Tracy's professed concern for empirical analysis as against speculative philosophy. A number of later commentators have made this point rather forcefully.

> Destutt de Tracy, in commenting on Montesquieu, discovered that the great historian remained too slavishly grounded in history, and he went about re-

> making Montesquieu's work by constructing the society that ought to be rather than observing the society that is.[68]

Such criticisms suggest that the conception of *la science sociale* envisaged by Tracy and his colleagues was closer to political philosophy than to a behavioural social science based on observation and the collection of data. The idéologues indulged in a good deal of speculative and deductive reasoning, and, with a few notable exceptions, not much empirical analysis. In their writings, a particular view of history emerges: history is seen in part as a moral tale of human misery, caused by ignorance, superstition, and oppression; this is followed by a progressive liberation and redemption through the flowering of reason, which allows mankind to control nature and to establish social institutions which secure their happiness, prosperity and freedom.[69] Historical data, in this view, is tainted by its association with the dark ages of domination and prejudice; history could thus all the more readily be ignored as a source concerning appropriate patterns of social behaviour.

The idéologues wanted to create a new set of social facts, a new pattern of social organisation, to be shaped by an enlightened élite of politicians, administrators, entrepreneurs and educators, in accordance with the rationalist tenets of idéologie. "Social science" was invoked as a set of principles concerned with the perfection of social and political institutions, judged by the criteria of reason, freedom, happiness and justice (which for Tracy were interdependent). Politics, wrote Tracy, is the "science of human happiness".[70] The economic, political and educational content of such principles will be discussed in the last four chapters of this study.

Tracy's discussion of how to establish a rational moral order, and his emphasis on the importance of the general interest, show clear links with the utilitarian stream of political and moral writings. Is it possible that he derived his terminology from Jeremy Bentham, who clearly also wanted to be a Newton of the science of man? There was a clear overlap of approach and language on many levels, as Tracy's disciple Joseph Rey implied in his writings.[71] It is very unlikely that Tracy was directly influenced by Bentham, since Tracy did not read English and Bentham's works did not begin to appear in French translation until Etienne Dumont edited and translated some of Bentham's legal writings in 1802. Tracy may have heard about Bentham from Gallois, or indirectly from his reading of other authors. But it seems unnecessary to suggest this, since Tracy shared many ideas with the physiocrats, Helvétius, Beccaria (whose most influential work on crimes and punishments was translated into French in 1766 and was republished many times), and Condorcet (who had experimented with mathematical solutions to the problems of rational calculation of political choices). Tracy's version of utilitarianism is all the more interesting for its critical attitude to quantitative methods in the calculation of individual and public interests or in other aspects of the human sciences.

LIMITS OF SOCIAL MATHEMATICS

We have already seen (chapter three) that Tracy developed an early suspicion of arithmetical or algebraic calculations applied to explain human behaviour. In 1801, in the first volume of his *Eléments d'idéologie*, Tracy pointed out that quantitative measures were the only forms of absolute truth, but they could not readily be applied to all types of phenomena.[72] Aspects of time, space and motion could be measured with great precision and certainty, even in relation to human beings: their age, location, volume, weight, etc. could be calculated and compared. But their other aspects, beauty and goodness for example, could not be measured precisely in quantitative terms.[73] The *intensity* of our desires could not be measured, Tracy had noted in his first mémoire.[74] In the moral and political sciences

> We have no precise measures to evaluate directly the degrees of energy of men's sentiments and inclinations, their goodness or their depravity, the degree of utility or danger of their actions, the consistency or inconsistency of their opinions. That is what makes research in these sciences more difficult and their results less rigorous.[75]

However, Tracy continued, it might be possible to make some use of calculation by measuring opinions, actions and sentiments indirectly, in terms of their *effects*. An accurate measurement of these effects might serve to evaluate the causes. Even in cases where considerable uncertainty remained, there were boundaries within which one might be sure of the truth.

> Thus, for example, it may be impossible to determine how much more preferable is a particular sentiment or social institution over another; but it is impossible not to recognise that one leads to absolutely bad results and another to absolutely good results; and that is enough to stop us saying that these (moral and political) sciences are completely uncertain ... (The degree of certainty of all the various sciences) depends on the extent to which the objects of each science are reducible to quantities measurable by exact units ...[76]

The use of calculus in the various sciences thus depended on whether the objects could readily be measured in terms of fixed quantitative units. The use of numbers and calculus in subjects where they were *not* appropriate was merely a case of charlatanism and bogus scientism.[77]

Tracy returned to some related questions in writing a "Supplement to the first section of the Elements of Ideology" (1805), published as an introduction to his *Traité de la Volonté* (1815). He included a twenty-page discussion on the "theory of probability" (developed by Condorcet and Laplace), and on its limited uses in the human sciences.[78] This theory, he said, should not be seen as a separate science in itself nor as a substitute for a sound logical basis of enquiry. The theory of probability consisted of two parts: (i) the collection and evaluation of relevant data, and (ii) the calculation or combination of the data. In the case of historical events, the collection and evaluation of data depended on knowledge of the circumstances in question, and of the authors who had described them; it thus depended on, and was part of, the science of history.[79]

In the case of examining the probable results of a social institution or of the deliberations of a political assembly, the relevant facts are the details of the social organisation, and the dispositions and intellectual operations of these men. Thus, it depended on knowledge of "social science", morality, or idéologie.[80] The collection and evaluation of data, then, should be recognised as highly variable, depending on the subject matter to which the theory of probability is applied. The mathematicians who developed the calculus of probability applied it with great success to simple fields like games of chance, lotteries, or interest on money—fields where the choice and evaluation of data presented no difficulties.[81] But when they tried to apply their theorems to more subtle and complex areas, their results became distorted by neglecting those considerations which are not amenable to quantification.

> This is why we have seen great calculators, after the most learned combinations, give us forms of voting which are quite defective, for they have not taken account of a thousand circumstances inherent in the nature of men and things, attending only to their numerical circumstances. That is why Condorcet himself, when he tried to apply the theory of probabilities to the decisions of assemblies and especially to the judgements of tribunals, either dared not to make any claims about actual institutions, limiting himself to reasoning on imaginary hypotheses, or was often led to expedients which were absolutely impractical or which had inconveniences worse than those he sought to avoid.[82]

Condorcet had placed great hopes upon mathematical methods for the future development of the human sciences, but had recognised that much work remained to be done in perfecting such methods. Tracy argued that Condorcet's hopes for the utility of a social mathematics could be realised only by severely restricting the scope of calculus. The theory of probability was concerned to determine the likely effects of a given set of causes, or to determine the likely causes of a given set of effects. Now since only those objects which could be assigned a numerical or quantitative value could be successfully subjected to calculus, it followed that there were many objects which could not be analysed in that way, even when the data collected was very detailed. Tracy noted the particular problem of the human sciences.

> Assuredly the degrees of capacity and probity of men, the energy and strength of their passions, their prejudices and habits, are impossible to evaluate in numbers. The same is true of the degree of influence of certain institutions or certain functions, the degree of importance of certain establishments, the degree of difficulty of certain discoveries, and the degree of utility of certain inventions or processes.[83]

If we attempted to determine numerically the "frequency and extent of their effects", we would not only be obliged to aggregate as similar a multitude of quite different data, but we would also find it impossible to "clarify the changes and variations in concurrent causes, influential circumstances, and a thousand essential considerations".[84]

In order to avoid the pitfalls of a false calculation, it was first necessary to understand which subjects could not properly be subjected to quantitative analysis of this kind.

> It is for the science of the formation of our ideas, the science of the operations of our intelligence, in a word for sound idéologie, to identify these cases, make known their nature, and show us the reasons why they are so refractory. And it will render a great service to the human mind in preventing it in future from making erroneous usage of one of its finest instruments.[85]

Tracy asserted that, despite these limitations, the utility of probability theory in the moral sciences was not entirely destroyed:

> ... for if the various shades of our moral ideas cannot be expressed in numbers, and if there are many other things relative to social science which are equally incapable of being estimated and calculated directly, these phenomena are related to others which often make them reducible to calculable quantities ...[86]

While, for example, the degrees of value we attach to desirable things cannot be directly measured in figures, some objects have other qualities which are calculable or comparable, in terms of their weight, size, etc. And while the energy and durability of our bodily faculties cannot be directly estimated, we can judge them indirectly by their effects.

In the moral sciences, wrote Tracy, many phenomena are susceptible to quantitative calculation, but many are not; the important thing is to discriminate carefully between the two. There are also situations where the facts are an inextricable mixture of types, some refractory and some amenable to calculation, in which case the use of such calculation is likely to produce great distortions.[87] We must be aware, he noted, of "how delicate and subtle is the calculation of all moral and economic quantities, how much precaution it requires, and how imprudent it is to want to apply indiscreetly the rigorous scale of numbers".[88] Where quantitative calculation is inappropriate, we must have recourse to ordinary language for our analysis.[89]

Tracy, despite his sensationalism, had reached an awareness that human actions and feelings were qualitatively different from purely physical phenomena. His philosophy of sensibility, despite its materialist nuances, avoided the implication that human behaviour could be ordered and judged by quantitative criteria alone. A felicific calculus standing alone would always remain incomplete, and present a distorted picture of social reality. Nevertheless, Tracy clearly felt that this limitation on the utility of mathematical reasoning was unfortunate for the "scientific" status of the moral and political sciences. While insisting that a great deal of human action and feeling could not be measured, he appeared to regret having to abandon his positivist enthusiasm of 1796: "let us imitate the mathematicians".[90]

Having rejected the mathematised model for social science, what alternatives did Tracy have? He had already rejected an historical approach, modelled on perhaps Ferguson or Montesquieu. He had rejected a conservative social theory of the type put forward by Burke, wherein men's reason was embedded in their slowly evolving institutions and habits of thought (rather than exemplified by a capacity for rational critique of that system). For Tracy, the variety exhibited by human societies did not disturb his conception of a single unfolding human nature, the unity amid the diversity. For the rationalist philosophes, societies could be "arranged in an 'ideal' series, representing the 'natural order' of the development of mankind. This 'natural order' was accepted as applicable (both) to the progressive stages exhibited in the historical series and to the differences of culture discoverable in the present".[91]

Tracy's starting-point for his science of man and society was his view of human nature: man is a creature of biological and social needs. Finding the correct starting-point, he wrote, is the "most difficult" part of the task.[92] "In order for a single fact to become the indisputable basis of a vast system, it must be seen to be sufficient to produce all the observed phenomena".[93] Tracy's first and general fact was that man is located in a natural-social world where he begins with nothing but his needs and capacities, both of which are shaped by his environment. Just as an individual's capacities grow, as he acquires more abilities and understanding, so do those of the human species. Man begins with nothing but his perfectibility. History is the unfolding of his perfectibility. For Tracy, *la science sociale* attempts to demonstrate how to maximise man's successes or happiness in the economic, political and cultural realms. These form the subject of the remaining chapters.

Notes

1. B.W. Head, "The Origins of 'la science sociale' in France, 1770-1800", *Australian Journal of French Studies*, vol. 19 (1982), pp. 115-132.
2. Cf. R. Hubert, *Les Sciences sociales dans l'Encyclopédie* (Lille, 1923); P. Gay, *The Enlightenment* (London, 1973), vol. II: "The Science of Freedom", chapter 7; H. Gouhier, *La jeunesse d'Auguste Comte* (Paris, 1933-41), vol. II.
3. Cf. G. Bryson, *Man and Society* (Princeton, 1945); D. Kettler, *The Social and Political Thought of Adam Ferguson* (Columbus, Ohio, 1965); D. Reisman, *Adam Smith's Sociological Economics* (London, 1976); R. Meek, *Social Science and the Ignoble Savage* (Cambridge, 1976), chapters 4-6; A. Swingewood, "Origins of Sociology: the case of the Scottish Enlightenment", *British Journal of Sociology*, vol. 21 (1970), pp. 164-180. On the physiocrats, see G. Weulersse, *Le mouvement physiocratique en France de 1756 à 1770*, 2 vols. (Paris, 1910); H. Higgs, *The Physiocrats* (London, 1897); R. Meek, *The Economics of Physiocracy* (London, 1962); E. Fox-Genovese, *The Origins of Physiocracy* (New York, 1976). On Montesquieu, see W. Stark, *Montesquieu: pioneer of the sociology of knowledge* (London, 1960); R. Shackleton, *Montesquieu: a critical biography* (Oxford, 1961).
4. Cabanis, *Rapports*, in *Oeuvres philosophiques*, vol. I, p. 126.
5. "Mémoire sur la faculté de penser", p. 287.
6. *Elémens*, vol. I, p. 213. Tocqueville wrote, many years later, that in the French revolution, "the aim was to establish a social science, a philosophy, I might almost say a religion, fit to be learned and followed by all mankind": *Recollections* (New York, 1959), p. 75.

7. K.M. Baker, "The early history of the term 'social science'", *Annals of Science*, vol. 20 (1964), pp. 211-226; Head, "The origins of 'la science sociale'" (1982).
8. "Mémoire sur la faculté de penser", pp. 285-6.
9. *Ibid.*, p. 288.
10. *Ibid.*, pp. 318-319; "Dissertation sur quelques questions d'idéologie", p. 493.
11. "Mémoire sur la faculté de penser", p. 320.
12. D. Reisman, *Adam Smith's Sociological Economics*, p. 38.
13. Saint-Beuve, "Sieyès", *Causeries du lundi* (Paris, 1874), vol. 5, p. 196. E. Dumont, the collaborator of Mirabeau and of Bentham, reported Sieyès' claim to have perfected the science of politics: *Recollections of Mirabeau* ... (London, 1832), p. 53n.
14. Cited in W.M. Simon (ed.), *French Liberalism 1789-1848* (London, 1972), pp. 61-63.
15. Condillac, *Oeuvres philosophiques*, vol. I, p. 117.
16. "Mémoire sur la faculté de penser", p. 288.
17. *Ibid.*, p. 318.
18. J. Lakanal, 23 October 1794, in Hippeau (ed.), *L'instruction publique* ... (1881), p. 416.
19. *Ibid.*, pp. 416-417. Paul Dupuy suggests that this speech was largely the work of Garat, though delivered by Lakanal: *Le Centenaire de l'Ecole Normale* (Paris, 1895), pp. 54-71.
20. Cabanis, "Quelques considérations sur l'organisation sociale ..." (1799), in *Oeuvres philosophiques*, vol. II, p. 466. Condorcet's *Esquisse* was also a powerful source of faith in the certainty and progress of the human sciences: cf. *Sketch*, pp. 133, 173, 185-6.
21. "Mémoire sur la faculté de penser", pp. 387-8.
22. "Quels sont les moyens", in *Commentaire*, pp. 459-460, 473.
23. "Mémoire sur la faculté de penser", p. 389.
24. Cf. Condorcet, *Sketch*, 9th stage, p. 128.
25. "Mémoire sur la faculté de penser", p. 390; cf. p. 286. That the sciences were to be seen as "useful" was also assumed by Condillac: *Oeuvres philosophiques*, vol. II, pp. 234-5.
26. "Mémoire sur la faculté de penser", pp. 391-2.
27. Reprinted in A. Duruy, *L'instruction publique et la Révolution* (Paris, 1882), pp. 433-448; and in Tracy, *Elémens d'idéologie*, 5 vols. (Paris, 1824-1825), vol. IV, pp. 268-289; and *Ibid.*, 5 vols. (Bruxelles, 1826-1827), vol. IV, pp. 262-283.
28. Duruy, *op.cit.*, pp. 439-440.
29. *Ibid.*, p. 441.
30. *Ibidem.*
31. *Ibid.*, p. 442.
32. *Ibid.*, p. 441.
33. *Ibid.*, p. 443.
34. Cf. the memorandum cited by Duruy, p. 232, where an unfortunate teacher was criticised for failing to use a utilitarian and sensationalist theory of morality.
35. *Ibid.*, p. 433.
36. Daunou, 19 October 1795, in Hippeau (ed.), *L'instruction publique* ... (1881), p. 479: "freedom of domestic education, freedom of private establishments of instruction ... freedom of teaching methods".
37. Duruy, *op.cit.*, p. 434. Recommended authors included Dupuis, Chastellux, Ferguson, Voltaire, Condillac and Goguet (*ibid.*, p. 438).
38. *Ibid.*, p. 435.
39. *Ibidem.*
40. *Ibid.*, p. 293.
41. Volney's *Ruines* (1791) and *Loi naturelle* (1793) were highly rationalist; but his *Leçons d'histoire* (1795) have been called the first attempt to apply objective methods to the study of the human sciences: J. Gaulmier, "Volney et ses 'leçons d'histoire'", *History and Theory*, vol. 2 (1962), p. 65.
42. Daunou attained a considerable reputation as an historian after 1819 when he took a chair in history at the Collège de France. See his *Discours d'ouverture* ... (Paris, 1819), and the remarks by A.G. Lehmann, "Sainte-Beuve and the Historical Movement", in *The French Mind*, ed. Moore et al. (Oxford, 1952), pp. 259-260. For a more detailed and hostile view,

see B. Plongeron, "Nature, Métaphysique et Histoire chez les Idéologues", *Dix-huitième siècle*, no. 5 (1973), pp. 375-412.
43. Cf. similar remarks by Sieyès in Saint-Beuve, "Sieyès", pp. 193-4, and Bastid, *Sieyès et sa pensée*, pp. 386, 388.
44. *Observations sur l'état actuel de l'instruction publique* (1801), in *Elémens d'idéologie*, 5 vols. (Bruxelles, 1826-1827), vol. IV, p. 346.
45. *Ibid.*, p. 347.
46. *Ibidem.*
47. *Ibid.*, p. 362.
48. *Ibidem.*
49. *Analyse* (1804), pp. i, x.
50. Cabanis, *Rapports* (1830 ed.), vol. I, p. 23 ("Table Analytique" by Tracy).
51. *Logique* (1805), p. 438.
52. *Ibid.*, pp. 438-9.
53. *Ibid.*, pp. 441-2.
54. *Ibid.*, p. 442.
55. *Ibid.*, p. 443 (emphasis added).
56. *Ibid.*, p. 444.
57. *Ibid.*, pp. 393-4.
58. *Ibid.*, p. 395.
59. This is an obvious reference to Tracy's *Analyse* of Dupuis, his *Quels sont les moyens ...*, and his *Observations*.
60. *Traité de la Volonté* (1818 ed.), pp. 522-3. Tracy used the term social science in the *Traité*, p. 279 (1818 ed.), and pp. 33, 44 (1815 ed.).
61. Evidence for the date of composition appears in the text itself, pp. v, 65n, 91. See also Cabanis' letter to Maine de Biran, 8 April 1807, in Maine de Biran, *Oeuvres philosophiques*, vol. VII (Paris, 1930), p. 225. Cf. Lafayette, *Mémoires*, V, p. 288.
62. Philadelphia, 1811. On the events surrounding the American publication, from Tracy's sending the manuscript in June 1809, see G. Chinard, *Jefferson et les idéologues*, chapter 2, esp. pp. 43ff.
63. *Commentary* (1811), p. 1. That Jefferson himself wrote this prefatory letter by "the author to his fellow citizens" of the U.S.A., is shown in Chinard, *op.cit.*, pp. 62-63.
64. This is further shown by Tracy's letter to Jefferson, 11 April 1818, in Chinard, *op.cit.*, p. 180.
65. Cf. *Commentaire* (1819), p. 168n.
66. *Ibid.*, p. vii. In a letter to Jefferson of 4 February 1816, Tracy acknowledged that the *Commentaire*, together with his *Observations* on education, contained "the germ of all my ideas on legislation": Chinard, *op.cit.*, pp. 165-6.
67. *Commentaire*, p. viii. The term "science sociale" was also used on pp. 166, 187, 223, 224, 226, 237, 280.
68. H. Taine, *Les origines de la France contemporaine*, vol. I ("l'Ancien Régime") (Paris, 1876), p. 264. For similar remarks, cf. Georges Sorel, *The Illusions of Progress* (1908), (Berkeley, 1972), p. 96; Mignet, "Notice historique sur ... M. Destutt de Tracy", p. 277; Guillois, *Le salon de Mme Helvétius*, p. 104; G. Elton, *The Revolutionary Idea in France* (London, 1923), pp. 28-30.
69. See especially Condorcet's *Esquisse*; Cabanis' "Lettre sur ... la perfectibilité", in *Oeuvres philosophiques*, vol. II, pp. 512-519; Cabanis in *le Conservateur*, 30 September 1797, pp. 236-238: "Sciences, philosophie". Tracy noted in his *Discours* of December 1808 that Cabanis at the time of his death had been planning a major synthetic study demonstrating the means available for the improvement of man (pp. 19-20).
70. *Commentaire*, p. 308.
71. J. Rey, *Traité des principes généraux du droit et de la législation* (Paris, 1828); *Théorie et pratique de la science sociale* (Paris, 1842).
72. *Elémens*, vol. I, p. 194. (Cf. Condorcet, *Sketch*, pp. 181, 190-1, and Condillac, *Art de penser*, in *Oeuvres philosophiques*, vol. I, p. 768.)

73. *Ibid.*, p. 195.
74. "Mémoire sur la faculté de penser", p. 380.
75. *Elémens*, vol. I, pp. 198-9. Tracy in 1817 again noted that inherent variability of our moral ideas: *Principes logiques*, in *Elémens*, 5 vols., 1826-27, p. 246.
76. *Elémens*, vol. I, pp. 199-200. Tracy later followed Cabanis in describing moral certainties in terms of probabilities, a lesser degree of certainty than in the mathematical sciences (*Discours*, December 1808, p. 14).
77. *Elémens*, vol. I, p. 200n-203.
78. Cf. *Traité de la Volonté* (1815), pp. 30-50.
79. *Ibid.*, p. 33.
80. *Ibid.*, pp. 33-4.
81. *Ibid.*, p. 36.
82. *Ibid.*, pp. 37-8. The works of Condorcet to which Tracy refers are the *Essai sur l'application de l'analyse à la probabilité des décisions rendues à la pluralité des voix* (1785), and the posthumous volume *Eléments du calcul des probabilités et son application aux jeux de hasard, à la loterie et aux jugements des hommes* (1805). For discussion of Condorcet's views on "social arithmetic", cf. K.M. Baker, *Condorcet*, pp. 167ff, 330ff; G.-G. Granger, *La mathématique sociale du marquis de Condorcet* (Paris, 1956); C.C. Gillispie, "Probability and Politics", *Proceedings of the American Philosophical Society*, vol. 116 (1972), pp. 1-20.
83. *Traité de la Volonté* (1815), p. 41.
84. *Ibid.*, p. 42.
85. *Ibid.*, pp. 43-4.
86. *Ibid.*, p. 44.
87. *Ibid.*, p. 45-6, 48-9.
88. *Ibid.*, pp. 106-7.
89. *Ibid.*, p. 47.
90. "Mémoire sur la faculté de penser", p. 288.
91. F.J. Teggart, *Theory and Processes of History* (Berkeley, 1960), p. 98.
92. "Dissertation sur quelques questions d'idéologie", p. 512.
93. *Ibid.*, p. 493.

7. PRODUCTION AND ECONOMIC CLASSES

Economics, in Tracy's theory, is the science which studies "the effects and consequences of our actions considered as means to provide for our needs of all types, from the most material to the most intellectual".[1] Economic science, then, should be distinguished from the traditional connotation of economy as household management, and from its common meaning of carefully managing the goods in one's possession. The term "political economy" generally meant "the science of the formation and administration of the wealth of a political society".[2] It is true, wrote Tracy, that the science entitled, somewhat improperly, political economy has discovered "some important truths on the effects of property, industry and the causes which favour or hinder the formation and growth of wealth". But economics really should go back to the origin of our needs and of our power to act, for it is really the study of "the history of the use of our powers for the satisfaction of our needs".[3] (As if to express his dissatisfaction with the term "political economy", Tracy sometimes used the term "social economy". However, his major work on economics, *Traité de la Volonté* (1815), was republished in 1823 under the title *Traité d'économie politique*.)

THE CREATION OF WEALTH

Tracy's approach to economic theory is based on his view of man as a desiring and sentient being, whose actions consist in attempting to satisfy his needs or wants: material, social, intellectual. The concept of wealth is accordingly related by Tracy to this conception of man: "to be rich is to possess means for satisfying one's needs, and to be poor is to lack such means".[4] Something is useful or desirable, and thus an object of wealth, only by virtue of contributing in some way to the satisfaction of a need or desire. Without such desiring, the notion of possessing sufficient or insufficient means would not arise. The things which we regard as our riches, our means of satisfying our desires, do not consist only of physical objects such as precious stones, metals, landed property, a utensil, a dwelling, or a stock of food, as the physiocrats had implied.

> The knowledge of a law of nature; the habitual use of a technical process; the use of a language to communicate with our fellows and increase our powers by theirs, or at least not to be disturbed by theirs in the exercise of our own; the enjoyment of conventions made and institutions created in this spirit; these

> too, are riches for the individual and the species, for they are things useful towards increasing our means, ... and with the least possible obstacles, whether on the part of men or of nature, which is to increase their power, their energy and their effect.[5]

All such things which contribute to our well-being we call our "goods". These goods arise from the proper employment of our faculties, in accordance with the laws of nature. It is only by intelligent and careful application of our labour and energy to the materials at hand that we can find precious stones, make use of metals, produce crops, or fabricate a dwelling or a utensil.[6] Our original wealth and possessions consist simply in our physical and intellectual faculties. All our subsequent goods stem from the active application of these faculties to the satisfaction of our needs, and the value they have for us is created through our labours.[7] At this point, Tracy attempted to "deduce" the labour theory of value from his premise of man as a desiring and acting being. Given that our physical and moral faculties are our only original wealth, and that the use of these faculties (work or labour) is necessary to obtain all our goods, it followed, wrote Tracy, that the value of these goods arises from the labour involved.[8]

But labour itself has two kinds of value: "natural" and "conventional". The first, "natural and necessary" value, is measured by the amount of labour necessary to provide for the individual's basic needs of survival (whether he satisfies his own needs directly, or whether he labours for another in return for goods sufficient to satisfy these needs). This is the minimum necessary cost of labour, that which furnishes the subsistence of the individual labourer.[9] The second form of value is "contingent", generally "conventional", and much more "variable" than the first; it stems from the value of what is produced, rather than from the costs of sustaining the producer(s). The price of labour is agreed upon between contracting parties at the time. Moreover, it also depends on the wants and means of the employer who profits by it, rather than simply on the basic needs of the labourer himself.[10] Tracy allows, however, that not even the "natural" value of labour is entirely fixed and invariable. On the one hand, there is some variation in determining which needs are regarded as basic and indispensable in a given time and place, "and the flexibility of our nature is such that these needs are restrained or extended considerably by the influence of the will and the effect of habit".[11] On the other hand, favourable circumstances of climate and soil will allow basic needs to be satisfied more rapidly or by a smaller amount of labour; whereas in unfavourable circumstances, the amount of necessary labour will increase.

Tracy's emphasis on the role of individual and social labour in the production of wealth or enjoyments, was developed in opposition to the physiocratic theory of production. Tracy's concept of the desiring and acting self appeared to be incompatible with the physiocratic view that man's wealth was anchored in his dependence on rural production. In the same way, Tracy's emphasis on the importance of individual rights and education became incompatible at the political level with the physiocratic defence of a strong centralised monarchy to implement their economic doctrines. It is necessary to sketch the main lines of the debate between the defenders of physiocratic orthodoxy and its critics. The main point at issue concerned what should be called "productive" activities. The older doctrines were overthrown by a new version of the labour theory of value.

The idea that labour, applied to the raw materials supplied by nature, is the source or cause of wealth and enjoyments has had a long history, beginning with isolated remarks by the ancient philosophers and proceeding to a fuller development during the Renaissance. By the seventeenth century, many writers were underlining the connections between labour and wealth.[12] With Locke, the labour theory had been associated with a moral justification for property rights: one has a natural right to hold property by virtue of one's labour embodied in such property.[13] But the labour theory of value which emerged towards the end of the eighteenth century was quite distinctive, insofar as it assumed social conditions in which labour was freely available for purchase on the open market, and in which wages were seen as part of the cost of production of goods. In the writings of Adam Smith, the labour theory had become generalised into the notion that a society has an aggregate fund of labour which may be used in various ways to produce a range of useful goods and services, whose quantity depends on the availability of skills and on the proportion of people engaged in useful labour.[14] A full understanding of Tracy's views requires an outline of the physiocratic outlook and the new doctrines formulated by Adam Smith and Jean-Baptiste Say.

The physiocratic viewpoint developed largely as a critique of mercantilist doctrines, which had stressed that a nation without its own gold or silver mines should attempt to increase its national wealth by accumulating precious metals via a favourable trade balance, promoting exports and restricting imports as necessary.[15] Such preoccupation with a bullionist conception of wealth and its corollary of a permanently favourable balance of trade, were rejected by the physiocrats, who argued that the wealth of a society consists essentially in useful goods, not in money itself, which is merely a medium of exchange. But the physiocratic conception of wealth was itself restrictive, arguing that the only "productive" activities were those which resulted in a material surplus (*produit net*), and that agriculture was the fundamental producer of such goods. Manufacture and commerce were "useful" and "necessary", but were not genuinely "productive". Investment in agriculture, and the use of efficient large-scale techniques, were the best ways to increase national wealth; any surplus output could be traded externally for goods which were too difficult or costly to produce domestically. Physiocracy thus had a theory of economic growth, and definite policy implications for government. Whatever assisted agricultural investment and output should be encouraged; whatever diminished such investment should be discouraged.[16]

Society was divided by the physiocrats into three broad classes. First, the *productive* are those who are engaged in agriculture, fishing and mining; though the primary emphasis is on the agricultural entrepreneur rather than the labourers in the fields. Second, there are the *sterile* or unproductive, including manufacturers, artisans, merchants, professional men, and their servants: those who fail to produce a net surplus above their expenses (wages and profits are held to be included in such expenses). Third, the *proprietary* class consists of landowners, and others supported directly from the taxation levied on proprietary revenue (including the monarch and those who perform public functions in Church and State).[17] The growth of the public sector had to be limited for two main reasons: firstly, the physiocratic philosophy of free trade was inimical to a high level of government regulation of economic life. Secondly, since public expenditure had to be funded from taxation paid by the landed proprietors, a growing public expenditure would have to be met by rising taxes which would divert funds from agricultural investment.

The physiocratic outlook also assumed that society should reflect a natural order. "Political economy" was a quest for the natural laws of economic life. Government should follow these natural laws as far as possible; to flout them was to court economic and social disaster.[18] The natural order conception of economy and government was supplemented, however, by a psychological theory of wants and their satisfaction, a theory which was developed more fully by other writers (including Condillac in 1776), and which also underlay the utilitarian and post-Smithian political economy.

Smith and J.-B. Say began with the proposition that agricultural, manufacturing and commercial activities are equally productive of wealth; hence, the special status accorded to agriculture in the physiocratic doctrine was unjustifiable.[19] But although Smith believed that all goods and services having an exchange value or market price contributed to aggregate national wealth, he qualified this view by drawing a distinction between "productive" and "unproductive" labour, as between the labour of an artisan (who fabricates an object which can be sold) and that of a domestic servant (whose services, though deserving payment, "seldom leave any trace or value behind them").[20] For J.-B. Say, however, the notion of productive labour could be extended to include even the philosopher.[21]

Smith was largely responsible for the classical labour theory of value, distinguishing between use-value and exchange-value in a commodity, and regarding market price as determined primarily by the quantity of social labour embodied in the commodity.[22] Say was somewhat critical of this labour theory of value, regarding it as a one-sided response to the physiocratic doctrine that value is conferred only by the raw materials won in the agricultural and extractive industries, i.e. that values are conferred essentially by nature rather than by labour. For Say, value is conferred by some combination of labour, capital, and natural resources and powers.[23] Value, for Say, can only be determined by market exchanges. Underlying market prices, however, is the fact that goods can "satisfy the various wants of mankind" and this constitutes their utility. For Say, the production of wealth is the creation of utilities. But Say left aside the issue of whether market price reflects the actual utility of goods, save for his remark that the two measures will tend to coincide in proportion to the liberty of production and commerce.[24]

Tracy closely adhered to the "classical" tradition which followed the overthrow of physiocracy. Writing in about 1810, Tracy noted that some fine works of political economy had been produced by Turgot and Smith, but "no-one has shed more light on the subject than Mr. Say, the author of the best work I know on these matters."[25] According to Tracy, not even Smith and Say had been sufficiently rigorous in excluding all traces of physiocratic thought from their own superior systems.[26] However, Tracy willingly followed them in their conception of production in terms of utilities.

> What, then, do we do in our work, in our action on the things around us? Nothing but effect changes in their form or place, making them useful for the satisfaction of our needs. That is what we should understand by *to produce*; it is to give things a utility they did not have. Whatever our work, if it does not result in utility it is fruitless; if it does so, it is productive.[27]

Tracy therefore mounted a sustained attack on the physiocratic conception of the sole productivity of primary industry. It is "an illusion", he wrote, to believe that producing primary goods is more productive than their subsequent fabrication or transportation. The sowing of seed to produce crops is no more creative than producing flour and bread from wheat, or producing cloth from hemp. "In both cases, there is a production of utility, for all these tasks are equally necessary to fulfil the desired end, the satisfaction of some of our needs". In the same way, the man who nets fish is no more creative than he who dries or salts the catch, or takes the produce to market; and the man who digs in mines is similarly placed to he who smelts the metals, makes tools, or takes them to those who require them. "Each one adds a new utility to that already produced; consequently, each is equally a producer".[28]

The primary producer, the manufacturer and the merchant all must study the laws and the forces governing the objects of their activities, to turn them to the desired effect. "It is wrong, then, to have regarded agricultural industry as essentially different from all other branches of human industry, where the action of nature intervened in a unique manner."[29] Moreover, the very attempt to specify which activities should be included in the category of agricultural industry has always remained obscure. If one includes fishing and hunting, why not herding animals? If one includes the collection of salt from lakes dried by the sun, why not the production of salt by chemical and mechanical methods? If one includes the mining of ore, why not the extraction of the metal from the ore in refining? At what stage in the process of transformation does one draw a line between producing and fashioning? How shall we classify those who collect wood in forests, or peat from the fields: are they agriculturalists, fabricators or carriers?[30] To take cultivation in the strict sense, who is the true producer: he who sows or he who harvests? he who ploughs or he who fences? he who fertilizes the field, or he who shepherds the flocks? According to Tracy, they are all workmen who concur in the same productive process.

These confusions and mysteries arose from the falsity of the theoretical principle of the physiocratic *économistes*. They were poor metaphysicians, who had not understood the nature of man, especially his intellectual faculties, and had not seen that labour is our sole original wealth. They were led into many errors by their "false idea of a sort of magical virtue attributed to the land".[31]

> The truth is simply that all our useful labours are productive, and those relating to agriculture are the same (in all respects) ... A farm is a real manufactory; everything there operates in the same way, by the same principles and for the same end. A field is a veritable tool, or a store of first materials if you will ... In every case it is an instrument necessary to produce a desired effect, just like a furnace, or a hammer, or a vessel.[32]

Tracy conceded that primary industry in the most general sense was the most necessary activity and came first in time, since a thing must be produced before it can be used. But that did not mean it was uniquely productive, for most of its products still had to be worked up to become useful things. On the other hand, taking agricultural industry in a narrow sense, it did not come first in time (since men were hunters, fishermen and shepherds before farmers), nor was it the sole source of primary materials. It remained very important for our subsistence, but could not be regarded as uniquely productive. In short, agriculture "is a branch of manufacturing industry", and has no distinctive character which separates it from other industries.[33] "Let us conclude that all useful work is truly productive, and that all the labouring class (*la classe laborieuse*) of society equally deserve the name productive."[34]

In a neat reversal of the physiocratic doctrine, in which the unproductive or sterile class were mainly occupied in manufacturing and commerce, Tracy condemned as passive and sterile the landed proprietors and other wealthy investors who were not actively seeking to increase production. It is a criticism equally found in the opening pages of Sieyès' celebration of the Third Estate as the truly productive class,[35] and a doctrine taken up vigorously by Saint-Simon and the advocates of *industrialisme*.[36]

> The truly *sterile* class is that of the idle, who do nothing but live *nobly*, as it is termed, on the product of labours undertaken before them, whether this product is realised in landed estates which they lease or rent to a labourer, or whether it consists of money or effects which they lend for a premium, which is still leasing. They are the real *frelons de la ruche* ...[37]

According to Tracy, the labouring class, which directly produces all wealth, may be divided naturally into two groups: the manufacturers (including agriculturalists) who fabricate and fashion things; and the merchants, who transport them (for the utility of merchants consists in making goods available where they are wanted, otherwise they would only be parasitic speculators).[38] It is not clear from this division where Tracy wished to classify public employees and the professions, whose members neither fabricate objects, nor transport them, but provide services which he regarded as of immense importance for social progress.

Production is extremely varied, for there are many different kinds of "utility", some more solid and real than others. A thing may be termed "useful" if it is capable of procuring any advantage, even a frivolous pleasure. What we desire is to multiply our enjoyments and diminish our sufferings. These utilities can be graded in terms of how strongly we desire the object, and this degree of desire may be measured in terms of the sacrifices we are prepared to make to obtain the object. If I am willing to give three measures of wheat for one object, and twelve measures of wheat for a different object, it follows that I desire the second four times as much as the first.[39] Or even if I personally do not estimate their relative value in this way, I could not obtain them more cheaply, and that is the value generally attached to them. Market price is the real measure of value.

> In the state of society, which is nothing but a continual series of exchanges, the values of all the products of our industry are determined in this way. This fixation, no doubt, is not always founded on very good reasons; we are often poor judges of the real merit of things; but, in relation to wealth, their value is none the less that assigned by general opinion. It may be thus seen, incidentally, that the greatest producer is he who performs the most expensive type of labour, no matter if it be a branch of agricultural, manufacturing or commercial industry ...[40]

Tracy, as we noted above, subscribed to the labour theory of value on the grounds that labour, our physical and intellectual capacity, is our only method of creating utilities or satisfying our wants. Echoing the Lockean viewpoint, Tracy claimed that goods become the property of a person only "because he has previously applied some kind of labour, whose fruit is assured to him by social conventions".[41] In obtaining such goods by exchange, we are in effect paying for the owner's past labour, without which the goods would have no value. This "natural and necessary" value of labour "is the sum of indispensable needs whose satisfaction is necessary to the existence of he who executes the labour during the time he is working".[42] However, the "natural" values have little influence in modern market societies, in Tracy's view; hence the distinction between natural and conventional value is of little practical importance. There is no guarantee that the "natural" price of labour, in terms of the subsistence needs of the labourer, will be met. Tracy places the weight of his theory of value upon market prices:

> But here, where we speak of the value resulting from the free transactions of society, it is clearly a matter of the conventional and market value, that which

> general opinion attaches to things, rightly or wrongly. If it (the price of labour) is less than the wants of the labourer, he must devote himself to another industry or perish; if it is exactly equal to his wants, he subsists with difficulty; if it is greater, he becomes rich, provided however he is economical. In all cases, this conventional and market value is the real one in relation to wealth; it is the true measure of the utility of production, since it fixes its price.[43]

The actual determination of market price is not simply the abstract reflection of individual opinions about the value of an object. In other words, it is not a simple average of individual estimates. It depends on market conditions of supply and demand, or the relative needs and means of producer and consumer, buyer and seller. Market price depends on variable circumstances, and "the equilibrium of resistance between sellers and buyers."[44]

This depends in turn on a host of factors, including the relative scarcity of goods in demand and the ability of purchasers to pay a given level of prices.[45]

Tracy concludes his discussion of the value of labour by pointing to the historical importance of advances in productivity per unit of labour as a result of improved technology. For example, the invention of a machine which can manufacture in one day three times as many commodities as could a single craftsman, will boost the available social stock of goods and decrease the average cost per unit of output. However, the individual's income as a machine-operator is unlikely to be higher than his former income as a craftsman. This new technology is not "more productive" for that individual than previously, since his income remains constant, but it will be more productive for society taken as a whole, since the commodities are produced more cheaply. The consumers, who are the mass of the population, are the main beneficiaries of technical progress and the division of labour.

> That is the great advantage of civilised and enlightened society—everyone finds himself better provided in every way, with fewer sacrifices, because the labourers produce a greater mass of utility in the same time.[46]

That is the reason, wrote Tracy, why the standard of living of the poor classes in various historical periods should not be measured solely by the relation between a day's wages and the price of grain. Though bread may be the most important expense of the poor labourer, he also has other needs which may be better satisfied even when his ability to buy bread remains constant.

> If the arts have made progress, he may be better lodged, better clothed, and have better drink for the same price. If society is better regulated, he may find a more constant employment for his labour, and be more certain of not being troubled in the possession of what he has gained. ...(But) the elements of this calculus are so numerous that it is very difficult, and perhaps impossible, to make it directly.[47]

Tracy concluded that labour or industry is the fundamental "source of all our joys and riches'',[48] and the means by which historical progress has been achieved.

> Our manner of living is completely artificial. We owe to nature, that is, to our organisation, nothing but our sensibility and our perfectibility: we owe all the rest to our industry.[49]

But this emphasis on ''industry'' should not be confused with the later development of ''industrial capitalism'' or ''industrial society'', typified by machine production.[50] France at the beginning of the nineteenth century was still a largely agricultural society, with very few centres of machine manufacture. The concept of an industrial revolution did not emerge until the 1820s. Moreover, many of the families who profited from manufacture and commerce used their wealth to acquire noble offices and the attendant prestige of landed proprietors.[51] The debate between the defenders of physiocratic orthodoxy, urging the political and economic dominance of landed wealth, and the champions of the labour theory of value, was by no means resolved in a political way by the events of the Revolution. The *Dictionnaire de la Constitution Française* (1791),[52] the writings of Germain Garnier,[53] and even some members of the Class of moral and political sciences under the Directory,[54] continued to uphold the primary position of landed property in opposition to the mobile capital of the entrepreneur and merchant.

One policy upon which both theories could agree was the doctrine of freedom from most forms of government regulation—free trade, internally and externally; the abolition of corporative privileges and monopolies; allowing market forces to determine the costs and opportunities for each sector of the economy.[55] This was the ''liberal'' element in Tracy's economic theory: industry should be free from ''artificial'' or institutional restraints. Freedom of industry and commerce was regarded as the best way to ensure economic growth and progress. This was the main contribution of economics to the social science of happiness.

> Economic science is a major part of social science; it is even its goal insofar as we desire that society is well organised only because enjoyments (moral and material) are thereby more numerous, more complete and more peaceful ...[56]

In assuming an inter-relationship between wealth, happiness, and freedom of industry and commerce, Tracy was in accord with the notion of ''commercial society'' which had been developed by numerous writers in the second half of the eighteenth century. In the *Philosophie rurale* (1763) of Mirabeau and Quesnay, four kinds of societies were identified, in accordance with their different ''modes of life'' or socio-economic organisation: hunting, pastoral, agricultural and commercial.[57] For the physiocrats, the wealthy commercial societies were seen to develop alongside the agricultural, in an international division of labour. For Smith and his successors, however, commercial societies were a more advanced type in the evolutionary pattern, destined to supersede the purely agricultural societies, and promising a level of abundance far beyond that of previous social forms.[58] At the Institut, the evolutionary pattern was firmly endorsed, as in the paper read by Lévesque in February 1796 contrasting the opportunities for progress and civilisation in urban life (*la vie policée*) with the prior stages of savage and pastoral societies.[59] For Tracy, the "perfection of society", from an economic viewpoint, would be "to increase greatly our wealth while avoiding the extremes of inequality."[60] The physiocrats had also believed in the policy imperative of increasing abundance; the difference was that Tracy believed that further social wealth could not be expected from agriculture alone.

The new economic order which he saw gradually emerging in the last quarter of the eighteenth century involved a new class structure and division of labour. Production was not a process to which everyone contributed in the same way, nor from which all benefited to the same degree. The second section of this chapter takes up the question of economic classes, while the following chapter will discuss Tracy's analysis of the problems of material inequality.

ECONOMIC CLASSES

Tracy's critique of the physiocratic doctrine was developed on two levels. The first was a disagreement about the proper definition of "productive" activity. The second and related theme, which has not been sufficiently recognised by previous commentators, concerned the degree of economic and political importance which should be attributed to the "proprietary" class.

Firstly, Tracy did not disagree with the physiocrats' view that the tenant-farmers who were actually and directly responsible for agricultural production were genuinely "productive": he merely wanted to extend this concept to other branches of activity, to those activities in manufacture, commerce and services which had been called "sterile" industries by the physiocrats. As we have seen, Tracy's criterion of production was that of utility, as determined by market demand, instead of the physiocratic concept of an agricultural surplus.

Secondly, Tracy sharply criticised what he saw as the physiocrats' exaggeration of the economic and political importance of the "proprietary" class. In the physiocratic theory, this class contained a somewhat heterogeneous group of economic functions:

(i) the owners of rural estates, who leased their lands to tenant-farmers in return for some sort of rent;
(ii) the sovereign authority in the nation, responsible for law and order; and
(iii) servants of the sovereign, engaged in public instruction, defence or administration of the realm.

The latter two groups were supported from revenues derived from taxes paid by the landowners. According to the physiocrat Baudeau, whose explanation of the proprietary class was quite detailed, it could also be called "the class of nobles".[61] The identification of the proprietors with the nobility (and additionally with the monarchy and the ecclesiastics) raised grave doubts concerning the legitimacy of the proprietary class in the eyes of the liberals after 1789.

As Tracy wrote, the proprietary class were the idle (*les oisifs*) "who do nothing but live nobly, as it is termed, on the product of labours undertaken before them".[62] Here was the germ of a theory of exploitation: the idle landowners were seen as an unproductive and parasitical class, who themselves performed no important productive functions but retained an economic surplus in the form of rents. As will be seen later, however, Tracy does not develop the radical possibilities of such a theory; he rather urges that landowners use their capital in a more enterprising way, taking up active entrepreneurial functions instead of passive *rentier* functions. Our discussion will now focus on the differences Tracy recognised between the economic roles and incomes accruing to land-owners, entrepreneurs, and labourers. We may begin by noting some of the revisions in the physiocratic theory of economic classes made by economic thinkers after 1776, when Condillac's work on commerce and government[63] appeared as well as Smith's *Wealth of Nations*.

Unlike the three-class model of the physiocrats, Condillac had recognised only two major economic classes: the landed proprietors living on rents; and the *salariés*, among whom he grouped the entrepreneurial farmers who leased the lands of the proprietors, as well as the labourers who were employed by these farmers.[64] Condillac denied that the *salariés* were unproductive workers, for they added to the value of goods or provided valuable services.[65] Similarly, in the works of Adam Smith, classical political economy rejected the unique qualities attributed by the physiocrats to ownership of agricultural land, and attempted instead to show how land, labour and capital are inextricably united in the production of wealth. For Smith,

> The whole annual produce of the land and labour of every country ... naturally divides itself ... into three parts; the rent of land, the wages of labour, and the profits of stock; and constitutes a revenue to three different orders of people; to those who live by rent, to those who live by wages, and to those who live by profit. These are the three great, original, and constituent orders of every civilised society, from whose revenue that of every other order is ultimately derived.[66]

In the same way, J.-B. Say noted crucial differences in the functional roles and sources of income of landed proprietors (rent), labourers (wages), and capitalist entrepreneurs (profits). It was sometimes possible, according to Say, for a single individual to combine the roles of proprietor, labourer, and capitalist in certain circumstances; but usually the roles were divided among three functionally distinct classes of society.[67] In the writings of Say and Tracy, a particular emphasis was given to the active role of the entrepreneur in initiating profitable productive activities, in contrast to the passive role of the landowner or investor whose income (rent or interest) is essentially a return on idle capital.

For Say, all productive activity may be seen to involve three operations or aspects: knowledge of the properties of phenomena, and the laws governing them; application of this knowledge to a useful purpose; and the manual labour required to execute the task.

> These three operations are seldom performed by one and the same person. It commonly happens that one man studies the laws and conduct of nature, that is to say, the philosopher or man of science; of whose knowledge another avails himself to create useful products, being either agriculturalist, manufacturer or trader; while the third supplies the executive labour under the direction of the first two, this third person being the operative workman or labourer.[68]

According to Say, this division into "theory, application, and execution" is found in all branches of industry, and the wealth of a society depends upon the development of a high level of skill in all three types of activity.[69]

Tracy adopts Say's view that all branches of modern industry (agricultural, manufacturing and commercial) involve a functional division of labour between those specialising in scientific knowledge, organisational skills, and manual labour. "Theory is the work of the *savant*, application is that of the *entrepreneur*, and execution is that of the *ouvrier*".[70] (Significantly, Tracy here omits the role of the "mere" owner of land: this role is regarded as either redundant, or positively obstructive.) Each of these three types of worker derives an income from the profits resulting from their co-operative production. But each must bring to the production process a certain amount of investment (*avances*).

The *savant* is obliged to undergo a long and expensive education. The entrepreneur requires not only a certain education but must have enough money to obtain facilities and materials for production and to pay workers. Even the poor workman must have learned certain skills or acquired some tools of his trade, and must have been sustained for some years either by his parents or by a public institution. All these forms of capital investment are made possible by a surplus of production over consumption, a surplus which gradually builds up in a society as it becomes richer and more civilised.[71]

The various "capitals" of these three classes of productive worker give rise to "a great diversity in incomes (*salaires*)". The *savant*, whose knowledge can lower the costs of production and boost productivity, "will necessarily be sought after and well paid", so long as his knowledge is of practical utility and does not become commonplace.[72] The poor workman, who has only his physical labour to offer, will always be reduced to a very low wage, which can even fall below subsistence level unless manual labour is temporarily in short supply. The *savant* and the workman are both dependent financially on the entrepreneur. "This is in the nature of things", according to Tracy. For theoretical knowledge and manual labour are not enough for production:

> above all there has to be an enterprise, and he who undertakes it is necessarily the one who chooses, employs, and pays those who co-operate in it. Now, who is the one who can do this? It is the man who already has the funds by which he can meet the first expenses of establishment and supplies, and pay the wages until the moment of the first returns.[73]

The entrepreneur holds a special status in the political economy of Say and Tracy. Among French writers, the distinction between the passive owner of capital (receiving interest on his investment) and the entrepreneur (receiving profit on his enterprise)[74] was more carefully developed than among the British writers, who tended to use a single category of profit on capital or stock.[75] Richard Cantillon, in his *Essai sur la nature du commerce* (1755), stressed the role of the entrepreneur as a risk-bearer; Baudeau saw the agricultural entrepreneur as bringing together intelligent innovation and capital wealth; whereas Turgot emphasised the need for an industrial or merchant entrepreneur to commit large capital funds to initiate productive activity.[76] Say's concept of entrepreneurial activity highlights the planning, supervisory and co-ordinating functions, above the functions of supplying capital, making innovations, or bearing risks. The entrepreneur is the key element in production because he puts all the factors to work to achieve a given task. Moreover, he is a universal mediator between all the economic classes, and between producers and consumers; he is at the intersection of several economic relationships.[77] In this sense, Say's entrepreneur performs a universal social function, found in most historical stages of economic life and not specific to capitalist society. (On the other hand, Say also made a number of observations on how the entrepreneur mobilises capital and other resources in a competitive market society, where the typical economic enterprise is a one-owner operation, subject to market uncertainties with respect to levels of supply and demand for certain goods and services.[78])

Tracy largely adopts Say's explanation of the profit of the entrepreneur in terms of the market price of his specialist labour. Say had argued that the price of entrepreneurial labour is potentially very high because two main factors limit the supply of such labour: access to large funds, either his own or borrowed; and business acumen and managerial skills. Those who do not have "the requisite capacity and talent" are bound to fail, owing to the degree of risk in such enterprises.[79] In a similar way, Tracy argues that the essential determinant of profit is the quantity of utilities produced by the entrepreneur for which consumers are willing to pay a price which exceeds the costs of production:

> It is commonly said that the rewards of the entrepreneur, wrongly called salaries since no-one promises him anything, should represent the price of his labour, the interest on his capital and the recompense for risks undertaken ... (But) these are by no means the factors which cause his good or bad success; this depends solely on the quantity of utilities he has been able to produce, on the needs of people to obtain them, and on their ability to pay for them ...[80]

The entrepreneur's position is less predictable than that of the wage-earner who is bound by contract to receive an agreed income. The entrepreneur is "subject to uncertainty", for he may lose all his investments or may make a handsome profit.[81]

For Tracy, the role of the entrepreneur is starkly contrasted with that of the idle rich. The idle capitalist (*capitaliste oisif*) who receives nothing but a fixed income in the form of rent or interest on his capital, does not personally direct any productive labour. Rather, his capital (whether land, money or equipment) is hired to others whose *industrie* effects an increase in productive wealth. Indeed, says Tracy in mild indignation, the rent or interest received by idle capitalists is a levy or deduction from the products of the activity of *les citoyens industrieux.*[82] If these idle rich also happen to be employers, it is found that their employees are engaged in domestic service, or in catering for the luxurious tastes and enjoyments of their employers. The expenditure of this whole class of the idle rich is devoted to their personal satisfactions, and although they provide subsistence for many personal servants, the latters' labour is "completely sterile".[83]

This appears to be an inconsistency in the economic thought of Tracy and his colleagues. Production had earlier been defined in general terms as production of utilities for which there was a market. Domestic labour and production of "luxuries" seem to fall within the broad definition of production as creation of utilities, but Tracy rejects their proper inclusion. His reasons appear to be moral and political as much as purely economic. There had been a continual debate throughout the eighteenth century (not to mention earlier periods) concerning what constituted "luxury", and whether it was socially, morally and economically desirable. The consequences had been seen either as corrupting (Rousseau), a positive incentive to economic growth, employment, and useful arts (Montesquieu, *Esprit des Lois*, book VII), or as a product of human nature, of the inevitable desire for wealth and enjoyment (Saint-Lambert[84]). Most authors described luxury either as extravagant personal consumption, or more or less as that level of consumption typical of wealthy societies where basic needs had been met. The physiocrats described luxury in terms of expenditure by the proprietary and productive classes directed towards the "sterile" class, instead of being directed into rural investment and maintenance of their properties. Luxury, said Baudeau, is an "excess of sterile expenditure".[85]

Tracy's first discussion of luxury, in his *Commentaire* on Montesquieu, followed in the spirit of the physiocrats (allowing of course for their different concepts of "sterile" expenditure). "Luxury", wrote Tracy, "consists essentially in non-productive expenditure".[86] However, since most forms of consumption would fall under this heading, Tracy introduced a further notion of "unproductive" expenditure as purchase of goods or services which are "not necessary".[87] This raised further problems, since the concept of "necessary" satisfactions was so variable, according to circumstances;[88] yet Tracy persevered with the concept. His essential argument was that luxury consumption was not a source of national wealth, even if it was taken as a *sign* of individual wealth and prestige. A business could only increase its profits by savings and reinvestment, not by wasteful display. The same, wrote Tracy, was true of national wealth: a higher proportion of luxury expenditure would channel capital into areas of lesser utility from the viewpoint of economic growth.[89] The production of an economic surplus in society could only be achieved by careful management of resources (*économie* in the sense of savings) rather than by consuming everything immediately.

A better use of resources was that which produced things of "lasting utility".[90] In the case of a proprietor leasing his property, or lending his money at interest, the relevant questions concerned how the borrower made use of the capital, and what use the proprietor made of the interest or rent.[91] Generally speaking, proprietors had made poor use of their rental incomes; and therefore the *rentiers*[92] were engaged almost entirely in unproductive or luxury consumption. Under the *ancien régime*, wrote Tracy, most of the useful labour in France was directed towards providing the "immense revenues of the court and all the opulent class of society", revenues which were mainly used in luxury expenditure (e.g., employment of numerous servants to care for the gratifications of a small number of men). As soon as these resources were freed for productive uses, a great burst of national energy had taken place, with almost everyone engaged in some form of useful work.[93] Luxury, according to Tracy, was thus a cause of economic weakness and misery for the majority. "Its real effect is to destroy continually, by the excessive consumption of some men, the product of the labour and industry of others".[94] Luxury on a large scale was made possible only by vast inequalities of wealth: great fortunes, rather than mere idleness, were the main cause of excessive luxury. For this reason, industries which allowed sudden large accumulations of wealth in a few hands were less desirable than those where progress was steady, requiring skills, knowledge or other worthy qualities.[95]

In short, luxury, or "superfluous and exaggerated consumption",[96] is destructive of accumulated utilities and cannot be a source of further wealth. Luxury is also undesirable from the moral viewpoint, since it encourages vanity, frivolity, greed and various forms of depravity.[97] Tracy conceded that some degree of luxury was inevitable, since the taste for superfluous expenditure partly arises from man's natural desire for new kinds of enjoyments, which are made possible by industry and reinforced by habit.[98] However, the main point Tracy wished to emphasise was that the activities of proprietors or *rentiers* are generally "unproductive" insofar as their expenditures are devoted to personal gratifications and ostentatious display. Tracy's conception of liberty and happiness was tied to a view that productivity should be maximised. The economic functions of the old class of noble proprietors had become redundant, in his opinion, as soon as the social and political order sustaining their elevated and privileged position had been undermined. The "consumption of this species of capitalists is absolutely pure loss from the standpoint of reproduction",[99] and a diminution of acquired national wealth. Their revenues being fixed, there was no way they could increase the wealth of the community or employ an expanding work-force.[100]

Les capitalistes industrieux or active capitalists are quite different in their economic functions.

> The second class of capitalists, who employ and pay the wage-earners, consists of those we have called active. It includes all the entrepreneurs of every kind of industry, that is, all the men who, having more or less substantial amounts of capital, use their talents and industry in improving their capital rather than lending it to others, and who thus live neither on wages nor revenues but on profits. These men not only increase their own capital, but all those of the idle capitalists as well. They take on rental their lands, houses and money, and make use of them so as to derive profits greater than this rent. Thus they have in their hands almost all the wealth of society.[101]

By withdrawing from circulation only a modest amount of profit for their personal and family needs, the entrepreneurs return to the reproductive process the large and increasing amounts of capital they control. For their enterprises to grow, their profits must be higher than their costs, including both their private consumption and the rent or interest payable to the idle capitalists; if they are successful, they expand their business and engage a larger number of employees.[102] In this way, the production of active capitalists is responsible for initiating and maintaining the growth of wealth and its circulation among the various classes of society.

> The entrepreneurs of industry are really the heart of the body politic, and their capital is its blood. With their capital, they pay the wages to most of the *salariés*; pay rents to all the idle capitalists, owners of land or money; and through them pay the wages of all the other *salariés* ...[103]

The idle rich, on the contrary, are to be understood as destroyers of wealth, not creators. The source of wealth lies in production,[104] and not in the consumption of luxuries or in the employment of domestic servants to satisfy one's private whims. Consumption which does not generate further production is useless from the viewpoint of national wealth. The funds which pay for the employees of the idle rich are generated by *les hommes industrieux* who borrowed land or money from the *capitalistes oisifs*.[105]

> ... those who live on wages, those who live on rents, and those who live on profits, form three essentially different classes of men; and it is the latter who maintain all the others, and who alone increase the public wealth and create all our means of enjoyment. That must be so, since labour is the source of all wealth and since it is they alone (the entrepreneurs) who give a useful direction to current work, in making a productive use of accumulated labour.[106]

Capital which returns merely a fixed rent or interest can only be consumed, and is thus lost forever; capital which is put to use by productive entrepreneurs is the source of all increases in national wealth. Montesquieu had believed that the personal expenditure of the rich, derived from their rents, was the source of subsistence for the poor masses. But according to Tracy, Montesquieu did not understand the nature of these revenues, for they were really only rents levied on *industrie*, and were dependent on the productivity of industry.[107] "Economically speaking, then, luxury—exaggerated and superfluous consumption—is never good for anything". The only good consequence might be that such spending would bring about the ruin of *les oisifs* and release their capital into the hands of *la classe industrieuse*.[108]

Tracy noted that powerful men of property were hardly able to understand that their unproductive consumption was useless from the viewpoint of national wealth, or that their dissipation of great wealth rendered no great service to the state. Their exaggerated sense of their own importance had been largely accepted by their employees, who depended on such spending and could not envisage any alternative source of employment. Some landed nobility, obliged to abandon their landed estates during the Revolution, had wrongly believed that the villagers would lose their source of income, when in fact it was the tenant-farmers who hired most of the labourers; and the same nobility wrongly believed that the peasants who took over their property would be condemned to poverty. Tracy, while condemning any threats to "private property and justice", asserted that "the absence of a useless man" would make virtually no difference to the economic order, and that the suppression of feudal rights had greatly benefited the country by opening up more opportunities for the productive classes.[109]

We have examined in some detail the differences seen by Tracy between the economic roles of the *rentiers* and *entrepreneurs*. In the following chapter, we turn to examine the *salariés*, especially in relation to Tracy's view of the causes of and remedies for economic inequality.

Notes

1. *Logique*, pp. 437-8.
2. *Ibid.*, p. 437. On the origin of the term political economy, cf. W. Letwin, *The Origins of Scientific Economics* (Westport, 1975), p. 217; and J.-B. Say, *Traité d'économie politique* (Paris, 2nd ed. 1814), "Discours préliminaire", pp. xiii-xv.
3. *Logique*, pp. 391-2. For the term "social economy", see Tracy, *Traité de la Volonté* (1818), p. 289.
4. *Traité de la Volonté* (1815), p. 96.
5. *Ibid.*, p. 97.
6. *Ibid.*, p. 98.
7. *Ibid.*, p. 92-5.
8. *Ibid.*, p. 99. (Tracy's theory of value is praised by Victor Cousin, "Adam Smith", *Séances et Travaux de l'Académie des Sciences morales et politiques*, vol. 10 (1846), p. 449.)
9. *Ibid.*, pp. 100-1, 105.

10. *Ibid.*, pp. 101-2.
11. *Ibid.*, pp. 102-3.
12. R.L. Meek, *Studies in the Labour Theory of Value* (London, 1958), chapter 1.
13. J. Locke, *Second Treatise*, chapter 5.
14. A. Smith, *The Wealth of Nations* (1776), ed. Skinner (Harmondsworth, 1974), pp. 104-6.
15. J. Viner, "Mercantilist Thought", *International Encyclopedia of the Social Sciences* (New York, 1968), vol. 4, pp. 435-442.
16. A. Bloomfield and W.R. Allen, "The Foreign-Trade Doctrines of the Physiocrats", and J.J. Spengler, "The Physiocrats and Say's Law of Markets", in *Essays in Economic Thought*, ed. Spengler and Allen (Chicago, 1960); and the references cited in footnote 3 to chapter 6.
17. Mirabeau, *Leçons économiques* (Amsterdam, 1770), Leçon XXVI: "Classes sociales", pp. 112-119; Dupont de Nemours, *Abrégé des principes de l'économie politique* (1772), in E. Daire (ed.), *Physiocrates* (Paris, 1846), p. 376; Baudeau, *Première introduction à la philosophie économique* (1771), in Daire (ed.), *Physiocrates*, especially pp. 669, 692, 711; Baudeau, *Explication du tableau économique* (1767), in *ibid.*, p. 852.
18. Dupont de Nemours, *De l'origine et des progrès d'une science nouvelle* (1768), ed. Dubois (Paris, 1910), pp. 7, 11, 35; Le Mercier de la Rivière, *L'Ordre naturel et essentiel des sociétés politiques* (1767), ed. Depitre (Paris, 1910), chapter XLIV; Dupont de Nemours, *Abrégé*, p. 378; Quesnay, *Le Droit Naturel*, in Daire (ed.), *Physiocrates*, pp. 46, 52-55.
19. Cf. Say, *Traité d'économie politique*, book 1, chapter 2; M. Dobb, *Theories of Value and Distribution* (Cambridge, 1973), chapter 2; R.L. Meek, *Studies in the Labour Theory of Value*, chapter 2.
20. Smith, *Wealth of Nations*, book 2, chapter 3, pp. 430-1. Smith includes churchmen, lawyers and public servants among the "unproductive".
21. Say, *Traité d'économie politique*, book 1, chapters 7 and 13.
22. Smith, *Wealth of Nations*, book 1, chapter 5.
23. Say, *Traité d'économie politique*, book 1, chapters 4 and 5.
24. *Ibid.*, book 1, chapter 1.
25. Tracy, *Traité de la Volonté* (1818 ed.), p. 147. The reference is to the 1803 edition of Say's *Traité*. Tracy made a similar remark a few years earlier in his *Commentaire*, p. 285.
26. *Commentaire*, pp. 284ff.
27. Tracy, *Traité de la Volonté* (1818), p. 148.
28. *Ibid.*, p. 149.
29. *Ibid.*, p. 150.
30. *Ibid.*, p. 151.
31. *Commentaire*, pp. 281-3. Condorcet gave an extremely generous assessment of the physiocrats in *Sketch*, pp. 138-9, omitting to mention their doctrine of the primacy of agriculture.
32. *Traité* (1818), pp. 152-3.
33. *Ibid.*, p. 153; cf. pp. 201-3.
34. *Ibid.*, p. 154.
35. Cf. Sieyès, *Qu'est-ce que le Tiers-état?* (Paris, 1789), ed. Zapperi (Genève, 1970), pp. 121ff.
36. Cf. B.-C. Dunoyer, "Esquisse historique des doctrines auxquelles on a donné le nom d'*industrialisme ...*", *Revue encyclopédique*, vol. 33 (February 1827), pp. 368-395; Saint-Simon, *Selected Writings*, ed. K. Taylor (London, 1975), Part III.
37. Tracy, *Traité* (1818), pp. 154-5; cf. pp. 290-2. The phrase "frelons de la ruche" (drones of the hive) had previously appeared in Tracy's *Commentaire*, p. 294.
38. *Traité*, p. 155; cf. *Commentaire*, p. 287. (For Tracy's views on the productivity of commerce, cf. *Traité*, pp. 205-215. He is in accord on this point with Say, *op.cit.*, book 1, chapter 2.)
39. *Traité*, p. 157.
40. *Ibid.*, p. 158.
41. *Ibid.*, p. 159.

42. *Ibid.*, p. 160.
43. *Ibidem.*
44. *Ibid.*, p. 161.
45. Cf. *Commentaire*, pp. 290-1.
46. Tracy, *Traité*, p. 163. Cf. Say, *op.cit.*, book 1, chapter 7, who makes this point forcefully.
47. *Traité*, p. 164.
48. *Ibidem*; cf. *Traité* (1815), p. 99.
49. "Mémoire sur la faculté de penser", p. 401.
50. On the term "industry", cf. F. Brunot, *Histoire de la langue française*, tome VI, p. 379f; R. Williams, *Keywords* (London, 1976), pp. 137-8.
51. Cf. G.V. Taylor, "Non-capitalist wealth and the origins of the French Revolution", *American Historical Review*, vol. 72 (January 1967), pp. 469-496; R. Price, *The Economic Modernization of France* (London, 1975); F. Braudel and C.E. Labrousse, *Histoire économique et sociale de la France*, tome III: 1789-années 1830, vol. I (Paris, 1976).
52. *Op.cit.*, article "industrie", p. 253f.
53. Cf. E. Allix, "L'oeuvre économique de Germain Garnier", *Revue d'histoire économique et sociale*, vol. 5 (1912), pp. 317-342; Allix, "La rivalité entre la propriété foncière et la fortune mobilière sous la Révolution", *ibid.*, vol. 6 (1913), pp. 297-348.
54. Cf. Cambacérès, "Discours sur la science sociale", *Mémoires de l'Institut National, Classe des sciences morales et politiques*, vol. III (1801), pp. 3,5.
55. Cf. Baudeau, *Première introduction*, in Daire (ed.), *Physiocrates*, p. 723: "*Laissez les faire*, as a famous *intendant du commerce* (Gournay) said, that is the whole of legislation for the manufactures and sterile arts ... *Qu'on les laisse faire*, that is the true legislation, i.e., the function of the guarantor authority".
56. *Commentaire*, p. 280 (and p. 280n).
57. Cf. the extracts in R.L. Meek (ed.), *Precursors of Adam Smith*, especially pp. 108ff.
58. For a detailed account of the French and Scottish contributions to the "four-stages" theory of historical development, cf. R.L. Meek, *Social Science and the Ignoble Savage* (Cambridge, 1976).
59. P. Lévesque, "Considérations sur l'homme, observé dans la vie sauvage, dans la vie pastorale et dans la vie policée", *Mémoires de l'Institut*, vol. I (1798), pp. 209-246. Lévesque (born 1736) did not, however, make a clear distinction between a society whose major "industry" was agriculture and one whose "industry" was increasingly oriented towards manufacturing, commerce and "useful arts".
60. Tracy, *Traité* (1818), p. 322.
61. Baudeau, *Première introduction*, pp. 669, 691.
62. Tracy, *Traité* (1818), p. 154. For the origin of "class" terminology, cf. Brunot, *Histoire de la langue française*, tome VI, pp. 191f.
63. Condillac, *Le Commerce et le Gouvernement considérés relativement l'un à l'autre* (1776), in *Oeuvres philosophiques*, vol. II, pp. 241-367. See also I.F. Knight, *The Geometric Spirit*, chapter 9.
64. *Ibid.*, pp. 311-2.
65. *Ibid.*, pp. 258-62. Condillac's heretical view was strongly attacked by the physiocrat Le Trosne, *De l'intérêt social* (1777), in Daire (ed.), *Physiocrates*, especially pp. 929ff.
66. Smith, *Wealth of Nations*, p. 356; cf. p. 155.
67. Say, *Traité*, book 1, chapter 5.
68. *Ibid.*, book 1, chapter 6 (*Treatise*, New York 1880, p. 80).
69. *Ibidem.* (*Treatise*, p. 81.)
70. Tracy, *Traité* (1818), pp. 166-7; cf. pp. 176-7, 214.
71. *Ibid.*, pp. 167-9.
72. *Ibid.*, pp. 170-1. Cf. Say, *Traité*, book 2, chapter 7 (*Treatise*, pp. 327-9), who claims that the *savant* is typically underpaid for the important services he provides.
73. Tracy, *Traité* (1818), p. 171.
74. Cf. Say, *Traité*, book 2, chapter 8, section 2 (*Treatise*, p. 354).
75. M. Dobb, "Entrepreneur", *Encyclopedia of the Social Sciences* (New York, 1931), vol. 5,

pp. 558-560.
76. Cf. Bert Hoselitz, "The early history of entrepreneurial theory", in *Essays in Economic Thought*, ed. Spengler and Allen (Chicago, 1960), especially pp. 247-8.
77. Say, *Traité*, book 2, chapter 7, section 3 (*Treatise*, p. 332).
78. Hoselitz, *op.cit.*, pp. 250-3; G. Koolman, "Say's conception of the role of the entrepreneur", *Economica*, vol. 38 (1971), pp. 269-286; M. James, "P.-L. Roederer, J.-B. Say and the concept of 'industrie'", *History of Political Economy*, vol. 9 (1977), pp. 455-475.
79. Say, *Traité*, book 2, chapter 7, section 3 (*Treatise*, pp. 330-1).
80. Tracy, *Traité* (1818), pp. 172-3.
81. *Ibid.*, p. 172; cf. pp. 214-5.
82. *Ibid.*, p. 333.
83. *Ibid.*, p. 334.
84. Saint-Lambert, "Luxury", in Diderot et al., *Encyclopedia: Selections* (New York, 1965), especially p. 230.
85. Baudeau, *Principes de la Science morale et politique sur le luxe et les loix somptuaires* (1767), ed. Dubois (Paris, 1912); and for the quote, see his *Première introduction* (1771), in Daire, p. 736.
86. *Commentaire*, p. 79.
87. *Ibid.*, pp. 80-1.
88. As he was well aware: *ibid.*, pp. 81-3.
89. *Ibid.*, pp. 83-4.
90. *Ibid.*, p. 85; cf. *Traité*, (1818), p. 343.
91. *Commentaire*, p. 86.
92. The term *rentiers*, meaning "idle" capitalists living from rent or interest, is used in *Traité* (1818), pp. 290, 342, 347. Tracy also used the term *rentiers oisifs* in 1798: "Quels sont les moyens", in *Commentaire*, p. 470.
93. *Commentaire*, pp. 92-3; *Traité*, pp. 356-363.
94. *Commentaire*, p. 88.
95. *Ibid.*, pp. 97-8.
96. *Traité*, pp. 345, 349.
97. *Commentaire*, p. 99; *Traité*, p. 368.
98. *Commentaire*, pp. 95-6; *Traité*, p. 364.
99. *Traité*, p. 335.
100. *Ibid.*, pp. 290-1.
101. *Ibid.*, pp. 335-6. Cf. *Commentaire*, p. 55, where Tracy points to the perceived need by dominant classes in earlier societies to repress industrious lower classes which could otherwise accumulate all the wealth by their talent and industry.
102. *Traité*, pp. 336-7.
103. *Ibid.*, pp. 338-9.
104. *Ibid.*, p. 353. Cf. Smith, *Wealth of Nations*, book 2, chapter 3.
105. *Ibid.*, p. 346.
106. *Ibid.*, p. 341.
107. *Ibid.*, p. 348. Moreover, non-agricultural industry was even more productive: *ibid.*, pp. 202-3.
108. *Ibid.*, p. 349.
109. *Ibid.*, pp. 354-5 and 355n.

8. THE PROBLEM OF ECONOMIC INEQUALITY

Tracy saw economic inequality as a problem to be understood and tackled, not simply as an eternal fact of life. He recognised that there were different levels of inequality, some more readily overcome than others. What types of inequality were least acceptable to him? As a political liberal, Tracy was particularly troubled by social conditions which prevented men from exercising their natural rights to life, liberty and property. Slavery or bondage was the worst form of inequality; it was incompatible with "civilised" society, in Tracy's view. The second type of inequality which he attacked was inequality of instruction, skills or knowledge. While it was obvious that everyone had different talents and instructional needs, it was necessary for all men and women to receive a basic instruction to equip them for citizenship and their occupation. Ignorance was the servant of repressive élites.

Thirdly, there was economic inequality, examined in the present chapter. This form of inequality arose mainly from the different prices commanded in the market by different types of labour. Tracy was concerned, on the one hand, that extremes of wealth and poverty led to moral corruption and to material misery or stagnation. On the other hand, he opposed all doctrines of economic egalitarianism, owing to his belief in the sanctity of private property, and to his desire to encourage talents and industry. But Tracy wished to see a levelling of the extremes: reducing the prodigal extravagances of some types of luxury expenditure, and ameliorating the deprivations of the poorest classes who lacked skills or opportunities for work.[1] He wished to see a system in which higher wages were accepted as desirable both for the wage-earners and for the expansion of the market economy. His strategies for attaining a more equitable distribution of wealth were not, however, thoroughly developed. Other than his proposal that inheritances be equally distributed among the children of a marriage, and his great emphasis on increasing the availability of general and specialist education, Tracy's liberalism allowed little more than appeals to reason and philanthropy, on the one hand, and faith in the benefits of economic growth, on the other.

In accordance with the labour theory of value, Tracy recognised the economic importance of manual workers and he endowed their labour with a certain moral dignity denied by physiocratic notions of the sterility of industry. The manual labourer could even be said to have a small amount of capital (his tools, and skills) but he was always bound to depend for wages on an employer. Generally speaking, the market price of his labour was likely to be very low, because his skills were not very scarce or highly developed. Having nothing to offer but his manual labour, his wages were likely to remain near a subsistence level, and were in danger of falling even lower in some circumstances.[2] It is a general law of the market, wrote Tracy, that while the "most necessary" labour is the most constantly required and employed, "it is in the nature of things that it is always the lowest paid: it cannot be otherwise."[3] Production of commodities in common usage required only a relatively low level of skills, whether in fabricating or agricultural industries. It was indeed important that the price of such commodities should be kept low, for it was the poor who, as consumers, were most dependent on such items: the poor could not afford higher prices. But there was a vicious circle implicit in the situation of the poor, because

> it is on the lowest price to which these (commodities) can be reduced, that the lowest price of wages is regulated; and the workers, who labour in their manufacture, are necessarily included in this latter class of the lowest wages.[4]

Tracy argued that there was a "natural" and inevitable inequality in the distribution of wealth. Every individual held some property by virtue of possessing his own individuality and his faculties; but a natural inequality prevailed because individuals had different talents and abilities. Modern societies facilitate the differential development of such abilities and consequent inequalities. "This natural inequality is extended and manifested in proportion as our means are developed and diversified".[5] It is impossible to eliminate inequality, Tracy believed, since it is grounded in human nature for individuals to possess property and to have unequal talents. Could anything be done to reduce inequality? Tracy held that it was not the task of governments to enforce economic equality. Such measures could not succeed, for they were too much against "nature" to be durable. Conflicts over the distribution of communal goods, or over the sharing of communal toil, would replace disputes over the defence of private property, and the general result "would be to establish an equality of misery and deprivation, by extinguishing the activity of personal industry".[6]

Tracy was aware, then, that there were inherent tendencies towards economic inequality stemming from the division of labour in modern society. What is more, he conceded that a conflict of interests was inherent in the operation of market forces:

> The frequent opposition of interests among us, and the inequality of means, are thus conditions of our nature, as are suffering and death ... I believe that this evil (inequality) is a necessary one, and that we must submit to it ...[7]

In a society based upon "the free disposition of the faculties of the individual, and the guarantee of whatever he may acquire by their means", everyone exerts himself in various directions and all are involved in exchange relationships. "The most able gain, and the most economical amass wealth".[8] The system of private property usually entailed a freedom of disposal. Tracy was concerned that inherited wealth was a means of acquisition without labour; it was a mechanism for perpetuating and aggravating inequalities. Tracy believed that there were simple legislative remedies, such as equal inheritance, which could ensure that these unearned riches were more evenly divided.[9]

In a new and industrious nation such as the United States, where the land had not all been taken up, the ordinary citizens could obtain vacant land and live in relative comfort. But where such land was entirely occupied, scarcity dictated that those who had few resources were obliged to work for those with larger resources.[10] Competition for jobs diminished the price of labour, and their problems were compounded by producing more children. The poorest families could scarcely manage to eke out a precarious subsistence.[11]

In such conditions, could it be said there was a major social division between proprietors and non-proprietors? Tracy rejected this proposition, together with the physiocratic proposition that the landless poor could be termed non-proprietors. The poor, he claimed, are proprietors at least of their individuality, their labour and the wages of this labour. They have a need to conserve such property, and thus they have an interest that property be respected. No-one, even those who commit crimes against property, can afford to deny the right of each individual to security of property.[12] Moreover, the physiocrats had wanted to restrict the term proprietors to those owning landed estates: whereas land is actually just one form of capital among others, including money and industrial equipment. "It would be more reasonable", continued Tracy, "to divide society into the poor and the rich, if one knew where to draw the line of demarcation".[13] But this would be misleading in relation to property, since "the poor man has as much interest in the preservation of what he has, as the most opulent man".[14]

The conflict of interests in society is a many-sided phenomenon. One can detect in the division of labour and unequal rewards

> the germ of opposing interests, which are established between the entrepreneur and wage-earners, on the one hand, and between entrepreneur and consumers, on the other hand; among the wage earners themselves, among entrepreneurs ..., and finally among consumers themselves ...[15]

An examination of these diverse interests and the passions they arouse, shows that all groups "seek the support of force" to buttress their interests and conceptions, or at least they seek "prohibitive regulations to constrain those who obstruct them in this universal conflict".[16] The consumers, being the whole of the population, cannot form a special interest group: their interest is the "universal interest", and they can be protected only by general laws or by universal liberty. But those who have a particular over-riding group interest form a separate body and appoint agents to further their cause.[17] Tracy particularly had in mind the lobbyists of wealthy interests. Wage-earners had been forbidden the right to organise trades unions by the legislation of 1791, on the grounds that all "corporate" interests should be suppressed. The poor, noted Tracy, could nevertheless be "formidable" in time of trouble "when the secret of their strength is revealed to them and they are excited to abuse it".[18]

If the major social division was not that of proprietors versus non-proprietors, what could it be? Tracy claimed that the key division of interests in society was "that between the *salariés* on the one hand and those who employ them, on the other".[19] The "two great classes" were thus the employers and those receiving salaries and wages.[20] The defect of this classification, he said, was that somewhat different types of people were included in each category: a minister of state would rub shoulders with a day-labourer among the *salariés*, and the smallest master-workman would be bracketed with the richest idle capitalist. But there was one essential difference of interest between the two classes: the wage-earners wanted to maximise their wage levels, and the employers wanted to pay low wages. Tracy claimed that the entrepreneur's apparently clear interest in paying low wages was not really as obvious as might be assumed, for he also required the consumers to be able to afford to buy the commodities he put on the market. If they did not have enough money, the level of demand would fall, and the entrepreneur might not be able to sell his products at above his costs of production.[21] Here was an underconsumptionist notion of economic recession.

Tracy was far from championing the interests of entrepreneurs against the consumers. He remarked that since the interest of consumers if that of everyone, it is to be regretted that

> modern governments are always ready first to sacrifice the *salariés* to the entrepreneurs by constricting the former with apprenticeships, corporation privileges and other regulations; and secondly, to sacrifice the consumers to these same entrepreneurs by granting the latter certain privileges and sometimes even monopolies.[22]

Tracy thus defended the general interest (consumers) and the majority interest (*salariés*) against certain restrictive practices which interfered with the operations of the free market. He had noted the inherent tendency of the market to depress the price of labour, and believed it was incumbent upon public authorities to adopt policies of economic liberalisation in order to promote an expanding economy and to relieve the worst aspects of poverty.

In common with the physiocrats, and most liberal writers of his day, Tracy strongly denied that there were any permanent and legitimate bases for class antagonism in society, on which a serious conflict of interests might emerge. The physiocrats had asserted a unity of objective interests among the three classes, based upon economic prosperity: the interest of the "cultivator" or producer should prevail.[23] Condorcet had regarded conciliation of interests as one of the highest tasks of the "social art", and he argued that "all the classes have only one interest": to protect the right of everyone to enjoy and increase his property.[24] Tracy also denied there were permanently hostile class interests:

> ... although each of us has particular interests, we change so frequently our roles in society, that often we have in one respect an interest contrary to that which we have in another, so that we find ourselves linked with those to whom we were opposed the moment before. This means, fortunately, that we cannot form groups which are constantly enemies.[25]

This notion of changing and cross-cutting loyalties, taken up via Tocqueville into modern political sociology, is one of Tracy's arguments against a class analysis of modern society. People are bearers of several economic roles, which draw them in different directions, both at any given moment and over a longer period of time. Tracy also proposed a second argument against the conception of a fundamental clash of class interests: the importance of shared or common interests which underlie all our social and economic life.

> ... in the midst of all these momentary conflicts, we are all constantly united by our common and immutable interests as proprietors and as consumers; that is, we all have a permanent interest, first, that (private) property be respected, and secondly, that industry should be perfected, or in other words that manufacturing and transport should be in the best possible state.[26]

In short, everyone has a general interest in seeing that the economy is expanding, through the free development of the faculties of each individual.[27]

However, the problem of economic inequality could not be entirely resolved through the natural operation of market mechanisms. What other options were available? Tracy did not condone the political or industrial mobilisation of the masses to influence market forces or public policy in a direct manner.[28] Instead, he argued that the community as a whole should be made to understand that everyone benefits in the long term by a system of relatively high wage levels. He also enunciated the general principle that "the laws should always tend to protect the weak, whereas too often they are inclined to favour the powerful."[29] Tracy never showed in detail how this principle should be applied in particular cases. But in the present context of income distribution, the implication is fairly clear: there should be a wage structure high enough to alleviate poverty and to generate consumer demand, yet not so high as to undermine the profitability of business.

Tracy's primary concern appears to be a limited defence of the interests of *les pauvres* or *les simples salariés*: "humanity, justice and policy equally require that, of all the interests, that of the poor be the most consulted and the most respected."[30] In other words, Tracy felt that the interests of the poor majority were of a different order from the particular advantages and desires of other groups and individuals, whose needs were not matters of physical survival. While it was true that the poor also had many wants of a petty kind, more importantly they shared a precarious economic existence. "Humanity", wrote Tracy, "does not allow interests of that kind to be placed in the same balance with simple conveniences''.[31] Justice, he continued in a utilitarian vein, obliges us to take account of the relative numbers of interested parties (*le nombre des intéressés*).

> Since the lowest class of society is always by far the largest, it follows that whenever it is in opposition with the others, what is useful to it should always be preferred.[32]

Policy (*la politique*) also demands that the interests of mere wage-earners be protected, because whenever the lowest class of society is too miserable, ''there is neither activity, industry, knowledge, nor real national strength; ... nor interior peace well established.''[33]

Assuming a distinction between desires and interests,[34] Tracy claimed that the ''true interests'' of the poor were consistent with reason and the general interest. This perspective dissolved those ''prejudices'' according to which the struggle between the poor and the rich was seen as an eternal part of the social order.[35] The first interest of the poor man, insisted Tracy, was the maintenance of the right to hold property, an interest he shared with the rich man even though their relative wealth was very different. Property, he repeated, included personal as well as fixed and moveable property. Security of property was valuable to the poor man not only to guarantee his own actual possessions, but to protect the capital of his employer. ''Thus he has a direct interest not only in the conservation of what he himself possesses, but also in the conservation of what others possess''.[36] Since property in one's own person is the ''source'' of all other forms, Tracy derives the moral maxim that one should respect the other's person in the same way one wishes other forms of property to be respected. ''Leave him the free disposition of his faculties and their employment, as you wish him to leave you that of your lands and capitals''.[37]

The second interest of the poor man is that he should receive a high price for his labour. Tracy understands how unpopular such a doctrine would be with employers.

> All the superior classes of a society—here including even the smallest owner of a workshop—desire that the price of wages be very low so they can obtain more labour for the same amount of money. They desire it with such passion that, whenever they can and the laws permit them, they even use violence to attain this end. And they prefer the labour of slaves or of serfs because it is even cheaper. These men do not fail to say, and persuade, that what they believe to be their interest is the general interest, and that the low price of wages is absolutely necessary for the development of industry, for the extension of manufacture and commerce, in a word for the prosperity of the state.[38]

Tracy conceded that if the price of labour was so high that goods could be imported for a much cheaper price, domestic manufacture and employment would collapse. Such a wage level would not be in the interest of the poor because it would lead to vast unemployment. However, this situation would only be temporary, for market forces would rapidly lower the price of labour, and the labourers would be willing to work for smaller wages. If wages were too high even where labour was in plentiful supply, the cause lay in bad workmanship and inefficiency. It would then be necessary to combat "the lack of skill, the ignorance and the laziness" of the workers, which are the "true causes of languor in industry wherever it is encountered".[39]

Such defects among workmen were typically the product of economic and moral misery. The greed of employers blinded them to this fact. The northern parts of the United States, for example, were characterised by high wages and a general vigour and prosperity; whereas the southern states employing slave labour were relatively stagnant even though they produced valuable commodities. Such examples illustrated a general truth of all societies:

> Wherever the lowest class of society is too wretched, its extreme misery and resulting abjectness is the death of industry and the principle of infinite evils, even for its oppressors.[40]

The slavery of the ancient world, the slavery in contemporary European colonies, and the serfdom of feudal Europe, had led to enormous "errors in economy, morality and politics". The popular disturbances in many nations of Europe, and even the problems caused by the enormous poor tax in England and by the large numbers of wretched men who had to be restrained by force, were all evidence of the general proposition:

> that when a considerable proportion of society is suffering too greatly, and is consequently too brutalised, there will be neither repose, nor safety, nor liberty possible even for the rich and powerful. On the contrary, these first citizens of a state are much more truly great and happy when they are at the head of a people enjoying an honest comfort, which develops in them all their moral and intellectual faculties.[41]

Tracy was vague concerning how such a system of moderately high wages might be introduced or maintained. He rejected the tactic that the poor should employ violence to obtain the desired level of payment, for their first interest was to respect the property of everyone. But equally he did not want the rich to determine wage levels in a one-sided way. He simply hoped that the free disposition of labour, and the free market, would ultimately become a more humane mechanism for determining the price of labour; yet he had earlier shown that market forces generally tended to depress wage levels.

The third interest of the poor man was that his wage or income should be constant. This was more useful to him than any temporary or extraordinary increase in his income, which might encourage improvidence and wasteful consumption and soon turn into misery. The constancy of wage-levels was part of a wider interest, namely, that the price of basic commodities should vary as little as possible. "For it is not the price of wages in itself that is important, it is their price compared with that of the things necessary for life".[42] The lowest wage levels were closely related in the long run to the price of goods necessary for subsistence. If the cost of necessities fell, the labourer benefited temporarily but without lasting utility. If their price increased, the poor suffered great distress; consequently, they would become more anxious to offer their labour, which unfortunately would drive down the price of labour even further, so that they were paid less at the very time they needed to be paid more. In times of distress, noted Tracy, it was always found that wage levels declined, because there was a surplus of labour on the market; "and this lasts until the return of prosperity or until they perish".[43] In short, it was desirable that the price of commodities, especially those important for subsistence, should be "invariable". The best method of achieving this goal was not to urge government regulation of prices, as had occurred both during the *ancien régime* and under the Jacobin régime of 1793-4 (the law of the *maximum*).[44] It was better

> to leave the most complete liberty to commerce, because the activity of speculators and their competition make them eager to take advantage of the smallest fall to buy, and the smallest rise to sell again; and in this way they prevent either one or the other from enduring or from becoming excessive. This method is also that which is the most consistent with the respect due to property, for the just and the useful are always united.[45]

The sudden expansion or contraction of particular industries could have a similar effect upon the employment and fortunes of the poor as did variations in the prices of basic commodities. Tracy alluded to a contemporary debate about the relative prosperity and stability of agricultural and commercial nations, and he cast doubt upon the qualities attributed to agricultural nations.[46] The latter were more exposed, in his opinion, to large fluctuations in the price of grain because, in the event of a domestic crop failure, the cost of transporting imported grain to inland regions was extremely high. Imported supplies were little more than a psychological consolation, for they did not resolve the problems of hardship and misery. Security of existence would be greatly facilitated if foodstuffs could be reduced to a small bulk for easy transportation.[47] In contrast with agricultural nations (which usually had large landlocked hinterlands), commercial nations had sufficient seaports to ensure that all areas could be readily supplied by imports in a time of trouble. On balance, commercial nations provided a better standard of living: they were less prone to the threat of starvation caused by crop failures; and, providing their industry and commerce developed "naturally" rather than by a forced and "exaggerated extension", severe fluctuations in prosperity could be avoided.[48]

Such a conclusion tied in with Tracy's general assumption that society, understood as "continual commerce", was the source of all our power, resources and happiness.[49] Wherever a commercial nation was found to be stagnant, the cause was not commerce itself, but such factors as a very unequal distribution of wealth, which is "the greatest and most general of evils".[50] Such cases only illustrated the truth that "the human race gains happiness from the development and increase of its means, but is ever ready to become unhappy from the bad use it makes of them".[51] Tracy summarised the major interests of the poor as follows:

> the poor man is a proprietor as well as the rich; in his role as proprietor of his person, his faculties and their product, he has an interest that he be allowed the free disposition of his person and his labour, that this labour should procure sufficient wages for him, and that these wages should vary as little as possible. That is, he has an interest that his capital should be respected, that this capital should produce the revenue necessary for his existence, and that this revenue if possible should be always the same. And on all these points, his interest is consistent with the general interest.
> But the poor man is not only a proprietor, he is also a consumer, for all men are both. In the latter role, he has the same interest as all consumers, that of being provisioned in the best and cheapest way possible. It is necessary for him, then, that manufacture should be very skilled, communications easy, and relations multiplied; for no-one has a greater need for being supplied cheaply than a man with few means.[52]

Some writers had argued that the development of machine technology, simplifying the labour process and increasing the productivity of industry, should be seen as opposed to the interests of the poor. J.-B. Say and Tracy disagreed with this argument.[53] By reducing the labour time embodied in a commodity, production costs were reduced, and the market price for the poor consumer was lower. Tracy argued against those who complained that machines would replace labourers and create vast unemployment. Wage-earners were paid, he claimed, out of the total capital funds available to the employers. If there was a saving of funds in one area, those funds would be diverted into new channels of investment, and the same number of workers could thereby retain employment (if the new investment was profitable). The best way to increase the total funds available for new investment, and thus for employment, was to *make manufacture more efficient and productive*; this was the only way in which social wealth could increase. (Otherwise, one might advocate the proliferation of useless labour to keep everyone employed. But this would actually divert funds away from productive labour, and no useful goods would be produced to satisfy our needs and to increase our social wealth.)[54]

The argument in favour of machines and other technical advances was extremely simple, said Tracy: useful labour is more useful than useless labour.[55] Tracy used the same arguments to refute criticisms of the construction of roads and canals, or improvements in communications and commercial relations. The poor could only benefit from the development of commerce and transportation, in the same way they benefited from the development of industry. Moreover, a highly developed commerce was more likely to make prices more constant, protecting the interest of the poor and of society at large. Even if there were short-term fluctuations as a result of industrial and commercial innovations, this was not enough to outweigh the long-term substantial benefits of such progress.[56]

We have seen that Tracy acknowledged a "necessary opposition between our particular interests", but he emphasised that "we are all united by our common interests as proprietors and consumers". It would, therefore, be "wrong to regard the poor and the rich, or the wage-earners and those who employ them, as two essentially hostile classes".[57] The true interests of the poor coincided with those of society at large. But while men's interests may be objectively united, it was necessary to take account of another "condition of our nature", namely, our inequality of means. It had sometimes been asserted, wrote Tracy, that inequality is a useful benefit for which we should thank Providence. On the contrary, he said, inequality is an evil "because it is a powerful support to injustice". Justice, our "greatest good" and sole means of conciliation, is on the side of the weak.[58]

In the case of brutal and savage society, inequality of power is manifested directly in the physical subjection of the weak by the strong, and severely limits the extent of social relations. In civilised society, such personal subjection and inequality tends to be greatly reduced, for "the object of social organisation is to combat the inequality of power" typified by the Hobbesian state of nature.[59] Those cases where slavery had been introduced were even more repugnant than primitive societies. But in general, society manages to reduce inequality of power among men, and thereby establishes security. This allows a development of men's faculties and of their wealth, or means of existence and enjoyment—such are the advantages of society. These benefits are particularly facilitated by modern societies ruled by representative government.[60] But economic growth brings inequalities of new kinds: the more our faculties are developed, the greater are their inequalities and soon there exists "inequality of wealth, leading to inequalities in education, capacity and influence".[61]

Having reduced the effects of personal and physical inequalities, and provided security for individuals to develop their abilities, society should attempt to overcome the worst effects of the tendency towards inequality of wealth: always by gentle means, eschewing force, and remembering that "respect for property is the fundamental base of society and its guarantee against violence".[62] Inequality of wealth is an evil because it brings about inequalities of education, capacity and influence, and tends to re-establish an inequality of power, thus undermining the advantages of civil society.

Tracy here underlined his distinction between active and idle capitalists, arguing that the "great fortunes" are held by the idle rich, who employ no labour except for their pleasure, instead of being held by the entrepreneurs of industry who are the only ones able to increase the national wealth.

> Wherever you see exaggerated fortunes, there you will see the greatest misery and the greatest stagnation of industry. The perfection of society, then, would be to increase greatly our riches while avoiding their extreme inequality.[63]

But even if the general principle is clear, the means and difficulties of implementation will differ markedly in each society according to circumstances. A poor agricultural society with limited commercial relations might well avoid gross inequalities for a long period. But in the case of conquest, or if very scarce commodities are produced, a part of the population will benefit disproportionately. Various other factors influence the degree and the distribution of national wealth:

> the different characters of peoples, the nature of their governments, the greater or smaller extent of their knowledge, and above all of their understanding of the social art at those moments which decide their fortune ...[64]

While nations may differ in circumstances, the terms of the problem remain the same. Society, having provided security for persons and their property, brings about the development of their faculties and their wealth; this growth leads towards a very unequal distribution of wealth and thus towards that inequality of power which society was originally established to constrain.[65] In short,

> all may be reduced to the following truth, which has not always been sufficiently understood: the multiplication of our means of enjoyment is a very good thing, their too unequal distribution is a very bad one and the source of all our evils. On this point also, the interest of the poor is the same as that of society.[66]

We have seen that for Tracy, the tendencies towards economic inequality should be resisted, in the interests not only of the poor but of the community as a whole. The material standard of living of the wage-labourers should be protected, by adequate wages, stable employment, and constant prices of commodities. Public instruction and vocational training could improve the price of wage-labour in the market. Employers should be made to understand that everyone benefits from a well-trained workforce and from moderately high wages, for the circulation of wealth is thereby raised and demand for goods is maintained. Moreover, if the poor are assured of their subsistence, they are less likely to seek violent solutions to their economic problems, and social harmony is thus ensured.

Tracy and other liberals believed that *philanthropy* was also necessary to deal with the poverty caused by temporary fluctuations in various sectors of agriculture and manufacture or by problems in trade and commerce.[67] Beggary and vagabondage were another matter— they were a social evil, to be eliminated by rational education, laws and institutions.[68] But the overall solution to the problem of poverty lay in continuous growth in productivity and national wealth. The entrepreneurs were the key to such economic growth, and the idle rich *rentiers* who obstructed the optimal use of productive capital were the main brake upon economic progress. Tracy believed that economic growth was paradoxically both the cause of inequality of wealth, and equally the only peaceful solution to the problem of inequality. Tracy did not examine the paradox in any systematic way, nor suggest reasons why the labourers would be led to understand that their *sectional* interests as the suffering poor were outweighed by their *universal* interests as proprietors and consumers. Unlike Say,[69] Tracy did not envisage a society where wage-labourers could achieve anything more than frugal comfort; and even this would be possible only in a society which had an abundance of resources and industry. He looked forward to a society in which the various forces of production could develop rapidly, unrestrained by the landowning class of the *ancien régime*, or by government interference with the natural operation of market forces. He identified the sufferings and vulnerability of the labourers under the market system, and proposed some general humanitarian principles to protect them from material deprivation and moral degradation.

Tracy believed that the complete liberalisation of commerce and industry, and the application of science to productive processes, would be the best guarantee of general prosperity. The division between men of skill and education, as well as of capital, on the one hand, and the ordinary labourers on the other, was seen as the major feature of the modern division of labour. This division between the educated and uneducated, even more than that between the rich and the poor, was also a prominent theme in Tracy's political and educational theorising. This theme will be developed in the following chapters.

Notes

1. Cf. Condorcet, *Sketch*, pp. 174, 179-184, on the need to reduce economic inequality. That Tracy regarded some kinds of inequality as reversible may be judged from the following: "When we deal with legislation, it will be seen further that the extremes of inequality and of luxury are much more the effects of bad laws than of the natural course of events". (*Traité de la Volonté*, 1818 edition, p. 354 n.1.)
2. *Traité*, pp. 168-171.
3. *Ibid.*, p. 175.
4. *Ibid.*, p. 176.
5. *Ibid.*, p. 262.
6. *Ibid.*, p. 263.
7. *Ibid.*, p. 264; cf. pp. 288, 513.
8. *Ibid.*, pp. 264-5.
9. "Quels sont les moyens", in *Commentaire*, pp. 464, 466. Tracy gave no philosophical justification for such measures; it was more a matter of pragmatic intervention.
10. *Traité*, pp. 270-4.
11. *Ibid.*, pp. 265-6; on population pressures, cf. *ibid.*, chapter 9, and *Commentaire*, book 23. Tracy argues that there is no duty to populate the world with miserable and unwanted children, and that the welfare of individuals is more important than their multiplication. Having recognised the Malthusian problem of resources in relation to population, he prescribes no remedies, apparently believing that rates of growth and decline in numbers are determined by economic factors. Tracy's position here is close to that of Condorcet, *Sketch*, pp. 188-9.
12. *Traité*, p. 266.
13. *Ibid.*, pp. 267-8.
14. *Ibid.*, p. 268.
15. *Ibid.*, p. 173.
16. *Ibid.*, p. 174.
17. Cf. Smith, *Wealth of Nations*, pp. 357-9.
18. *Traité*, p. 175. On the Le Chapelier law of 1791, see J. Godechot, *Les Institutions de la France sous la Révolution et l'Empire* (Paris, 1951), pp. 181 ff.

19. *Traité*, p. 268.
20. *Ibid.*, p. 290.
21. *Ibid.*, p. 268. For a more detailed discussion of underconsumptionist doctrines in the history of economic thought, see M. Bleaney, *Underconsumption theories* (London, 1976), especially chapters 1, 3, 5.
22. *Traité*, p. 269.
23. Cf. Dupont de Nemours, *Abrégé des principes de l'économie politique*, p. 383; Baudeau, *Première introduction*, pp. 740ff, 803ff.
24. Condorcet, *Sketch*, pp. 128, 184 and especially 192; Condorcet, "Que toutes les classes de la société n'ont qu'un même intérêt", *Oeuvres complètes* (Paris, 1804), vol. 18, pp. 43-50.
25. *Traité*, p. 269. For a view that class interests are in conflict, cf. Mably, *Doutes proposés aux philosophes économistes* (c. 1768): "In a society where landed property and inequality exist, no social order can be considered by everyone as the best. Society is divided into classes and these classes have antagonistic interests": cited in Morelly, *Code de la Nature* (1755), ed. Volguine (Paris, 1970), Introduction, p. 17.
26. *Traité*, pp. 269-70.
27. *Ibid.*, p. 288.
28. Cf. *ibid.*, p. 302.
29. *Ibid.*, p. 264.
30. *Ibid.*, p. 294.
31. *Ibid.*, p. 295.
32. *Ibid.*, pp. 295-6.
33. *Ibid.*, p. 296.
34. Cf. Dupont de Nemours, *Abrégé*, pp. 382-3, for the view that one may be misled or mistaken about one's desires, but one's interests are objectively given. Cf. *Traité* (1815), p. 86.
35. *Traité* (1818), p. 296.
36. *Ibid.*, p. 297.
37. *Ibid.*, p. 298.
38. *Ibid.*, pp. 298-9.
39. *Ibid.*, pp. 299-300.
40. *Ibid.*, pp. 300-1.
41. *Ibid.*, p. 302.
42. *Ibid.*, p. 305.
43. *Ibid.*, p. 306. I have omitted Tracy's discussion of the inflationary effects of paper money, found in *ibid.*, chapters 6 and 12; similarly, I have omitted his discussion of types of taxation, in *Commentaire*, chapter 13.
44. On the price-fixing regulations of this period, see Godechot, *Les Institutions* (1951), pp. 349ff.
45. *Traité* (1818), p. 307.
46. Cf. *ibid.*, p. 327, where he rejected the identification of commercial nations with greed and agricultural nations with moderation.
47. *Ibid.*, pp. 309-310.
48. *Ibid.*, p. 311.
49. *Ibid.*, p. 312.
50. *Ibid.*, p. 313.
51. *Ibidem.*
52. *Ibid.*, pp. 313-4.
53. Cf. Say's criticism of Sismondi, in Say, *Traité de l'économie politique*, book 1, chapter 7 (*Treatise*, especially p. 90n-91).
54. Tracy, *Traité* (1818), p. 315.
55. *Ibid.*, p. 316.
56. *Ibid.*, p. 317.
57. *Ibid.*, p. 318.
58. *Ibid.*, p. 319.

59. *Ibid.*, p. 320.
60. *Commentaire*, pp. 57-8.
61. *Traité* (1818), p. 321.
62. *Ibidem.*
63. *Ibid.*, p. 322. (cf. *Commentaire*, p. 97.)
64. *Ibid.*, p. 325. Tracy illustrates the last remark by comparing the sad fate of the Spanish Americas, with later developments in North America under the influence of "Locke and Franklin".
65. *Ibid.*, p. 326.
66. *Ibid.*, p. 329.
67. On the liberal and idéologue belief in philanthropy and sympathy for the deserving poor, cf. Chamfort, *Oeuvres complètes* (Paris, 1808), vol. II, pp. 116-120; R. Fargher, *The 'Décade Philosophique'*, pp. 291ff; J. Kitchin, *Un journal 'philosophique'*, pp. 201-3.
68. Cabanis, *Quelques principes et quelques vues sur les secours publics*, in *Oeuvres philosophiques*, vol. II, pp. 1-63. For the eighteenth-century background to the discussion of poverty, cf. M. Leroy, *Histoire des idées sociales*, vol. II, chapter 12; O. Hufton, "Towards an understanding of the poor in eighteenth-century France", in *French Government and Society 1500-1850*, ed. Bosher (London, 1973), pp. 145-165.
69. Cf. Kitchin, *op.cit.*, p. 198.

9. LIBERAL POLITICS AND ELITISM

Tracy's political theory may be seen as an attempt to find a balance between principles of democracy and enlightened leadership. He advocated a system of representative government, founded on liberal-constitutional principles and individual rights, which would extend public instruction and civic-mindedness among the people, and which would be led by an enlightened élite. Tracy claimed that this type of political system was the most likely to produce a prosperous, contented and energetic nation, where individual merit would be rewarded, and the least talented would nonetheless receive a basic education in citizenship and a trade.

ENLIGHTENED DEMOCRACY

Tracy was firmly convinced that progressive change had to be initiated by élites, in particular by *savants* of various kinds, politicians and educators. In an age before the rise of modern political parties, parliamentary government was largely a system of rule by notables.[1] Under the Directory (1795-99) the notables included certain idéologues and men sympathetic to that outlook. For Tracy, the essential quality of the élite should be its understanding of the "social art" and the science of "legislation" or social science.[2] The essential test of good government was its principles: was it devoted to the general interest, individual rights, and the security and happiness of the people? He was scarcely concerned about the "politics of experience" in the sense intended by philosophical conservatism.[3] Experience in the narrow technical sense was useful, in the idéologue view, because it implied efficiency. But experience in the broad sense of historically evolving social practices and traditions, was of small relevance to the idéologues: this type of experience had been found guilty by its association with the mass ignorance and oppression of the past.[4] It was the task of the liberal notables to create the institutional, legislative and educational bases of the society, and shape a social consensus around the new institutions. In time, ordinary citizens might understand the practical wisdom, if not the theoretical principles, embodied in the rational social arrangements. But Tracy never speculated on a future in which a more participatory form of democracy would be made possible by generalised enlightenment.

Tracy's conception of government is essentially that of implementing certain principles; it is not a matter of compromises and bargaining among various socio-economic interests. Given his insistence on a politics of principles, he was almost inevitably bound to desire that men of principles (indeed, his own principles) should occupy the positions of authority and influence. The élite should be a knowledge élite rather than a propertied élite, knowledge here being defined in the sense of the social art or social science. Another way of describing Tracy's views is to say that he believed in a meritocracy whose task was to reconcile order, progress, and individual liberty. The democratic element of his thought emphasised parliamentary government, free elections, civil liberties and legal equality; the élitist element emphasised the role of leadership, guidance, knowledge and principles in achieving a rational society.

Pierre Flourens, speaking at Tracy's funeral in March 1836, made the illuminating remark that Tracy had been born into a hereditary nobility, but eventually sought a nobility of merit.[5] If the qualities of the élite were uppermost in Tracy's mind, one might wonder why he professed democratic principles of any kind: why not seek an educational autocracy? The short answer is that he strongly believed in the doctrine that legitimate government is based on the sovereignty of the people. He believed in the superiority of representative government as the form best able to secure the Rights of Man and the general happiness and progress of society. He did not claim that its superiority stemmed from the intrinsic value of political participation, or from an effective articulation of group interests.

According to Tracy, the uneducated masses could not be expected to make any useful contribution to government decision-making: government should be responsible to the people, and govern in their interests, but it should be conducted by an educated élite.[6] Mass political mobilisation had no place in Tracy's outlook, other than for the limited objective of patriotic defence of national boundaries. Social stability was a value which he never under-estimated. This viewpoint had been reinforced by experience of the Terror in 1793-4, when Tracy and several colleagues spent many months in their prison cells reflecting on the dangers of populist demagoguery replacing a stable structure of authority with constitutionally defined procedures and due process of law. The idéologues in 1795 were content with those provisions of the new Constitution which introduced a property qualification for the franchise, declared that private property was the basis of wealth and of the social order, and defined equality as a legal category with no economic implications.[7]

Most liberals in the period before the late nineteenth century held serious reservations about the wisdom of universal suffrage: they generally recommended that voters should have certain qualifications of property, gender or education. Tracy shared their scepticism and caution. He was unwilling, in the first place, to acknowledge that women should play an active role in public life. He argued in his *Commentaire* that although women had the same rights and probably the same capacities as men, they were most usefully occupied in domestic functions, in which they excelled. Men were the "natural" representatives of families in public affairs.[8] The sexes were not "unequal", simply endowed by "nature" with different functional roles. He provided no evidence, however, for his assumption that the division of tasks between men and women was "natural" (thus irreversible) rather than a social convention (and even an oppressive convention). Tracy's view that public life was, and should remain, a sphere of exclusively male influence set him apart from Condorcet, who had vigorously supported equality of education for girls and boys, and encouraged the movement of women into various spheres of public life.[9]

Tracy's conception of a "natural" differentiation of functions, based upon supposed differences in needs, inclinations, and abilities, was potentially open to abuse. Tracy had avoided one possible inconsistency in his discussion of political and legal equality by arguing for the equal rights of blacks in the French colonies; this was an extension of his condemnation of slavery and his support for the implementation of the Rights of Man. On the issue of universal suffrage, however, Tracy found it necessary to invoke restrictions. These were justified by an appeal to a functionalist version of utilitarianism. It was not in the general interest of society, he claimed in 1806, that everyone should participate in every kind of activity. Rather, they should specialise in those activities for which they are best fitted.[10] The problem with this doctrine, of course, is to determine what is the optimal, or the natural, division of labour and to determine whether the actual role occupied by a particular individual or category of individuals is the result of natural talents or of social and cultural conditions. Tracy's doctrine of the paramount influence of education might have suggested to him a more critical analysis of any allegedly "natural" division of labour.

Tracy invoked his principle of utilitarian specialisation in a second area of political influence: he was unwilling to allow the uneducated and the propertyless citizens a decisive voice in determining the composition or the policies of the national legislature. Tracy recognised the need to maintain the principle of popular sovereignty; but he also saw a tension between that principle and the need for expert leadership. He resolved the dilemma in the following way. In discussing the procedures by which a new constitutional convention should be elected, Tracy made two important claims:

(i) no man should be excluded from participating in the electoral process merely by virtue of his birth, wealth, or social rank;

(ii) however, the poor and uneducated masses should participate only in *primary* assemblies; these would elect representatives to intermediate bodies, whose task in turn would be to elect the national representatives.[11]

Those chosen to represent the local assemblies would generally be better educated citizens and less subject to local prejudices, according to Tracy. Such men would be best suited to choosing the membership of a national convention: *c'est là la bonne aristocratie.*[12] The "best" political leadership would emerge from such a tiered structure of representation.

By this indirect method of election, the actual capacities of men might best be correlated with the functions to be performed. All men were fit to participate in primary assemblies;[13] but only a select few had enough knowledge and experience to be suitable electors at a higher level. One advantage of an indirect method of election was that there would be little need to specify precise property qualifications for membership of the intermediate body; equality of rights was preserved without odious restrictions on political participation. Tracy believed that education was more important than property as an index of political wisdom. Although it was empirically true that property and education usually co-existed, the correlation was not perfect. Hence, "reason" would not be best strengthened by giving special privileges to certain "fractions of society" whose material interests might sometimes be contrary to it.[14]

Tracy was willing to allow universal male suffrage providing that the method of election remained indirect. He believed that class legislation would best be avoided by refusing to differentiate between the political rights of various socio-economic groups. The best strategy, he implied, was to emphasise common rights and interests, not differential class qualities, which would only encourage social conflict. Reason was more likely to prevail when not formally attached to the destiny and interest of any social class.[15] He also assumed that the civil equality embodied in the Rights of Man would pose difficulties for discrimination upon the basis of property.

Tracy's primary political orientation was the liberal-constitutionalism of the first Assemblée Nationale of 1789-91. The doctrines of civil equality, universal legal principles and rights, abolition of traditional privileges, separation of Church and State, limited powers of government, defence of private property, and minimal regulation of industry and commerce: these were some of the main articles of political faith among the liberals of 1791. Tracy remained committed to these doctrines throughout the following decades of political upheaval. However, the overthrow of the monarchy, the changing fortunes of the republican régimes, and the rise of the Napoleonic Empire, led him to modify his views on some points and placed strains on the consistency of his outlook. He sometimes felt obliged to make concessions in order to enhance, as he saw it, the long-term success of his principles. It is necessary to return briefly to Tracy's reactions to political events in the 1790s.

Tracy's early political career saw him championing a reformed system of constitutional monarchy, which would incorporate guarantees of various legal and political rights of citizens; which would rationalise the administrative and taxation system; and which would acknowledge the fundamental right of the governed, through elected representatives, to make laws and levy taxes. Tracy's belief in the advantages of representative government in protecting the natural rights of the citizens owed much to the American examples of constitution-making in the 1770s and 1780s, as well as to the general stream of philosophical opinion critical of autocracy and privilege. Tracy assumed, with Locke and Rousseau, that the sovereignty of the people was the basis of legitimate government. During the period of the first Constituent Assembly of 1789-91, Tracy was a firm adherent of a compromise between monarchy and democracy, which finally took shape in the 1791 Constitution.[16] There was no hint of republicanism in the views he expressed. On the contrary he agreed with Lafayette on the importance of maintaining public order[17] and on protection for the royal family at times when popular sentiments seemed to threaten their security; and he criticised all manifestations of "mob" rule in the streets and demagoguery in public journals.

The (unsuccessful) flight of the royal family towards the border in June 1791, widely understood as attempting to rally foreign support to defend the king's prerogatives against the encroachments of the Assembly, caused many of the liberals to reassess their loyalties towards the Crown. Further doubts about the king's sympathies were raised in Tracy's mind six months later when he returned to a military command under Lafayette; when calling upon the king to pay his respects before departing for the front, he was disappointed to find Louis absorbed in the activities of an aristocrat preparing to flee abroad.[18] When the dispute between the liberal constitutionalists (including Lafayette) and the Jacobins reached total breakdown in mid-1792, Tracy resigned his command to seek a more tranquil life of study and domesticity away from the turmoil of public life. The monarchy, alleged to be in collusion with the foreign powers, was declared overthrown after the riots of 10 August, and a National Convention was elected in September 1792 to frame a republican Constitution. The king was executed in January 1793.

Tracy was undoubtedly appalled by these events of 1792-3. During the early months of the Republic before his arrest in November 1793, Tracy maintained an aloof propriety, eschewing political involvement, but doing whatever was necessary to demonstrate his continued "patriotism" and to avoid being condemned as an erstwhile aristocrat of dubious *civisme*. His experience in prison apparently did not colour his later attitudes to republicanism or to monarchy as such, but it undoubtedly reinforced his earlier concerns for public order and political stability. As will be seen later, however, Tracy had become extremely critical of the principle of hereditary power by 1806 when he wrote his *Commentaire*, doubtless in reaction to the development of Napoleon's autocracy.

The idéologues gave their support to the Directorial Constitution of 1795, until 1799 when they supported the installation of Bonaparte as First Consul in a new constitutional system. They naively believed this new régime would contribute to progress in the moral and political sciences, and advance the idéologues' own political and philosophical aspirations. However, Bonaparte's régime rapidly neutralised their political influence, and increasingly isolated them from the social consensus being forged by the First

Consul's domestic and foreign policies. The deterioration in political and personal relationships between Bonaparte and the idéologue members of the Tribunate and Senate, and the evolution of the Consulate into the Empire with a hereditary ruling family, have been documented by many historians and require no further discussion here. Tracy's energies under the Directory had been largely channelled into his work on educational administration and the further development of his theory of idéologie; he was not directly involved in the political struggles of the period. It is difficult to know how far he shared the optimistic illusions of his colleagues. His nomination to a life-tenure position in the Senate suggests that he was known to be a supporter of the new Bonapartist order. Tracy's views on the constitutional problems raised by the Directory, Consulate, and Empire were made known indirectly through his commentary on Montesquieu, commenced two years after the coronation of Napoleon as Emperor in 1804. In the following section, the main lines of Tracy's critique of Montesquieu are discussed, focusing on the main forms of government, their sources of legitimation, and their social effects. The chapter concludes by noting Tracy's celebration of representative government and its supposed connections with happiness, reason and liberty.

CRITIQUE OF MONTESQUIEU

Tracy's major work of political theory was his *Commentaire* on Montesquieu's classic text, *l'Esprit des Lois* (1748). Tracy's work was written during 1806-7 under the Empire, and contained a number of veiled criticisms of Napoleon's régime as part of a critique of the principle of hereditary authority. The circumstances of the publication of the *Commentaire*, and the light it throws on Tracy's view of social science, have already been noted in chapter six. It is now necessary to discuss Tracy's political theory in a more systematic way on the basis of the principles elaborated in the *Commentaire*.

Tracy, following the structure of Montesquieu's work, began by discussing the concept of *law*. Rejecting Montesquieu's proposition that laws are necessary relations deriving from the nature of things, Tracy substituted the idea that a law in society is

> a rule prescribed for our actions by an authority we regard as having the right to make this law: this last condition is necessary, for otherwise the prescribed rule is no more than an arbitrary order, an act of violence and oppression. This idea of law implies that of a penalty attached to its infraction, of a tribunal which applies this penalty, and a physical force which puts it into operation. Without all that, the law is incomplete or illusory.[19]

The "positive" laws made by men in society, "artificial and conventional laws", are to be distinguished from the "laws of nature", which are the necessary expression of the operation of phenomena in specified circumstances. Natural laws are unchangeable, whether those governing falling objects, or those governing the sensible qualities of animate beings including their capacity for happiness and misery. Here again we find Tracy claiming that our "natural" capacities form a kind of substructure of human action, on which a social science of needs and their satisfactions could be built. Natural laws, he claimed, could be discovered through the observation of phenomena; how such observation could yield laws of "human nature" was left to the science of idéologie.

Tracy posed the question of the relation between the positive laws of a society and the natural laws governing our behaviour and capacities. He claimed, in a way reminiscent of the "natural law" theory of the physiocrats, that the "good" and the "just" laws in a society are those which conform most closely to the natural laws.[20] The difficulties of detecting, or facilitating, such a correspondence between the social and natural realms were glossed over. It was for idéologie to demonstrate the basic faculties and needs of man, and for the various human sciences to deduce the social and political institutions which would maximise individual satisfaction within a social framework of authority. The naturalistic terminology disguised the speculative character of the enterprise: the search for natural laws, to which social practices should conform, was a form of political philosophy disguised as an empirical "natural history" of man.

Tracy regarded the science of politics as concerned to find those institutions and practices which would increase and secure human "happiness". Good and just laws were those which were directed towards this objective. Tracy noted that concepts of the "good" and "just" were applicable only to one class of laws, those created by men. These laws should be judged in accordance with their effects upon human happiness (understood in terms of reason and liberty). Natural laws, on the other hand, were not subject to moral judgements: a law of nature was simply "necessary", since it could not be changed by our actions.[21] A genuine discourse on the spirit of laws, said Tracy, should investigate the degree of correspondence between positive laws and the natural laws of human action, in relation to the circumstances and organisation of various societies.[22] Montesquieu was found inadequate for failing to undertake such a project.

Tracy examined Montesquieu's division of government (republic, monarchy, despotism) and found it of little use for his purpose of assessing how various institutional forms contributed to the happiness of man or conformed to the natural laws of human behaviour. Tracy noted that Montesquieu's first type, *republic*, was commonly stretched to cover a multitude of diverse historical cases, including various kinds of democracy, oligarchy and aristocracy. Moreover, the term republic was not an appropriate contrast to monarchy, for there were nations like the United States or Holland, usually called republics, which had a single chief magistrate.[23]

Montesquieu's second type, *monarchy*, should strictly denote a government where executive power was held by a single person; but this fact alone, said Tracy, did not sufficiently describe the essence of that social organisation, and could be found to co-exist with many other diverse characteristics. In Great Britain, for example, authority resided in some respects with a noble aristocracy; and the *ancien régime* of France was really an ecclesiastical and feudal aristocracy, of both robe and sword.[24] In fairness to Montesquieu, it should be pointed out that Tracy's two examples were not inconsistent with Montesquieu's own view of monarchy, wherein a single person governs by fixed and established laws, and where power flows through intermediate bodies, particularly the nobility and judiciary.[25]

According to Tracy, Montesquieu's third type, *despotism*, should not be regarded as a separate type of government, but rather as an abuse of power which may enter to some extent into all political forms, whenever the rule of law gives way to the arbitrary will of one man or of a group. No government is ever established with arbitrary rule as its guiding principle; it is rather a degeneration which may occur when people have not taken adequate precautions against its emergence. The nearest approximation, said Tracy, would not be the Oriental empires, but Denmark, where the king had been granted unlimited discretionary power in order to prevent a restoration of influence by the nobles and clergy. Yet his rule had been so moderate that it seemed a misnomer to call his government a despotism. Even the old French monarchy, with its claims to hold authority from God alone, was not a despotism, despite its enormous abuses: it was always a limited monarchy. The term despotism, then, could not stand as a separate type of government. In practice it usually meant simply a brutally conducted monarchy.[26]

The threefold classification of republic, monarchy and despotism, Tracy concluded, was completely unsatisfactory, producing many confusions, and was not applicable to many of the states commonly contained in each category. What alternative classifications were available? Tracy equally rejected a division of governments which had been attributed to Helvétius in a letter allegedly written to Montesquieu.[27] According to this conception, all governments could be simply divided into "the good", which do not yet exist, and "the bad", which variously enrich the governors at the expense of the governed. Tracy's main objection to this dichotomy was that since each government may produce some good and some bad practical effects, it could be placed in one or other category at various times.[28] Moreover, Tracy professed to adopt a more detached and objective attitude than Helvétius, claiming he did not seek to judge the intrinsic merit of a government's theoretical principles. His *Commentaire* was said to be more akin to Montesquieu's work, in being descriptive and analytical: Tracy wanted only to "describe what exists, show the different consequences arising from the various modes of social organisation, and leave to the reader the task of drawing his own conclusions in favour of one or another form".[29]

After his claim to be presenting only the facts, Tracy proposed his own twofold classification of the "fundamental principles" of governments (leaving aside the "diverse forms" which they might take). The first was called *gouvernement national ou de droit commun*, and the second was called *gouvernement spécial ou de droit particulier et d'exceptions*. Tracy added in a note that "we could also say *public* or *private*, not only because one is founded on the *general* interest and the other on some *private* interest, but also because the one effects *publicity* in all its deliberations and the other, *mystery*".[30] The reader could be left in no doubt concerning the preference of the author.

Tracy's first type of government, however organised in detail, was based on the principle that "all rights and powers belong to the whole body of the nation, reside in it, emanate from it, and only exist by it and for it". Such a government would proclaim the principle (asserted in the *Parlement* of Paris in October 1788) that holders of public office, *qua* officials, have only duties, while the citizens alone have rights. A "national" government of this type might take one of many possible forms, such as absolute democracy (where the whole nation strictly exercises all powers); representative government (where power is delegated to officials elected periodically); various forms of aristocracy (where power is granted wholly or partly to groups of men, whether for life, whether hereditary, or with powers of co-option); or it might even be a monarchy (where power is entrusted to a single man, with hereditary rights or otherwise). Beneath this diversity of possible forms, there would remain the fundamental principle that the system might be *changed* or abolished if the nation so desired, and that no-one had the right to oppose the general will as manifested in the recognised manner.[31]

The second type of government included all those forms whose authority was based on sources of legitimacy other than the general will— such as divine right, conquest, birth in a certain place or caste, mutual capitulation, or an agreement of some kind. As with the general will, these diverse sources of particular rights could also give rise to many forms of democracies, aristocracies and monarchies: but different kinds of rights would be recognised. The organisation of a "special" government was difficult to alter by legal methods because this would require agreement by groups with very different interests and beliefs.[32]

Tracy reiterated that he was not concerned to judge the relative merits of each type of particular right, nor the merits of national and special governments. His point of departure was, with Montesquieu, to examine the nature of "the laws which tend to conserve each form".[33] It soon became evident, however, as the comparative analysis proceeded, that Tracy was a strong advocate of national government based on the general will, and especially a champion of representative government as that form most likely to develop the talents and protect the interests of its citizens. In his distinction between two main forms of government, it is noteworthy that he was less concerned with details of institutional organisation than with types of legitimacy and the effects of policies upon the citizens.

Tracy criticised Montesquieu's discussion of the cultural sources of legitimacy and stability (the *sentiments* which must be held by the citizens) in relation to each of the forms of government. Montesquieu had claimed that the sentiments of virtue, honour and fear corresponded to his classification of governments: republic, monarchy and despotism. Tracy found this list of sentiments misleading and inappropriate. He conceded that a sentiment such as virtue, honour or fear might be seen as the *principe conservateur* of a political society, enabling it to continue over time; but that was quite different from the *principe moteur* of a society, which arose from the actions of its governing power.[34] For example, fear among the population might well facilitate and encourage despotism, but that cannot make fear the "principle" of this government; despotism is a tendency towards the abuse of power found in all types of government, and stems therefore from a variety of sources. Moreover, a reasonable man might prefer to suffer arbitrary abuses and thus forestall even worse suffering, but his decision could be seen as motivated by reason and not by fear. In the same way, in seeking to avoid greater levels of suffering, it may be that citizens would voluntarily grant a government greater powers in response to a temporary crisis.

Montesquieu's principle of honour (and ambition) in a monarchy, and the principle of virtue (and moderation) in a republic, are also found to be deficient by Tracy. All these sentiments may take contradictory forms, some of which are elevating and some of which are despicable. Honour may be either dedicated to the good it produces, or may be merely a glittering exterior indulging in fashionable vices. Ambition may take a generous form, content to obtain the gratitude of one's fellows, or a selfish and power-hungry form which uses any means available. Moderation may likewise vary, being wise or weak, magnanimous or dissimulating, according to circumstances. As for virtue, why is it appropriate only to republics? Would it be out of place in other governments, and is that desirable or inevitable? Does Montesquieu really believe that the vices he portrays in court life are as useful and necessary to monarchy as other more virtuous qualities?[35]

Having interrogated and rejected Montesquieu's classification of the types of government and the sentiments which sustained them, Tracy pursued his own view of the types of government and their consequences, beginning with the diverse forms comprised in the type called "national" (where sovereignty lay with the whole nation). The first of these forms was "pure democracy" or "absolute democracy". According to Tracy, this system could be relevant only to a very small territory, and could last for only a short period of time. It was thus an "almost impossible" system of government, confined to a few primitive tribes and peoples in a remote corner of the earth. As soon as social relations became more highly developed, it rapidly fell into anarchy and, in its quest for peace, was led to aristocracy or tyranny. Even the ancient Greek democracies were of short duration, and were not self-sustaining— they were always protected by their federative links; and in another sense, they were really aristocracies of free citizens, considering the huge numbers of slaves excluded from public life.[36]

If the "original democracy" was transformed into an aristocracy, and thereby into a relation between superior and inferior classes, the *principes conservateurs* of the latter system came to consist in the pride and competence of one class and the humility and ignorance of the other. In the same way, if direct democracy was transformed into a monarchy (having a single ruler, whether hereditary or for life), the government was stabilised by such sentiments as the monarch's sense of dignity and superiority; by the arrogance, ambition and devotion of the courtiers, and their scorn for the inferior classes; and finally, by the superstitious respect among the lower classes for all this grandeur and their desire to please those who were decked out in it.[37]

All these sentiments, said Tracy, were functionally useful for the maintenance of monarchy, whatever may be our judgement of such ideas from other viewpoints and whatever their other effects on society at large. He suggested that an aristocratic or a monarchical form of government was in theory possible for a "national" type of government, so long as general respect for the rights of man and the sovereignty of the citizens as a whole still predominated. In practice, however, respect for the rights of citizens tended to be soon forgotten. These governments would quickly turn into "special" governments based on the legitimacy of particular rights, as soon as a general respect for the rights of man was abandoned.[38] The only form of "national" government which promised to be long lasting and consistent, in Tracy's view, was representative government.

Tracy assumed that a government whose *principe conservateur* most closely conformed to the sentiments of "human nature" would not only have the best chance of survival, but would be the most likely to encourage the development of individual talents and thereby the prosperity and happiness of all. Tracy's discussion therefore turned rapidly away from Montesquieu's functionalist preoccupation with the sentiments needed to sustain a government,[39] towards a concern with the social consequences of each type of government. Tracy looked primarily at the kinds of sentiments, opinions, and knowledge typically engendered and fostered by each type of government: these social and cultural effects, said Tracy, were "much more important for the happiness of men".[40]

Perhaps the most important area for an idéologue like Tracy was the extent to which the various governments tried to curtail or to encourage the development of knowledge and its diffusion among the citizens. Tracy first examined the monarchical and aristocratic forms of "special" government. He gave a scathing portrait of the type of education fostered by a hereditary monarchy.[41] Whether its legitimacy was based on conquest, ancient possession, social pact, or divine right, the hereditary monarchy

> is bound to inculcate and propagate the maxims of passive obedience, a profound veneration for established forms, confidence in the permanence of these political arrangements, a great antipathy to the spirit of innovation and

> enquiry, and great aversion to the discussion of principles.[42]

To this end, the monarch would draw support from religious ideas which, influencing the mind from infancy, formed lasting habits and firm opinions before the age of reflection. Priests would have to be made dependent upon the monarch's power in order to be a source of stability instead of undermining his authority. And among the religions, the monarch should promote the interests of that which is most concerned to dominate minds; prohibit enquiry; preach the sanctity of precedent, tradition and hierarchy; uphold faith and credulity; and spread the greatest number of dogmas and mysteries.[43]

In the realm of culture and society, the monarch would seek to induce gay and superficial qualities of mind and manners, whether in the fine arts and literature or in the graceful reaches of high society. Erudition and the exact sciences might be safely encouraged; indeed, remarked Tracy, the success of the French in these accomplishments, and their corresponding fame and vanity, long diverted them from serious business and philosophical research, matters which a monarch should seek to repress or discourage. If he succeeds in all these methods of social control, there is little more to be done, to protect his power and stability, than

> encourage in all the classes of society a spirit of individual vanity and a desire for distinction. For this purpose it will suffice to create a multiplicity of ranks, titles, privileges and distinctions, in such a way that the most esteemed honours are those which are most closely associated with his person.[44]

These measures, according to Tracy, captured the general spirit in which the education of the subjects should be directed in a hereditary monarchy. It was necessary that precautions be taken

> to provide only a limited instruction among the lowest classes of the people, and to restrict it virtually to religious teachings. For this class of men needs to be kept in a degraded state of ignorance and crude passions, so that they do not progress from an admiration of all that is above them in society, to a desire to escape their miserable condition; or even to conceive of the possibility of change, which would make them the blind and dangerous instrument of reformers of all kinds, whether fanatical and hypocritical or benevolent and enlightened.[45]

Similarly, the aristocratic form of "special" government, where the nobility claim legitimate authority over the rest of the nation, would be concerned to restrict the content and diffusion of education. However, wrote Tracy, there were two main differences, one concerning the role of religion, and the other concerning the need for serious education among the nobility themselves. In the first place, the noble aristocrats are less imposing and less united than a monarch; they therefore cannot plausibly claim the authority of divine right, nor can they with confidence manipulate religious ideas and the priesthood. Religion, as an instrument of social control, must therefore be used with more caution and discretion. Religious ideas should not be unduly encouraged by the nobility lest the priests turned it to their advantage; but neither should the nobility combat religion by fostering "reason and enlightenment", for that would "soon destroy the spirit of dependence and servility".[46]

Secondly, the interests of the aristocracy differed from those of a monarch also in regard to the education of *la classe supérieure* of society. Whereas the nobles and courtiers in a monarchy could be encouraged to adopt a spirit of vanity, levity and lack of reflection, the governing body of an aristocracy required in its members qualities of solid knowledge, hard work, business acumen, capacity for reflection, a circumspection and prudence even in their pleasures, and a certain gravity and simplicity of manners. The ruling nobles had to understand man and society and the interests of various states, if only the better to combat them when necessary. Their principal study and occupation should be *la science politique* in all its dimensions. Insofar as such knowledge was cultivated, the aristocracy had a strong interest in confining it to themselves. They had even more to fear from an enlightened *tiers-état* than did a monarch, though the latter also was most threatened from this quarter.[47]

Tracy ignored the educational doctrines appropriate to pure democracies because the latter were largely theoretical or "imaginary" systems, and because those which had existed were operated by primitive peoples among whom there was no "education in a strict sense". Tracy equally passed over what Montesquieu had called despotism because such a government was generally only a brutal form of monarchy.[48] Tracy had a little more to say about the monarchical and aristocratic forms of "national" government, whose interests would be largely the same as those discussed above as "special" governments. The difference was that, as national governments, they would have to demonstrate more respect for the governed since they claimed to derive their legitimacy from the general will. They could not brutalise the people, nor weaken and impair the minds of *la classe supérieure*, without undermining their own character as a national and patriotic government based on the rights of man, and without thus reverting to a form of "special" government. In the latter case, their legitimacy would be weak if the citizens had previously experienced the benefits of a government of universal rights where "reason and truth" were not neglected.[49]

Tracy regarded legislation as one of the key influences shaping the ideas and behaviour of citizens: all laws had the effect of inspiring certain sentiments and discouraging others, tending to produce certain actions and restraining others of an opposite kind. In the long term, the laws thereby guided the *moeurs* and habits of men[50] The question posed by Tracy is what type of laws are most conducive to the various forms of government. Having once more criticised many of Montesquieu's views as inconsistent, imprecise, based upon faulty classification, and inattentive to the requirements of human nature,[51] Tracy again adopted his own nomenclature to tackle the question of how forms of law were related to forms of government.

Monarchy, in the sense of the authority of a single ruler, had its origins in a condition of ignorance and barbarism. It tended to be despotic, with its administration and revenue-raising conducted by force rather than by a system of legislation. The ruler was obliged to control the nomination of his successor and also to make use of religious authority where possible to control his ignorant subjects. To transcend this precarious form of social organisation, the ruler must elaborate a more systematic and complete form of authority, perhaps establishing a precise line of hereditary succession confined to a sovereign family. But such authority would be too isolated to survive unsupported for long. It was necessary to create around it a great number of ennobled families, whose permanent interests were tied to those of the monarchy: the term "honour", said Tracy, was merely a mask for their real interest in securing the obedience of the whole people.[52]

The private rights of the monarch should be buttressed by the private (but subordinate) rights of a nobility who were strong yet submissive. The monarch should make use of respected and established forms, while making them dependent on him; everything should have a certain plausibility that avoids recourse to discussions of original rights and authority. Montesquieu's functionalist advice to monarchs on how to preserve their system was thereby vindicated, according to Tracy. Even the most contentious point, the need for venality of offices, was confirmed by this analysis, because the monarch was still able to maintain his choice of officials, his revenue was increased, and the successful purchasers were sure to uphold that external show and grandeur which was so important in a monarchy.[53]

Finally, this venality helped to impoverish the *tiers-état*, profit the treasury, and swell the fortunes of *la classe privilégiée* by the entry of new wealth from below. This was an important consideration, since in this system, all the wealth of society was produced entirely by the industry, commerce and useful arts of *la classe inférieure*. Members of the latter class would rapidly become the most wealthy and powerful in society, were they not constantly repressed and exploited, for they had already accumulated the most knowledge and wisdom by virtue of their occupations. If the members of *la classe moyenne* (i.e., the more wealthy and educated sections of the *tiers-état*) were not tempted by foolish vanity to seek entry into the nobility, they might soon take hold of all the benefits in society. The intermarriage between rich plebeians and poor nobles was one way of preventing this from occurring.[54]

Montesquieu's advice to an aristocracy on how best to preserve their authority[55] was also endorsed by Tracy as accurate, except to warn that Montesquieu's prohibition against aristocratic fortunes should be balanced by ensuring that members of *la bourgeoisie* did not accumulate great wealth; otherwise, the richest commoners would have to be absorbed into the ranks of the aristocracy itself. Monarchies and aristocracies claiming to be based upon popular sovereignty had the same interests and the same available methods as the "special" forms already discussed, except that they had to be more circumspect in their tactics, for they should be seen to rule in the interests of the whole people. It was clear enough, noted Tracy, that all those methods designed to protect the "particular" interests of the governors were "contrary to the general good and to the prosperity of the masses".[56]

This account of Tracy's critique of Montesquieu may be concluded by discussing the "great problem" of arranging the institutions of authority so that "none of them may trespass on the limits prescribed by the general interest", and so that the authorities be kept in line by "peaceful and legal means".[57] Montesquieu had devoted considerable attention to the "balance" of power among the executive, legislature, and judiciary, taking England as the best example of such a system of checks and balances. Tracy found that the English system operated in a somewhat different manner from that envisaged by Montesquieu. Tracy also claimed that the freedoms enjoyed by Englishmen had little to do with these institutional checks and balances. His critique of Montesquieu and of the English Constitution was inspired partly by his dislike of the influence enjoyed by the Crown and the hereditary nobility in that country, and partly by his admiration for the United States constitutional arrangements. These antipathies and enthusiasms naturally endeared his work to Jefferson, whose interpretation of Montesquieu as an Anglophile coincided with Tracy's reading.[58]

The principle of the "division of powers" as a bulwark against arbitrary government was accepted by the idéologues as a major triumph of the social art. There were obvious dangers to the liberty of citizens if two or more of the branches of authority fell into the same hands. The difficulty, wrote Tracy, was not to perceive this manifest fact, but to discover the methods of avoiding it. Montesquieu, said Tracy, "spared himself the trouble of seeking out these methods; he preferred to think he had found them", namely in his idealised conception of the English system of government.[59] Montesquieu had too quickly forgotten that legislative, executive and judicial functions are really only delegated trusts, and that authority flows by right from the will of the nation. Montesquieu had been preoccupied with his view of these powers as independent rivals, which need only to be mutually restrained for public liberty to be protected. He had failed to note the crucial importance of executive power, and thus conceded it too readily to a single man, even on a hereditary basis, purely because an individual was alleged to possess more unity of action than a plurality. He should have asked whether such a man would permit free action to exist around him, and whether a ruler chosen by chance would have the necessary wisdom for governing. Montesquieu had given no satisfactory reason for the continued existence of a privileged hereditary chamber in the legislature with a veto power over decisions by the freely elected chamber. The judicial functions of the House of Lords did not give that chamber an independent regulative function: it was really "an appendage and advance-guard of the executive power, ... and to give it a veto power and judicial authority only strengthens the party of the court ..."[60]

The English system, according to Tracy, continued to operate not because of any "balance", but because of public sentiments and the ability of the executive to control the machinery of authority. Public attachment to personal liberty and a free press, and the existence of certain civil and criminal procedures, were what protected the citizens from their government. Public opinion could be made known; and when the king had abused his power, he had been overthrown. This deposition of the monarch, wrote Tracy, is a last resort forced upon a civilised people, who will endure many evils before turning to such a remedy. They may even become so conditioned to servility that they lose the desire or capacity for change. Tracy added, in a note to the 1819 edition, that when he had written these remarks under the Napoleonic régime, "we greatly feared that the oppression would last so long that people would become accustomed to it".[61] The problem of the division of powers was better resolved in the United States than in England, according to Tracy; the United States Constitution prescribed what should be done where the executive and legislature were in opposition, where one exceeded its authority, or where constitutional amendment was necessary.[62]

Tracy's remarks criticising hereditary monarchy were coloured by his attitude to the Napoleonic régime; the defender of the 1791 compromise had become a mordant critic of the hereditary principle. In England, said Tracy, the monarch was really "a parasite, a superfluous wheel in the machine, augmenting its friction and expense".[63] The monarch depended on his ministers, who actually governed the country, and his own influence depended on controlling part of the legislature. Tracy rejected the belief that unity in the executive was best obtained by granting it to a single individual: this had been the doctrine of the physiocrats. On the contrary, a plural executive, e.g. a council of ministers, could still reach united decisions by majority; it was better able to implement them than an individual, and would be more consistent in policy.[64] Tracy outlined what he saw as the distinction between the American presidency and the Napoleonic régime. There was a great difference, he claimed, between a single chief executive who was answerable to the electors at intervals, whose powers were circumscribed, and who remained "the first magistrate of a free people" rather than a monarch; and, on the other hand, a single chief executive whose fate was tied to that of the régime as a whole, whose powers were much broader, and whose succession was established in a governing family. The interest of this second type of ruler becomes separated from that of the people: they want peace and happiness, while he thrives on discord and military adventures. Such a man clings to power, or loses it only amid public calamity.[65]

For Tracy, the hereditary principle is false in both theory and practice. It is absurd, he jested, that a man will unthinkingly obey a hereditary monarch, when "he would be considered deranged if he declared hereditary the functions of his coachman or his cook".[66] Rare is the man who could not be corrupted in time by unconstrained power; and it is even less likely that his eldest child would be capable of wise and modest rule. The greatest problem, however, is that the principle of hereditary power tends naturally to be exclusive and unlimited, and thus inconsistent with the principle of the general will, which tends to be temporary and revocable. Liberty and monarchy are antithetical principles.[67] Montesquieu had been correct to detect corrupt tendencies in monarchist government: luxury, disorder, conquest, and contempt for the knowledge found in moral philosophy. Hereditary power "divides the nation in different classes to dominate some by means of the others, subjects them all by illusions, and consequently produces misery and error in theory and practice."[68] For Tracy, then, the problem of ensuring the liberty and happiness of citizens could not be resolved "so long as one gives too much power to one man", such that he could not be removed without violence and without changing the whole system.[69] Tracy's remarks on the defects of those governments not based on the general will, serve as background to his discussion of the system he saw as most in accordance with human nature, reason, liberty and happiness: representative government.

The conception of representative government outlined by Tracy in his *Commentaire* is an ideal-type construction, not a description of any existing system nor an average of historical examples.[70] Representative government, in his view, may be demonstrated to be the most advanced form of political organisation, and the most in accordance with fully developed human capacities. It is the system created by free and rational men in order to maximise that same liberty and reason. It is the fulfilment of the science of politics, taking that science as concerned with social happiness.[71] Unlike earlier forms of democracy, founded in ignorance, representative government is "the democracy of enlightened reason".[72]

In representative government, said Tracy, all the citizens participate in electing their delegates, and limit the extent of public authority in accordance with the provisions of an agreed constitution. Whereas direct democracy belongs to primitive peoples in a confined territory and is of short duration, representative government is a democratic form capable of continuous existence and is suitable for states of all sizes. It is the state of *la nature perfectionnée*.[73] Representative government, in Tracy's view, is "a new invention", still unknown in the time of Montesquieu. It could scarcely have been created before the great effects of the invention of printing had been understood, and in fact was not conceived until three centuries after the discovery of "that art which has changed the face of the world". The written word, Tracy pointed out, facilitates both communication among the citizens, and the delegates' accounting for their actions.[74]

The *principe conservateur* among the citizens living under representative government, according to Tracy, is "love of liberty and equality, or if one likes, of peace and justice".[75] The spirit of the citizens is opposed to the spirit of conquest and usurpation (an obvious critique of Napoleon, and an anticipation of Benjamin Constant's famous brochure[76] of 1814). They are more concerned to protect their possessions, and seek to extend them only through the development of their own talents and industry, never through violating others' rights or through appropriating public wealth. They feel threatened themselves by an injustice suffered by their neighbour at the hands of the public authorities. They are not deflected from their concern for the rights of all by any prospect of personal gains or favours; for in the latter case, they would soon be led to condone arbitrary actions by the government in the hope of obtaining personal reward.[77]

These sentiments sustaining representative government are closely linked to Tracy's conception of human nature. Man's "natural" sentiments are held to consist in "simplicity, the habit of work, scorn of vanity, and love of independence".[78] Tracy did not explain why such qualities were more inherent in man than vanity, idleness and submissiveness. His viewpoint was based on an assumption, held by Rousseau and many philosophes, that "natural man" was unpretentious and uncorrupted. That so many men were victims of "unnatural" sentiments was an indictment of the social institutions and culture which facilitated such practices and values. The metaphor of "nature" as a pristine form of goodness is a frequent theme in the writings of Tracy and the idéologues. They simultaneously argued that society is the product of art and labour, but also that a fully developed society in some way recaptures and extends a "natural" archetype. In any case, men's "natural" sentiments need to be nurtured and encouraged in order to survive and develop. These simple and industrious qualities, he claimed, are so much "in our nature" that they can be "infallibly and necessarily produced" in us through "a little habit, good sense, some wise laws, and the experience that violence and intrigue seldom bring success". The virtuous qualities arising from human nature were quite different, in his opinion, from the sentiments demanded by Montesquieu's "republican virtue", because the latter was based on self-renunciation, a motive which Tracy saw as contrary to human nature and which could thus be sustained only for a temporary period and by fanaticism.[79]

One of Tracy's main criteria for good government is the extent to which reason and knowledge are protected and encouraged. Unlike the governments founded on various kinds of privilege, representative government was closely linked with the pursuit and protection of reason and truth.

> (Representative government) can in no way fear the truth; its constant interest is to protect it. Founded solely on nature and reason, its only enemies are error and prejudice. It must always try to foster sound and solid knowledge of all kinds; it cannot subsist unless they prevail. All that is good and true is in its favour, all that is bad or false is opposed to it. Thus, it should encourage in every way the progress and especially the diffusion of knowledge, for it has a greater need of spreading knowledge than of making new discoveries. Being essentially united with equality, justice, and *la saine morale*, it must constantly attack that most dangerous kind of inequality, connected with all the others: the inequality of talents and knowledge in the different classes of society. It

> must continually try to protect *la classe inférieure* from the vices of ignorance and misery, and *la classe opulente* from those of insolence and false knowledge. It must try to bring them both nearer to *la classe mitoyenne*, which is naturally imbued with the spirit of order, work, justice and reason, since, by its position and its direct interest, it is equally distant from all excesses.[80]

This is clearly a philosophical claim about social and political perfectibility rather than an empirical analysis of institutional structures and historical practices.

According to Tracy, the "only thing which makes one social organisation preferable to another is that it is better able to make happy the members of the society".[81] However, if there are established ways in which the citizens' desires can be made known, this makes it more likely that they will be governed in accordance with their will.[82] These arguments show that Tracy ultimately rejected the *dirigiste* solution which had lurked in the background of idéologue thought in regard to the reconstruction of society and culture. He declared that politics is about subjective wants, not objective interests. This was to place a considerable distance between his liberal political theory and the centralist solutions of both the physiocrats and the egalitarian Jacobins.

Tracy argued that an abstract ideal must undergo considerable change if it is to be implemented in a society. In the case of France, he concluded (in a note added after the Restoration, in the 1819 edition of the *Commentaire*) that

> constitutional monarchy, or representative government with a single hereditary leader, is now, and for a very long time to come, despite its imperfections, the best of all possible governments for all the peoples of Europe and especially for France.[83]

Was Tracy simply inconsistent and opportunistic in making this relativist concession? He denied it, claiming that he was "only establishing the very important difference ... between the abstractions of theory and the realities of practice".[84] Tracy's *Commentaire* was nevertheless seen by liberals as an important contribution to the political debate in Restoration France. The publisher of the anonymous 1817 edition had claimed that publication of a French edition, several years after the American edition, was "a true service to the liberals of all countries".[85] While Tracy's critique of the hereditary principle may have appeared misplaced in the context of the Restoration, his defence of individual liberty and free speech, his emphasis on the principle of popular sovereignty, and his view of the need to constrain the powers of the executive, and restrict the role of the state in economic regulation,[86] marked his work as belonging to the main currents of liberal thought.

The *Commentaire* also showed that Tracy's thought had become more firmly gradualist in outlook under the Empire: the inculcationist perspective of 1796-1801, seeking to hasten the spread of reason, gave way to a long-term evolutionary viewpoint. Tracy did not withdraw his view that reason would ultimately triumph, or that representative government was the highest form of social organisation. There was an implication, however, that the gap between ideal and reality, though diminishing, remained large. The subjective wants of men seldom coincided with theoretical analysis of their objective interests as rational beings. Tracy also appeared to agree that the stability and security of established forms of authority were a "good" in themselves, especially if these forms enjoyed the support of their citizens.

The source of progress in human societies was knowledge and the rational shaping of social experience. Education was the means of bridging the gap between ideal and reality; it was the means by which a society sustained itself (socialisation) and advanced the happiness of its citizens (economic, political and technological progress). The importance of education in the idéologues' thinking can scarcely be underestimated. This is the subject of the final chapter.

Notes

1. Cf. Max Weber, "Politics as a Vocation", in *From Max Weber: Essays in Sociology*, ed. Gerth and Mills (New York, 1946), pp. 100ff.
2. In the sense discussed in chapter six.
3. Cf. the writings of Professor Michael Oakeshott, and the collection of essays edited by P.T. King and B.C. Parekh, *Politics and Experience* (Cambridge, 1968).
4. This was also the viewpoint of the physiocrat Mirabeau, and of the idéologue Sieyès: cf. P. Bastid, *Sieyès et sa pensée*, p. 388.
5. J.-P.-M. Flourens, *Discours* (1836), p. 9.
6. Cf. the remark by Amaury Duval, editor of *la Décade*, on 29 January 1797: "the inequality of talents would serve the equality of happiness". Cited in M. Régaldo, "Lumières, Elite, Démocratie", p. 203.
7. Cf. text of Constitution in J. Godechot, *Les Constitutions de la France depuis 1789* (Paris, 1970), pp. 101f. The property qualification operated at the second level of a three-tier structure of representation. See also G. Lefebvre, *The Thermidoreans* (London, 1965), chapter 9; J. Godechot, *Les institutions* (1951), pp. 395f.
8. *Commentaire* (Paris, 1819), pp. 177-8. For another instance of Tracy ascribing certain qualities of mind and temperament to women, cf. *De l'amour*, pp. 50-1. Tracy, however, condemns social systems in which women are domesticated slaves, "the playthings and victims of men": *Commentaire*, p. 299. Tracy argues that it is only in countries guided by liberty and reason that women escape various forms of oppression and indignity: *ibid.*, p. 103.

9. For Condorcet's views, cf. *Selected Writings*, pp. 97-103, 134-140; the latter extract is also reprinted in C. Hippeau (ed.), *L'instruction publique* (1881), pp. 279-288. For a strong statement of the traditional distinction between male (public) and female (domestic) roles, cf. the "Discours de Mirabeau sur l'instruction publique" (1791), in Hippeau, *op.cit.*, especially pp. 12-14. This *discours* is usually attributed to Cabanis who was the doctor and friend of the comte de Mirabeau (not to be confused with his father, the physiocratic marquis de Mirabeau). The report on public instruction by Talleyrand in September 1791 made similarly traditionalist distinctions: see Hippeau, *op.cit.*, especially pp. 175-181.
10. *Commentaire*, pp. 177, 179.
11. *Ibid.*, pp. 170-6, 179-180.
12. *Ibid.*, p. 180. For the meaning of the term "aristocracy" in this context, see also Cabanis, *Oeuvres philosophiques*, vol. II, pp. 467, 472, 475.
13. Tracy made a few obvious exceptions on grounds of age, infirmity of mind, criminality, or employment by foreign powers: *Commentaire* p. 177.
14. *Ibid.*, pp. 175-6.
15. *Ibid.*, pp. 174-6.
16. Cf. *M. de Tracy à M. Burke* (1790), p. 9.
17. *Tracy à Burke*, p. 13.
18. Mignet, "Notice historique sur ... Destutt de Tracy", p. 252.
19. *Commentaire*, pp. 1-2.
20. *Ibid.*, pp. 2-4, and 220.
21. *Ibid.*, pp. 4-5.
22. *Ibid.*, p. 6.
23. *Ibid.*, p. 7.
24. *Ibid.*, p. 8.
25. Montesquieu, *De l'esprit des lois* (1748) (Paris, 1922), vol. I, book 2, chapter 4.
26. *Commentaire*, pp. 8-10. For further discussion of the three forms, cf. *ibid*, pp. 63-6. See also Cabanis, *Oeuvres philosophiques*, vol. II, pp. 466-473.
27. It has been shown that the letter was probably a forgery, written by the editor of the 1795 edition of the *Oeuvres* of Helvétius, the abbé Laroche: cf. R. Koebner, "The authenticity of the letters on the 'Esprit des lois' attributed to Helvétius", *Bulletin of the Institute of Historical Research*, vol. 24 (1951), pp. 19-43. Tracy had reprinted the letter in the American edition of his work: *A Commentary and Review of Montesquieu's Spirit of Laws* (Philadelphia, 1811), pp. 285-9.
28. *Commentaire*, pp. 10-11; cf. *Commentary* (1811), p. 288 for the distinction attributed to Helvétius.
29. *Commentaire*, p. 12.
30. *Ibidem*.
31. *Ibid.*, pp. 13-14.
32. *Ibid.*, pp. 14-15.
33. *Ibid.*, p. 15.
34. *Ibid.*, p. 16.
35. *Ibid.*, pp. 17-19.
36. *Ibid.*, pp. 21-2.
37. *Ibid.*, pp. 25-6.
38. *Ibid.*, pp. 26-7.
39. *Ibid.*, p. 31.
40. *Ibid.*, p. 27.
41. Tracy also allowed for an "elective monarchy", *ibid*, p. 38: one possible example was Bonaparte's authority as Consul for life, and later as Emperor, both ratified by plebiscite. Tracy, however, possibly would have initially included these systems under his category of national governments, owing to their profession of respect for the rights of man, but would have argued that the rights tended to be undermined by the form of authority itself.

42. *Commentaire*, p. 35.
43. *Ibid.*, pp. 35-6. It would be of some interest here to compare and contrast the advice to a prince given by Machiavelli, Montesquieu and Tracy.
44. *Ibid.*, p. 37.
45. *Ibid.*, pp. 37-8.
46. *Ibid.*, pp. 39-40.
47. *Ibid.*, pp. 41-2.
48. *Ibid.*, pp. 42-3, 64.
49. *Ibid.*, pp. 43-4.
50. "Quels sont les moyens", p. 463; *Commentaire*, p. 46.
51. *Commentaire*, pp. 47-50.
52. *Ibid.*, pp. 51-2.
53. *Ibid.*, pp. 53-4.
54. *Ibid.*, pp. 54-5.
55. Montesquieu, *De l'esprit des lois*, book 5, chapter 8; Tracy, *Commentaire*, pp. 48-9.
56. *Commentaire*, p. 56.
57. *Ibid.*, p. 159.
58. Cf. Chinard, *Jefferson et les idéologues*, chapter 2; Lafayette, *Mémoires*, IV, p. 350-1.
59. *Commentaire*, pp. 150-2, 226.
60. *Ibid.*, pp. 152-4.
61. *Ibid.*, pp. 156-7 and 157n.
62. *Ibid.*, pp. 159-160.
63. *Ibid.*, p. 186. Tracy even argued (pp. 111-2) that representative government would be "cheaper" to operate because the court and idle aristocracy would not be a drain on public funds. Max Weber, a century later, argued that democratic egalitarianism breeds an increasingly expensive bureaucratic structure: cf. *From Max Weber*, p. 224.
64. *Ibid.*, pp. 185-9.
65. *Ibid.*, pp. 190-2.
66. *Ibid.*, p. 194.
67. *Ibid.*, pp. 194-7.
68. *Ibid.*, p. 198.
69. *Ibid.*, pp. 226-7.
70. I mean to suggest a parallel with Weber's concept of an ideal-type: cf. Max Weber, *Methodology of the Social Sciences* (New York, 1949), p. 90. Tracy's model of representative government is doubly an ideal-type, given his passionate attachment to that particular type of government.
71. *Commentaire*, p. 308.
72. *Ibid.*, p. 57.
73. *Ibid.*, p. 22.
74. *Ibid.*, pp. 23, 115.
75. *Ibid.*, p. 23. (The American translation by Jefferson used the words "country and equality": *Commentary*, p. 19.)
76. B. Constant, "De l'esprit de conquête et de l'usurpation", in *Oeuvres*, ed. Roulin (Paris, 1964), pp. 949ff. Constant's ideas also were originally developed in 1806: see p. 1570.
77. *Commentaire*, pp. 23-4.
78. *Ibid.*, p. 24.
79. *Ibid.*, pp. 24, 29-30.
80. *Ibid.*, pp. 44-5. The notion of a "middle class" characterised by reason, work and education is rather similar to Aristotle's discussion in *Politics*, sections 1221-1222. Tracy's theory on this point is to be distinguished from the somewhat self-congratulatory conception of a *classe moyenne* in the work of F. Guizot, who succeeded Tracy in the Académie française: see, for example, Guizot's *Discours de réception* (1836), p. 17 and the reply by Ségur, p. 30.
81. *Commentaire*, p. 149.

82. *Ibid.*, p. 150.
83. *Ibid.*, p. 211.
84. *Ibidem*. Cf. a similar distinction in his letter to Jefferson of 14 July 1814, in Chinard, *Jefferson et les idéologues*, p. 125.
85. *Commentaire* (Liège, 1817), p. v ("Avertissement de l'éditeur").
86. On the proper role of the state in economic affairs, cf. Tracy, *Traité*, pp. 350-2, 358-363, chapter 12; and *Commentaire*, chapters 13 and 22. A more activist conception appears in Condorcet's *Sketch*, pp. 131-2, 180-1. Tracy's position is close to that of Adam Smith in most respects: cf. Reisman, *A. Smith's Sociological Economics*, chapter 7.

10. PUBLIC INSTRUCTION AND IDEOLOGY

Tracy had argued in 1798 that legislators and rulers were the true teachers of humanity, and that a sound moral instruction was dependent on a proper framework of legislation and administration.[1] It was necessary, however, that these authorities should be suitably enlightened in their actions: "truth is the sole road to well-being", and truth consisted in a knowledge of the laws of our own nature and those governing our environment.[2] The élitist character of the educational writings of Tracy and other idéologues arose partly from their environmental determinism and partly from their scientism. Progress could be achieved by modifying the institutional environment which conditioned the people's actions and beliefs; but only an élite equipped with scientific knowledge of man and the social environment could intervene in a decisive manner to control the direction of social change.

It had become a commonplace in eighteenth-century social philosophy that education was the key to reforming moral and political practices and improving the material prosperity of the people. Ignorance and habitual prejudice were taken to be the main obstacles to human improvement, for they were seen as the pillars supporting all forms of oppression, injustice, inequality and superstition. If individuals' ideas were shaped, as Helvétius[3] had emphasised, by their social milieu, this implied that the cycle of repression and determinism would be reproduced by each generation unless an "external" force intervened to alter the institutional pattern. This was the role of the *savants*. The determinist theory implied the possibility of social engineering by the élite. A different pattern of values and beliefs could be encouraged by carefully modifying the social and cultural environment, so that virtue, honesty and co-operation would be rewarded, for example, instead of selfish and dishonest behaviour. It was this theory of education and environment which Marx later summarised in his critical claim that the "materialist doctrine concerning the changing of circumstances and education forgets that circumstances are changed by men and that the educator must himself be educated. This doctrine has therefore to divide society into two parts, one of which is superior to society".[4]

IDEOLOGICAL EDUCATION

The educational theories of Tracy and the idéologues were directly related to their project of making the people "free and happy".[5] Education was what "made" man, and education could change him for the better if properly planned. Instruction in the art of making correct judgements was essential for moral and social behaviour as well as for advances in the sciences of physical nature. Tracy's conception of knowledge in terms of propositions derived by "ideological" deduction from the observation of man's natural capacities, and his emphasis upon the diffusion of a scientific model of thought, led to a "transmission" conception of education. The task of the enlightened élite of legislators and educators was to frame rational institutions, distil the essential principles of scientific knowledge, and ensure that these ideas were widely extended throughout the society. Public instruction was the necessary adjunct to rational political and legal authorities.

It was no accident that the idéologues were deeply involved in the educational projects of the 1790s: the diffusion of science, and especially of "scientific" approaches to social and moral questions, was central to their reforming enterprise. Moreover, developments in the sphere of public instruction after Thermidor, especially in the new system of *écoles centrales*, may be regarded as essentially idéologue in character. This chapter is concerned to discuss Tracy's contribution to the "ideological" principles which infused the schooling system of 1795-1801, and Tracy's defence of that system when it was about to be disbanded under Bonaparte's Consulate. It is now necessary to examine the educational writings and activities of Tracy during this period, and the extent to which idéologie actually became embodied in the curricula.

Tracy emphasised the importance of institutional practices as the main agency in shaping moral judgements and actions. Moreover, he argued that formal schooling or instruction was only one part of an individual's educational life-experience, and that it was not necessarily the most effective agency of moral socialisation for most people. Where direct instruction could not succeed, it might still be possible to arrange social circumstances in such a way that individuals were indirectly prompted to value certain forms of action and to avoid other forms. Tracy assumed that what is true of men's linguistic usage is also true of their social behaviour, namely, that people are primarily creatures of habit (rather than of ratiocination). This assumption led to his distinctive statement of the foundation of progressive education: the essential thing, said Tracy, is "to make correct judgements habitual".[6]

The practical task of the science of idéologie in formal education was to provide a pedagogical methodology, by means of which students could be taught how to draw correct judgements from the basic data of experience. The truths or principles which emerged from this procedure were held to be capable of demonstration (proof) and of systematic presentation as a series of connected propositions stemming from a scientific understanding of human nature. Idéologie, applied to the content of the schooling system, could provide a systematic demonstration of the rationality and social wisdom embodied in the Rights and Duties of Man and Citizen, thereby helping to stabilise the new social and political order and preserve republican institutions. What was the proper relationship between government and education? To what extent should the system of public instruction be used by the government as a functional support for the political régime?

Montesquieu had argued in Book IV of *l'Esprit des lois* (1748) that the educational laws of a society are always in fact related to the principles of the government; education within the private family will mirror the content of the education received in the *grand famille* of society as a whole; both levels prepare us to be citizens in our own type of community.[7] Tracy in his *Commentaire* agreed in general that our education should "dispose us to have sentiments and opinions which are not in opposition with established institutions; otherwise, we would want to overthrow them".[8] The three levels of education—our parents, our teachers and the world around us—should complement each other if they are to act effectively; a wise government will take quiet measures to ensure that the three levels tend to operate in the same direction and tend to maintain the principles of the system of government.[9]

The limits of interference had to be carefully defined. No government, said Tracy, should ever interfere with the natural authority and custody of parents over their children. Hence, the Jacobin proposals for compulsory state boarding-schools could not be tolerated. Nor should any religious doctrine be enforced, for this should be a matter of family concern. However, it was legitimate, in Tracy's view, for a government to try to influence, but not control, public opinion. If public opinion could be enlightened, this would have some effect upon even the private or family sphere of education, and would certainly affect the general education which people received from their institutional environment. The other type of education, in the schooling system, was more open to direct influence because the majority of children attended government schools and the minority at private schools would still be influenced by the tendencies followed in the state schools. Tracy concluded that all three levels of education were subject to the direct or indirect influence of government principles.[10] The unstated premise of Tracy's analysis is that all governments will in practice try to influence the opinions both of children and of adult citizens, but that this attempted influence is really legitimate only where the content is in accordance with "reason" and social happiness. Tracy undoubtedly believed that reason, happiness and liberty had a special status as goals of politics and education. However, he stopped short of autocratic schemes to enforce his own "ideological" view of these goods. Even under the Empire, he professed his faith that reason and truth would triumph over prejudice by peaceful means.[11]

The line between reasoned supervision and autocratic control was sometimes very fine indeed under the Directory. It is of considerable interest to trace the supervisory role played by Tracy and other idéologues in the education system after 1798, when the "ideological" influence over the content of curricula and the operation of the schools became more noticeable. As we saw earlier, Tracy became directly involved in state supervision of the *écoles centrales*, owing to his membership of a Council of public instruction established by the Minister of the Interior, François de Neufchâteau. The work of this Council, during the twelve months following Tracy's appointment in February 1799, provides invaluable insights into the general conceptions of public education held by Tracy and the idéologues, and more particularly the ways in which they tried to devise pragmatic methods for remedying the widely perceived defects of the *écoles centrales*.

In his first brief term of Ministerial office in 1797, Neufchâteau had taken up the pressing question of elementary textbooks. He invited the professors in the *écoles centrales* to submit their *cahiers* for "examination by the Institut National, this great *jury d'instruction* of the French Republic", and promised rewards for those efforts judged worthy of being published as elementary texts at government expense.[12] Returning to the Ministry of the Interior in July 1798 after ten months as a member of the Directory, Neufchâteau took up the same problem. His creation of an advisory Council of public instruction, drawn from members of the Institut,[13] was evidently designed to facilitate the development of textbooks, through examining *cahiers* and offering constructive criticisms of each course and the overall programme of studies. The offical announcement of the creation of the Council on 6 October 1798 stated that its objectives were

> to examine elementary texts whether printed or manuscript, the *cahiers*, the views of the professors, and to be occupied continuously with the means of perfecting republican instruction.[14]

The members of the Council were *savants* rather than professional teachers, as one critic noted.[15] Tracy was appointed to strengthen the Council's supervision of the courses on *grammaire générale* and legislation.[16]

The work of the Council consisted largely of conducting an extensive correspondence with teachers and administrators in both the *écoles centrales* and primary schools, gathering information on the content and organisation of instruction, and drafting circulars and instructions for consideration by the Minister. There are several documents of particular interest for understanding the role of idéologie in public education: a series of four circulars to professors in the *écoles centrales* in August-September 1799, and a lengthy Report in February 1800 on the current state of public education and some suggested reforms. Tracy's publisher claimed in the last edition of his *Elémens d'idéologie* that all these documents were drafted by Tracy on behalf on the Council:[17] indeed, they were printed as his own work in volume IV of that edition. However, since they represent the collective views of the Council, and since Tracy's exact role in their production cannot be verified, all we may assume is that they reflect accurately both his own views and those of the other idéologues in the Council. The fact that the terms *idéologie* and *idéologique* appear in these documents adds further evidence of Tracy's intimate involvement.

The freedom given to teachers in the *écoles centrales* had resulted in an enormous diversity of course contents and teaching hours; in many cases this led to a lowering of teaching standards. There was a lack of co-ordination among teachers of related subjects, there was no coherent sequence of studies with appropriate pre-requisites set for more advanced courses, and teachers were often unsure what should be taught.[18] The invitations by Neufchâteau to the teachers to forward their *cahiers* produced few results, most of which were very disheartening to the members of the Council. Nothing worthy of reproduction as a student text had been forthcoming. The greatest problems occurred in the courses on ancient languages, *grammaire générale*, legislation and history. A circular, signed by the Minister, was therefore prepared for teachers in each of those subjects in August-September 1799. We have already examined the latter two circulars on legislation and history when discussing Tracy's conception of social science in chapter six. Here we will examine only those concerned with ancient languages and *grammaire générale.*

One practical problem with the teaching of ancient languages was that one appointee had been found insufficient to teach both Latin and Greek at various levels: an extra teacher had been recommended on a number of occasions, but without result except in the Paris schools. The Council seemed more concerned in its circular, however, with the content of such courses and their relationship to *idéologie* and *grammaire générale*. Each teacher of ancient languages was addressed in the following terms:

> You are not unaware, citizen, that the young cannot learn properly the principles of any language unless they are first given some notions of *grammaire générale*; and that they cannot understand the general rules of language unless one begins by explaining to them what goes on in their minds when they think and when they try to express their thoughts. This path is the only one to follow if the students are not to contract the fatal habit of being satisfied with words whose meaning they cannot grasp, and if the study of a single language is not to take up many years of repulsive and often fruitless labour ... Accordingly you see, citizen, that it is necessary for your course on the Latin or Greek language to be preceded by some treatment of *idéologie* and *grammaire générale*. No doubt, these two sciences do not have to be dealt with in great detail at this point, since the students will make a deeper study of them at a later stage when they take the course by the teacher of *grammaire générale*: but it is still necessary that they know the fundamentals, for therein is the true introduction to the study of languages.[19]

The circular recommended that suitable books might include works by "Condillac, Dumarsais, or some other *grammairien métaphysicien*". It repeated the earlier requests for the teachers to send their *cahiers* for examination, especially in regard to these preliminary studies which were the "most important" and the "most neglected" part of the course.[20]

The circular to the teachers of *grammaire générale* emphasised the importance of going beyond grammar as such, and recognising instead that the course should comprise four parts: "*idéologie*, *grammaire générale*, French grammar, and logic''. Understood in this broad manner, ''your course should be the complement and the completion of the courses on ancient languages, and the introduction to the courses on literature, history and legislation''. The teachers of *grammaire générale* were reminded that their courses were preceded by those on ancient languages, whose teachers should have commenced with instruction in ''some elementary notions of *idéologie*'' appropriate to their students' level of understanding, based on the principle of proceeding ''from the known to the unknown''.[21]

The later courses should build upon this elementary knowledge by providing ''more advanced lessons on *idéologie* and *grammaire générale*; for this is the stage where they should learn properly these two sciences''. These principles might then be applied to French grammar, necessary for the study of literature; and finally applied to the rules of the art of reasoning, or logic, which is the guiding thread helping the young ''to understand men and things, facts and institutions, in the courses on history and legislation, and which guides them for the rest of their lives''. The art of reasoning, or logic, was said to comprise the study of ''what constitutes the certainty of our knowledge, the truth of our propositions, and the correctness of our deductions''. Logic was based on ''the careful examination of our intellectual faculties, and of the effects produced by the frequent repetition of the same operations and by the constant use of the signs by which we combine and communicate our ideas''.[22]

Tracy's principles of idéologie clearly had the support of the Council of public instruction. Some unfortunate teachers of general grammar were upbraided by the Minister on the advice of the Council: their mistake was to have relied too heavily on Condillac's *Traité des sensations* (which Tracy and others regarded as in many respects too mechanistic), or to have proclaimed the immortality of the soul and the qualities of the Supreme Being. Such things were beyond empirical demonstration: ''the character of the new metaphysics is, and should be, to deal only with subjects which are clearly within the grasp of our intellect.''[23]

The acknowledged difficulties facing the *écoles centrales*, the public criticism of their performance, and the problems of making improvements in the absence of sufficient information about the abilities of the teachers and the achievements of the students, led the idéologues into a defensive campaign—to protect the *écoles centrales*, to rebut the more hostile critics, and to seek urgent reforms within the schools themselves. The pages of the journal *la Décade* in 1799-1801 contained many articles praising the more noteworthy *écoles centrales*, suggesting modifications, and attacking traditionalist critics.[24] In the early weeks of the Consulate, on the basis of further information obtained from the teachers and school administrations, the Council of public instruction was able to draw up a comprehensive Report to the Minister,[25] outlining

> the true state of public instruction in France, the hopes and fears which may be held for it, and the improvements which can be introduced, without, how-

> ever, giving too great a shock to the vast system which is established; for ... whenever a plea to change or reform the system of public education is announced in the legislature or in the acts of the government, this has been a signal in the departments for a coolness among the teachers, discouragement of students, and desertion of the schools.[26]

The Report, dated 5 February 1800, did not receive a reply from the new Minister of the Interior, Lucien Bonaparte, and the Council was quietly dissolved later in the year.[27] The Report, however, remains of interest, not only because Tracy claimed it as his own work in the 1825 edition of his writings, but also because the Report provided an account by the idéologues of how they interpreted the strengths and weaknesses of the education system begun in 1795, and it showed their willingness to modify their ideas in the light of practical experience.

According to the Report, the greatest defect of the *écoles centrales*, upon which there was a general agreement among the teachers themselves, was "the lack of liaison and relations between the different studies". Each course was isolated from those coming before and after it, and there were no pre-requisites for entry except a minimum age specified in the law of October 1795. This not only prevented able youngsters from entering the schools, thereby driving them into the arms of private tutors who were hostile to the *écoles centrales*; it also failed to tackle the important problem of ensuring that students had reached an adequate preparatory level before beginning any given course. Since the primary schools were not yet doing their job properly, it was incumbent on the *écoles centrales* to set aside some more time for elementary studies. The main defects of the law of October 1795 were the lack of structure in the course of studies, the minimum age regulations, and insufficient attention to ancient languages.[28] Teachers had also drawn attention to a number of other important reforms which could be implemented by centralised directives:

> that the government, by a general measure, should prevent students from taking too many courses at once; that it oblige them at the beginning of the school year to undergo an examination whose format is regulated by the government; that it determine the period of vacations, which are nowhere the same; that it establish the obligation to have passed a certain course in order to proceed to another; that it encourage, by all means in its power, the creation of *pensionnats* near the *écoles centrales* and the permanence of those already existing ...[29]

The notable feature of all these reforms is that they could readily be accommodated within the existing system. The idéologues were determined to improve the efficiency and co-ordination of the system in order to forestall larger criticisms of its whole philosophical approach. The Council's Report thus stressed that the system was improving rapidly and needed only minor changes to become completely satisfactory. Despite the organisational problems of a new system and the long interruption of public education caused by the years of turmoil, the evidence showed that there was good reason to have faith in the existing system of schooling.[30]

The Report reminded the Minister that the stability of the government could be derived "above all from the progress and diffusion of knowledge".[31] The Consulate, however, was not convinced by the idéologues' self-justificatory plea for continuing the existing system, albeit with several modifications; nor was it satisfied with the quality and quantity of the evidence alluded to in the Report concerning the viability of the *écoles centrales*. Chaptal reiterated in Bonaparte's Council of State in November 1800 many of the organisational criticisms made in the idéologues' Report, but argued that most schools were deserted, and recommended the creation of a different system of secondary education and the abolition of such courses as general grammar and legislation.[32]

In March 1801 an enquiry was ordered into national education, conducted by department prefects and members of Bonaparte's Council of State. Their replies[33] were generally unfavourable towards the *écoles centrales*, although several schools were undoubtedly of excellent quality. In April 1802, the *écoles centrales* were replaced by secondary schools and by a new élite of thirty state-financed *lycées*. In introducing the new legislation, Roederer accused the *écoles centrales* of having tried "to populate France with living Encyclopedias".[34] Fourcroy argued that, while the new institutions of 1795 had been inspired by "grander and more liberal ideas" than those of the *ancien régime*, they had met with little success or utility.[35]

In the meantime, Tracy had decided, probably as a result of his experience during 1799 on the Council of public instruction, to write a series of texts for students to overcome the absence of suitable course materials on general grammar. The first volume appeared in 1801, under the lengthy title: *Projet d'Eléments d'idéologie à l'usage des écoles centrales de la République française*. In the preface to this volume, Tracy noted that until the teachers themselves, through experience, could produce suitable student texts, there remained an important lacuna to be filled. The course on general grammar, he believed, would demonstrate that "all languages have common rules which are derived from the nature of our intellectual faculties", and that this knowledge is necessary "not simply for the study of languages but is also the only solid basis of the moral and political sciences". Hence, in teaching the philosophy of language, one would be providing an introduction to the course on private and public *morale*.[36]

But the intentions of the educational legislation of 1795 were now threatened, he noted: the Jacobin *fureur de tout détruire* had been replaced by the present government's *manie de ne rien laisser s'établir*.[37] The finest results of the revolution were being abandoned in the name of redressing the errors of the past. The wisdom of "practical knowledge" was now being championed as an antidote to "theories". But the critics had not troubled themselves to understand these theories and they wrongly attributed all the evils of the revolution to the philosophers whose ideas were embodied in the highly useful educational institutions. The production of excellent texts would require a number of years, taking account of experience in the classroom; this was an additional reason for hoping that the government would not halt

> the teaching of the ideological, moral and political sciences which, after all, are sciences like the others, with the difference that those who have not studied them believe so sincerely they know them, that they believe they are in a position to decide the issue.[38]

Tracy's worst fears were proving to be correct, and he rapidly wrote a last defence of the *écoles centrales*, based closely on the ideas contained in the Report of February 1800. His brochure, entitled *Observations sur le système actuel d'instruction publique*, appeared in about June 1801.[39] The *Observations*, said Tracy in his foreword, had been published out of sequence; he had wanted to wait until suitable texts had appeared for the courses on general grammar, and perhaps also for the courses on morals and legislation and history. Without such texts, a programme of studies was difficult to discuss or to justify, especially when the content was new and not well understood.[40] The *Observations*, he said, had to be published in haste owing to the imminent decision on the future of public instruction. Tracy's starting-point and general objective was:

> to prove that we have an excellent (system of public instruction); that its bases leave absolutely nothing to be desired; that it has already produced many good results and no bad effects; that to obtain from it all the advantages we have a right to expect, it is necessary only to know properly its character (*esprit*), in order to put successively into activity all the parts and to inter-relate them, and especially in order to avoid partial measures which, departing from the general system, disturb the totality and make it unrecognisable.[41]

This viewpoint was re-affirmed in his conclusion that, if the reforms proposed were carried out, it would become relatively easy "to spread among the mass of citizens a pure and quite extensive knowledge". The purpose of his pamphlet was

> to prove that the fundamental principles of our present institutions are excellent, and that to produce their best effects they have only to be completed. I would be happy if, by developing their character, I had forestalled their disorganisation![42]

DEFENCE OF THE 'CLASSE SAVANTE'

The *Observations* contain two inter-related kinds of arguments: the first and somewhat truncated argument concerned the relationship he saw between the schooling system and the class structure of society. The second concerned his detailed recommendations for reorganising the curriculum of the *écoles centrales*, based on a *plan d'études* which had emerged in 1799-1800 from the deliberations of the Council of public instruction.

Tracy began by asserting the existence of a permanent social division between two classes of men in terms of their educational needs and abilities:

> one, who draw their subsistence from their manual labour; the other, who live from the revenue of their properties, or from the product of certain functions in which the work of the mind is more important than the work of the body. The first is the *classe ouvrière*, the second is what I will call the *classe savante*.[43]

These two classes were regarded by Tracy as absolutely "invariable data" of social life, and as independent of human volition or intentionality: "they derive necessarily from the very nature of men and of societies; it is not in the power of anyone to change them".[44] These two classes differed from one another in all important respects: "*moeurs*, needs, means, everything is different between these two types of men".[45] Their educational needs and desires were therefore different. The children of the *classe ouvrière* were required for labour by their parents, and the children must acquire the skills and become accustomed to the habits of the "laborious toil for which they are destined". For these reasons, such children cannot spend many years in school; they must be given an abridged or summary education, complete in itself, before they enter the workshops or return to domestic or agricultural labour. Schools must be plentiful and easily accessible in every locality so that boarding schools are not required for these children, who are the vast majority.[46]

The educational needs and expectations of the children of the *classe savante* require a distinct set of educational responses. They are fortunately able to give more time to their studies; they are obliged to undertake a long period of education if they are to fulfil their social "destiny"; and they must study certain fields of knowledge which can be grasped only by minds with a certain maturity. Moreover, they are in a position to attend a more distant school or a boarding school, or to have private tutors; such arrangements are probably necessary, since their studies demand close supervision.[47]

The content of instruction for the two social classes should also be quite different, according to Tracy. The education of the masses should not consist simply in the first few years of the extended curriculum followed by the élite. Mass education should be an "abridgement" but not a "part" of the élite education. The objects and the methods of teaching should remain distinct. A carefully considered system of national education should really be two separate systems. Tracy claimed that this had been envisaged in the law of 1795:

> the primary schools and the apprenticeships in various trades, these are the education of the *classe ouvrière*; the *écoles centrales* and *écoles spéciales* are the education of the *classe savante*. And I would no more advise sending a child destined to be a workman to the latter schools, than sending to the former a child who would become a man of state or man of letters ...[48]

It was erroneous to believe that the primary schools were intended to form the first step in a graded system and thus to be linked to the *écoles centrales*. It might even be necessary to change the name "primary" in order to overcome this "false view". Children of the élite would have a private education in the family home until they could enter the *écoles centrales* at about the age of nine or ten; the majority of children would attend primary school from about the age of six, followed by vocational training of some kind as a skilled labourer or tradesman.[49]

Tracy's *Observations* are overwhelmingly concerned to discuss ways of improving the education of the *classe savante*, a class which he also describes as the *classe éclairée* and *classe supérieure*.[50] Tracy gave two reasons for this preoccupation. In the first place, the lower levels of education could not yet be fully organised for lack of "resources, teachers and students", and could only be established gradually over a long period.[51] Secondly, since the content of primary education should be a simplified resumé of the knowledge acquired by the educated élite, it was the task of the latter to propagate these "sound ideas and good methods" and to become the teachers of the whole society. The education of the élite, then, was a prerequisite for any generalised instruction of the "lowest classes of society". Tracy's transmission concept of education is well illustrated by this view of the relation between élite and the ordinary people. He drew an analogy between the diffusion of ideas and military instruction (with which he was very familiar), where the teaching of new exercises follows a chain of command from the senior officers, through junior officers, to the ordinary ranks.

> It is the same with all instruction. Once the education of the *classe savante* in society has been successful, one will see formed among them some excellent teachers for the *classe ouvrière*, see them provide many methods of instruction and instil in the latter the desire to profit from that instruction.[52]

Tracy's discussion of the education of the *classe savante* began by asserting that youths at the age of twenty years must take their place in the adult world, so that their formal schooling should be concluded by this time. Three stages could be specified as a "natural" division of instruction.[53] Young children, who are incapable of "sustained concentration", should not attend formal classes. Instead, the first eight or nine years of life should be spent under parental supervision, learning elementary skills of reading and writing, and acquiring those good habits of mind which result from the "company of men of good education and liberal *moeurs*".[54] A primary school was generally not a suitable place for acquiring the abilities and dispositions required by the *classe savante*, said Tracy. Primary schools were for the children of the working classes. Tracy did not explain why the latter should not also stay at home until the age of nine years: presumably it was a matter of wealth (the *classe savante* could employ private tutors) and not a matter of which children were more capable of "sustained concentration".

At the second stage of instruction, children of the *classe savante* would attend an *école centrale* for about eight years. Here, the student would learn "all those forms of general knowledge needed by every well-educated man". This would be followed by three or four years at an *école spéciale*, where he would learn professional skills for his career.[55] In the *écoles centrales*, it would be necessary to present a well-rounded education, covering all three areas of knowledge embodied in the three Classes of the Institut National: languages and literature, physical and mathematical sciences, and moral and political sciences. This tripartite division of studies appears to be largely a matter of convenience, since it does not rigorously correspond to Tracy's conception of the hierarchy of knowledge which we noted earlier.[56] Nor is there an obvious place for "literature" in a rigorous "ideological" schema: its inclusion in the curriculum of the *écoles centrales* was simply traditional. Tracy argued on practical grounds that these three areas are the "bases of all the learned professions", and that members of any learned profession really need some acquaintance with all such areas.[57] The education law of 1795 had established three divisions of the curriculum along broadly similar lines. The important thing, in Tracy's view, was to have a coherent and systematic plan of studies, whose content was carefully graded and mutually inter-related.[58]

The details of his plan need not concern us here, other than to note some of his remarks on the moral sciences. In years five and six, the students would study morals and legislation and public morality. The latter includes the origins of authority and the source of wealth, that is, the principles of "social organisation and political economy". In years seven and eight, the history course would be a "continual application of the ideological, moral, political and economic observations which have already been made". The student, while continuing to "learn the facts", would eventually be able to "make sound judgements on men and things in accordance with the true principles of the moral sciences". At the end of such studies, a student would be equipped either to proceed to a special school for professional training in one of the three fields described above, or simply to "live as a sensible man, as a good father of a family, as a sufficiently enlightened citizen—in a word, as a reasonable being ..."[59]

To ensure that courses conformed to the general intentions of the *plan d'études*, Tracy advocated the reactivation of a body such as the Council of public instruction, a body of learned men who would draw up detailed instructions for each course, and "while not positively dictating the teacher's lesson",[60] would give details of course content, the spirit in which it should be undertaken, its links with other courses, and a few words on teaching methods. The co-ordinating body would also invite teachers to send their written lessons, so the best might be printed as texts and the authors rewarded by the government; and it would publicise the general objectives and character of the *écoles centrales*. A wider understanding among the people of these goals would greatly contribute to the schools' success, for "the biggest obstacle to the implementation of the new public instruction arises from the fact that it is too far in advance of generally received ideas ...; such that few people have grasped the whole, and parents, students and even some teachers do not really know what is being propsed".[61]

The success of the education of the *classe savante*, in Tracy's view, depended partly on the public acceptability of the *écoles centrales*. One important step in this direction would be the establishment of privately-organised *pensionnats* so that students would receive additional supervised study,[62] a measure which had been advocated also in the Report of the Council a year earlier. *Pensionnats* should also be available for students at the *écoles spéciales*.[63] Students who successfully completed their studies at the *écoles centrales* should be able to pursue more advanced training in any of the three main fields they had already studied. For this purpose, it was necessary to open advanced institutions in the fields of the moral and political sciences, and in languages and literature, alongside the *école polytechnique* which already catered for the physical sciences.[64] In the short-term, it would suffice to attach additional positions to the *Collège de France* and the *Bibliothèque Nationale*. Tracy declared that an institution like the Collège de France should be preserved owing to its demonstrated excellence: "All my life I have proposed to increase what is good and never to destroy it; the long existence of an institution is part of its merit since this adds to its effect".[65] In a refashioned Collège directed towards perfecting the "ideological, moral and political" sciences, said Tracy,

> ... I would want not only teachers who demonstrated the principles of political economy or of social organisation in general. I would want there to be some who taught in particular the statistics of the various states, the theory of taxation, of the money system, of exchange, of the diverse branches of commerce, etc., for the individual utility of certain diplomats, administrators, merchants. There should also be some courses on the various parts of positive law, for the benefit of those destined for judicial positions ...[66]

There were many citizens, besides those in legal and judicial careers, who needed a detailed knowledge of the legal system. The course on morals and legislation at the *écoles centrales* was not intended to give this knowledge; a number of *écoles spéciales* for legal studies should thus be established. It should be borne in mind, however, that

> Positive law is a consequence, an application, of the principles of *morale* and of *la science sociale*. No field of study, with the possible exception of history, is more likely to damage the mind and seriously corrupt the judgement on the most essential points, if one gets used to confusing what *is* with what *should be*. And that is bound to happen if one is concerned with the positive before having enough knowledge of the principles. That is why the best lawyers have not always been the best legislators or the best judges of the wisdom of a legislative measure. It is then absolutely necessary to oblige young people to pass through an *école spéciale des sciences morales et politiques* before entering a professional school of law, just as one attends the *école polytechnique* before reaching a school of engineering, or, as in the medical schools, the courses on theory are done before taking those on clinical medicine.[67]

The idéologue position was clear: principles must precede detailed factual knowledge, in order to ensure that a proper framework of education is used by the students. It was the task of idéologie, in its application to the analysis of institutions, to elaborate the principles of a social science which could be used to judge the effects of various measures and practices upon the happiness and freedom of men. Tracy showed a boundless confidence that the principles were correct; indeed, that they were permanent laws governing the human condition, since they were derived from an analysis of human nature.

Tracy believed that a satisfactory framework already existed for the education of the *classe savante*: all that was needed was "stability, permanence and consistency".[68] On the other hand, public instruction for the *classe ouvrière*, which Tracy also called *la classe pauvre* and *la classe ignorante*, lagged behind considerably. Tracy's view of how the ideas of the lower classes are formed is highly suggestive for understanding his theory of education in general.

Of all the classes, the poor and ignorant are the most strongly influenced by everyday social institutions rather than by formal schooling. "The less a man receives explicit lessons, the more his ideas are due simply to his association with his fellows and to the chance circumstances of his life". Among the poor, almost all they learn is acquired "without their suspecting it". Tracy's image of the uneducated classes is one of passively accepting habitual ideas; they "invent nothing". Tracy assumes that their education is dependent entirely on the standards of those who write the almanacs used by the poor, and upon the knowledge of those who do business with them, namely, the educated élite. The education of the poor, he concludes, "is three-quarters accomplished if we have properly arranged that of *la classe savante*", who also provide the teachers and programmes of instruction. The material and intellectual possessions of the poor are "those which have become common" in a given society.[69] Through their ignorance, the poor are always several steps behind in accepting the truths discovered by the élite. "They are always behind the times: that is their only fault. And the task of those who attend to their instruction must continually and solely be to impart the ideas which have superseded those presently held by the people, on every point of theory and practice".[70]

Tracy makes the assumption that on every question, "there are a thousand ways of going astray, but only one way to decide correctly".[71] How can one avoid the errors and follow the truth? This is a difficult process, according to Tracy: a great deal of knowledge in related areas is required to be certain one has properly decided a question. The highly educated have enough difficulty in attaining certain knowledge, since no-one has the strength to suspend judgement on various matters until he has reason to be completely sure of his conclusions. The poor majority, by implication, are never in a position to know anything with certainty unless they are instructed by men who have gained such knowledge. Tracy's solution is not to attempt to educate the majority to a high level of knowledge (which could have been consistent with his environmentalist view of education), but to urge that the élite present the masses with a digest of truths about man, morality, social organisation, and productive technology. The poor have little time for instruction and little capacity for making correct judgements from subtle discussions. They should simply be given the sound results of modern science, in all three areas of knowledge: for the ignorant man has (erroneous) ideas on the same range of subjects as the most highly educated man.

Every man has his ideas of grammar and logic; history and morality; physics and arithmetic. It is thus necessary to shape opinions on all these points; otherwise one leaves such ideas to the fortuitous conjunctions of circumstances which have produced so much error and deception in the past.[72] In a perfect society, education of the masses could safely be left to the "slow but sure effect of the social organisation and private industry". This would be preferable to instruction given by the state, which might contain a serious flaw which was buttressed by the weight of public authority.[73] In the present circumstances, what should the government do about the instruction of the *classe ouvrière*? In regard to vocational training or apprenticeships, the best thing would be to help the employers become aware of modern scientific information and techniques: this would involve focusing on the *classe savante* rather than the workers themselves.[74] Secondly, the primary schools should be gradually improved as resources and teachers become available. But primary instruction should not be completely free, according to Tracy. Parents should pay fees amounting to perhaps half the operating costs of the schools. This was not only to lift some burden from the public treasury, but also because "no lesson is useful except where it is desired to receive it", and the best evidence of this desire was an agreement to contribute towards the costs.[75] Fees would also stimulate local interest in the school, ensure its economical operation, and lead to higher standards of achievement. Other improvements depended upon the prior education of the *classe savante* and the perfection of its own curriculum from which the instruction of the "less fortunate" would be extracted and distilled.[76]

Tracy corresponded with teachers in the *écoles centrales*, exchanging ideas, and rallying support, believing that the threat to the schools was motivated by political and religious prejudices.[77] The opinion of Tracy and the idéologues, that the main bases of the 1795 system should be preserved with a few changes in detail, was ignored in the reforms to the schools in 1802 and to the Institut in 1803. In the foreword to his *Grammaire* in 1803, Tracy expressed his sorrow that his texts could no longer be subtitled "for the use of the *écoles centrales*", and regretted that his second volume would be deprived of the stimulating exchange of ideas with teachers which arose from the first volume. Tracy also expressed his anger that idéologie, or "sound logic", which alone could throw light on all the other sciences, was no longer part of public instruction in France.[78] Tracy claimed that the scientific climate of opinion was now coming to demand the formulation of *la méthode des méthodes* or *la science des sciences* based on the theory of signs.[79] Finally, he expressed the hope that the Institut (which no longer contained sections on *analyse des idées* or on *grammaire générale*) would not come to regard "la philosophie rationnelle" as outside its proper concerns, nor occupy itself only with the French language to the exclusion of "the general theory of language".[80]

Tracy's defiant belief that his views were correct and irrefutable only increased during the period of the Consulate. In the 1804 reprint of his first volume, he declared that he was now convinced he had "reached the truth", that his later work had confirmed that his early opinions were well founded, and that his initial "hesitations and uncertainties" could now be abandoned.[81] In the three years of rapid change since 1801, he said, idéologie had given an "immense impetus" to knowledge, even though it had now been abolished in the Institut and the schools.[82]

Tracy, who had wanted to become, through his textbooks, "the secretary of all the enlightened men" of his time,[83] had lost the battle for an education system based upon rationalist principles of morality and politics. In his *Commentaire* of 1806, he ruefully joked that the only unproductive workers of any merit were those who studied the science of man: and they were the only ones persecuted. This, he said, was because they pointed out the errors of all *les oisifs*. Returning to this passage in 1819, Tracy noted that theorists were producers of the greatest of all utilities, that of truth.[84] The idéologue had not forgotten his dictum of 1798: "la vérité est le seul chemin du bien-être."[85]

Notes

1. "Quels sont les moyens", in *Commentaire*, p. 463.
2. *Ibid.*, p. 456; cf. *Elémens*, vol. I, p. 388.
3. Cf. Helvétius, *De l'esprit* (1758) and *De l'homme* (1773).
4. K. Marx, "Theses on Feuerbach" (1845) no. 3; and *The Holy Family* (1845), chapter 6, section (d) on French materialism.
5. "The most certain means of rendering a people free and happy is to establish a perfect method of education": Beccaria, cited on title page of Tracy, *Commentary* (1811).
6. *Elémens*, vol. I, p. 273; and chapter five, above.
7. Montesquieu, *De l'esprit des lois* (Paris, 1922), vol. I, pp. 29f.
8. Tracy, *Commentaire*, p. 28.
9. *Ibid.*, pp. 28, 33.
10. *Ibid.*, pp. 33-4. For a strong statement of the need for unity of principles between government and education, cf. Lakanal's speech on the *école normale* in Hippeau, *op.cit.*, p. 412.
11. *Logique*, p. 146.
12. Duruy, *op.cit.*, pp. 265-6.

13. The original appointees were Daunou, Garat, Jacquemont, Lebreton, Palissot, Domergue, Lagrange and Darcet; Daunou was replaced almost at once by Ginguené, and Tracy was added four months later: Duruy, *op.cit.*, pp. 241n, 266-7, 284f.
14. Duruy, *op.cit.*, p. 241n.
15. *Ibid.*, p. 286.
16. *Elémens*, 5 vols. (Bruxelles, 1826-27), vol. IV, p. 259.
17. *Ibid.*, pp. 257-8.
18. Cf. Duruy, *op.cit.*, pp. 235f.
19. Reprinted in the appendix of Duruy, *op.cit.*, p. 447.
20. *Ibidem.*
21. *Ibid.*, p. 444.
22. *Ibid.*, p. 445.
23. Cited in *ibid.*, p. 233: letter of about September 1799.
24. For secondary analysis, cf. Kitchin, *op.cit.*, pp. 179-192; Van Duzer, *op.cit.*, pp. 137-142.
25. Reprinted in *Elémens*, 5 vols. (Paris, 1824-25), vol. IV, pp. 294-324; or *ibid.* (Bruxelles, 1826-27), IV, pp. 288-318; or Duruy, *op.cit.*, pp. 391-411.
26. Duruy, *op.cit.*, p. 391.
27. Cf. letter by Lucien Bonaparte, 12 October 1800, cited in *Elémens*, IV, pp. 291-3 (Paris ed.) or pp. 285-7 (Bruxelles ed.).
28. Duruy, *op.cit.*, pp. 401-2.
29. *Ibid.*, p. 402.
30. *Ibid.*, pp. 403-5.
31. *Ibid.*, p. 411.
32. H.C. Barnard, *Education and the French Revolution* (Cambridge, 1969), pp. 199-202.
33. See the replies in Duruy, *op.cit.*, pp. 467-500.
34. Roederer, speech of 11 May 1802, in *Oeuvres*, vol. VII, p. 210.
35. Fourcroy, speech of 20 April 1802, in Hippeau, *op.cit.*, pp. 488-9.
36. *Elémens*, vol. I (Paris, 3rd ed. 1817), préface of 1801, pp. xxiii-xxiv.
37. *Ibid.*, p. xxv.
38. *Ibid.*, pp. xxviii-xxix.
39. Cf. the favourable review in *la Décade philosophique*, 10 messidor an IX (29 June 1801), pp. 14-31. The review is unsigned, but is attributed to Garat by J. Kitchin, *op.cit.*, p. 190n. A critical review appeared in the *Mercure de France* on 1 thermidor an IX (20 July 1801), pp. 192-7 (signed "P"): the critic believed that the moral and political sciences deserved to be omitted from the curriculum and that the Council of public instruction had been useless.
40. *Observations sur le système actuel d'instruction publique*, in *Elémens*, IV, pp. 319-375 (Bruxelles ed.), at pp. 321-2.
41. *Ibid.*, p. 325.
42. *Ibid.*, p. 375.
43. *Ibid.*, pp. 325-6.
44. *Ibid.*, p. 327.
45. *Ibid.*, p. 328.
46. *Ibid.*, p. 326.
47. *Ibid.*, p. 327.
48. *Ibid.*, p. 328.
49. *Ibid.*, p. 330.
50. *Ibid.*, pp. 368, 370.
51. *Ibid.*, pp. 329, 371.
52. *Ibid.*, p. 329.
53. *Ibid.*, pp. 329-330; the same idea had occurred in the circular to teachers of legislation, September 1799, in Duruy, *op.cit.*, pp. 440-1.
54. *Observations*, p. 330.
55. *Ibid.*, p. 331.
56. Above, chapter two.

57. *Observations*, pp. 331-3.
58. *Ibid.*, p. 336.
59. *Ibid.*, pp. 342-3.
60. *Ibid.*, p. 349.
61. *Ibid.*, pp. 350-1.
62. *Ibid.*, pp. 351-3.
63. *Ibid.*, pp. 364-6.
64. *Ibid.*, pp. 357-8. The legislation of 1795 had envisaged special schools for the moral and political sciences, but had not contemplated such an institution for language and literature.
65. *Ibid.*, p. 359.
66. *Ibid.*, p. 360.
67. *Ibid.*, pp. 361-2.
68. *Ibid.*, p. 367.
69. *Ibid.*, p. 368-9. Cf. *Elémens*, vol. I, p. 295, on the stunted intellectual development of the lower classes.
70. *Observations*, p. 370.
71. *Ibid.*, p. 369.
72. *Ibid.*, pp. 323, 344, 346-7, 370.
73. *Ibid.*, p. 371.
74. *Ibid.*, p. 372.
75. *Ibid.*, p. 373. Cf. "Quels sont les moyens", p. 476, on the importance of encouraging parents and students in the poorer classes, which comprised 90% of the people.
76. *Observations*, p. 374. Tracy's two-class approach was supported by Garat in his review of Tracy's pamphlet (see note 39 above); the more conservative reviewer in the *Mercure* was more critical of Tracy's distinction, regarding it as an overly strenuous reaction to the "equality of 1793" (*loc. cit.*, p. 193). Guizot in 1816 happily adopted a distinction similar to that of Tracy: cf. D. Johnson, *Guizot* (London, 1963), pp. 111-2.
77. Cf. Tracy, letter to Droz, 27 vendémiaire an X (19 October 1801), reprinted by A. Aulard in *la Révolution française*, vol. 58 (1910), pp. 361-2; and the fragment of a letter by Tracy cited in *la Décade*, 20 fructidor an IX (7 September 1801), pp. 496-7.
78. *Grammaire* (1803) (Paris, 2nd ed. 1817), pp. vi-vii.
79. *Ibid.*, pp. viii-ix.
80. *Ibid.*, p. xi.
81. *Elémens*, vol. I, foreword of 1804 (Paris, 3rd ed. 1817), pp. v-vi.
82. *Ibid.*, pp. vii-viii.
83. *Grammaire*, p. viii.
84. *Commentaire*, p. 97n.
85. "Quels sont les moyens", p. 456.

11. CONCLUSION: SOCIAL SCIENCE AND LIBERALISM

In these concluding remarks, I offer not a summary of the preceding chapters, but some brief reflections on the significance of the theory of idéologie in Tracy's social and political theory, with particular reference to his conception of scientific certainty and to the nature of his liberalism.

In the first place, I have noted on several occasions that the theory of idéologie held out the promise that truths about human behaviour could be determined with a degree of certainty similar to that of physics and chemistry. How was such certainty possible? It was premised upon

(a) following the same methods of observation, reasoning and calculation as the natural sciences;
(b) asking only those questions which could be answered on the basis of observational evidence; and
(c) discovering a general law-like proposition which was capable of explaining the multitude of social and political phenomena.

While Tracy was not the first theorist to insist on these aspects of scientific certainty (aspects which could perhaps be called naturalism, behaviouralism and scientism), he was more emphatic than most thinkers before Comte in wanting to apply them to the study of man and society. Rather than raising the issue of Tracy's influence upon such figures as Comte and his successors, I will indicate some of the implications of Tracy's view of social science for his liberalism and his social theory in general. Why was certainty regarded as desirable?

Tracy's desire for certainty in the social sciences may be understood as inherent in his view of science as control or mastery of one's environment. In seeking a secular alternative to the "metaphysics" of the past, Tracy found in positive science a model for theoretical knowledge and practical applications. A science of society would be characterised not only by the formal structure of theorems and methods of investigation mentioned above, but also by a central concern with public policy objectives. Science, man's rational mastery of nature and society, implied for Tracy a technology of control over natural processes for the benefit of man, and the possibility of social reform directed towards objectives dictated by reason.

This viewpoint was extremely ambiguous in regard to democratic control: it was perhaps more logical to support government by an élite ruling in the rational interests of the people than to support government directly controlled by the people. The more scientistic the theorist, the more was he concerned to protect the influence of the knowledge élite: the writings of Saint-Simon and Comte in the 1820s led to a technocratic conception of good government. Tracy resisted the latter solution, because he was strongly influenced by more traditional liberal conceptions of limited government, laissez-faire economics, the central importance of individual rights, and ultimately a belief that politics is about wants and not about objective interests. The élitism in Tracy's theories of government and education was sustained by two related sources. One was his scientism, with its meritocratic assumptions and its concern to give authority and leadership to the knowledge élite in government and education. The second was an argument from prudence, claiming that the masses had insufficient understanding and experience of the public sphere to play any useful role: their direct involvement had always had unfortunate consequences.

Tracy's conception of scientific certainty implied that once the truths about man's capacities and needs were known, it would be possible to deduce a set of social institutions which were most suited to his "human nature". Man's needs for sociality, for individual liberty, and for extending his rational control over his society and over nature, were held to be deducible from analysis of his basic faculties of thought and action. Representative government itself was justified in terms of its ability to meet the needs of civilised men for a free and secure existence. One of the problems with Tracy's approach was the inherently slippery concept of needs in relation to a doctrine of human nature. Which needs are central? Are they invariable or circumstantial? Can they be reconciled? How do they differ from interests, wants and passions? Even if these questions could be satisfactorily resolved, there was a second problem of establishing priorities, programmes and institutional frameworks to cater for such needs, and determining how far each type of need must be satisfied.

Tracy's theory of social science seemed to imply that public authorities should be involved in attempts to maximise the satisfactions of their citizens. However, Tracy contented himself with the view that government should provide only a rational framework of legislation and public instruction, beyond which it was the province of individuals to pursue their own satisfactions in accordance with their various talents and resources. Tracy's faith in scientific demonstration of truths about human nature sometimes led him towards a flirtation with the idea that there should be a progressive alliance of power and truth, government and education, politicians and *savants*. However, his recognition of the empirical diversity of men's opinions and desires, together with his appreciation of the abuses inherent in government control of censorship and propaganda, prevented him from urging this kind of educative autocracy.

Idéologie in its restricted meaning denoted a theory of signs or language, examining how simple units of sense-experience were variously transformed into complex and inter-related ideas. By uncovering the mechanisms of idea-formation and the operations of judgement, idéologie was supposed to provide techniques for improving men's reason, for eliminating erroneous and "metaphysical" ideas, and ultimately for making men understand better the basis of rational institutions and moral rules. Empirical and observational enquiry was not simply the most reliable method for describing and explaining social reality: it was used to buttress a view of human nature and to lend scientific credibility to the political and educational practices desired by the idéologues.

Idéologie was an instrument for discriminating between truth and error in concepts; by extension, it became an instrument for distinguishing between practices which enhanced and those which harmed men's liberty and happiness in society. Civic instruction, in "ideological" terms, involved transmitting selected packages of concepts which showed men their interests as rational and social beings. Thus, at the level of social and political theory, idéologie became a philosophy of perfectibility, defining progress in terms of the diffusion of knowledge and its embodiment in rational institutions. These institutions and practices were liberal insofar as they were designed to extend individuals' opportunities for satisfying their wants with the least interference from their fellows or from public authorities.

The theme of this study of Tracy's writings is that idéologie, as a science of thought and action, was concerned to propagate and actualise the Enlightenment ideals of reason and freedom, to destroy the sources of prejudice and traditional privilege, and to develop the policy sciences in law, government and education. Tracy's emphasis on conceptual reform was quite apposite in a doctrine which placed so much weight on education and on the leading role of *savants* and philosophers in social change. The road to further progress consisted in successfully influencing ideas at every level of society; the obstacles were identified as ideational rather than socio-historical or socio-economic. Like Condorcet, Tracy's view of history was that of man's gradual mastery of nature and social organisation, the unfolding of reason and social co-operation. Tracy's idéologie drew virtually no connections between systems of ideas and social groups (whether classes, estates, occupations, regional groups, etc.). There was no hint of a historical materialist theory of the relations between ideas and socio-economic forces, and little evidence of a concern for the sociological context of the formation of knowledges. Marx's theory of ideology, to which the modern discussions of this concept are deeply indebted, borrowed nothing from Tracy's theory except the name. According to Marx, Tracy's idéologie, far from providing a scientific account of the relationships between ideas, society and nature, was itself an example of a rationalist philosophy of liberalism posing as social science, urging men to adopt a rational and individualistic perspective, without understanding the historically developing social and economic forces which alone could bring into existence a rational society.

What Tracy and Marx had in common, apart from the word "ideology", was a grand conception of social science as a body of explanatory laws governing social phenomena and capable of predicting to some degree the happiness of men under particular forms of social organisation. For Marx, the obstacle to a free society was the power of the dominant economic class; for Tracy, it was the institutionalisation of ignorance and prejudice which made possible the survival of oppression. One of the most striking aspects of Tracy's work was his use of science as a type of all-encompassing explanatory system, amounting to a form of secular faith. It is interesting to note a remark by Dr Keith Thomas concerning the claims of astrology in England two centuries before Tracy's writings:

> Nothing did more to make (it) seductive than the ambitious scale of its intellectual pretensions. It offered a systematic scheme of explanation for all the vagaries of human and natural behaviour ...[1]

Tracy has many continuators of this kind in modern versions of behaviouralism and positivism, in which a theory of human nature is dressed up as social science.[2]

Notes

1. K. Thomas, *Religion and the decline of magic* (London, 1971), p. 324.
2. For a full bibliography of works relevant to the present study of Tracy's thought, see E. Kennedy, *A philosophe in the age of revolution* (Philadelphia, 1978) and B.W. Head, *The political and philosophical thought of Destutt de Tracy* (Ph. D. dissertation, London School of Economics, 1979).
   I hope to produce a further monograph which examines the social and political thought of the wider circle of idéologues.

INDEX